Java™ 2D Graphics

THE JAVA SERIES

Exploring Java™

Java™ Threads

Java™ Network Programming

Java™ Virtual Machine

Java™ AWT Reference

Java™ Language Reference

Java™ Fundamental Classes Reference

Database Programming with JDBC™ and Java™

Java™ Distributed Computing

Developing Java Beans™

Java™ Security

Java™ Cryptography

Java™ Swing

Java™ Servlet Programming

Java™ I/O

Java™ 2D Graphics

Enterprise Java Beans™

Also from O'Reilly

Java™ in a Nutshell

Java™ in a Nutshell, Deluxe Edition

Java™ Examples in a Nutshell

Java™ Power Reference: A Complete Searchable
  Resource on CD-ROM

Java™ 2D Graphics

Jonathan Knudsen

O'REILLY®

Beijing · Cambridge · Köln · Paris · Sebastopol · Taipei · Tokyo

Java™ 2D Graphics
by Jonathan Knudsen

Copyright © 1999 O'Reilly & Associates, Inc. All rights reserved.
Printed in the United States of America.

Published by O'Reilly & Associates, Inc., 101 Morris Street, Sebastopol, CA 95472.

Editor: Mike Loukides

Production Editor: Nicole Gipson Arigo

Printing History:

May 1999:	First Edition.

This book is printed on acid-free paper with 85% recycled content, 15% post-consumer waste. O'Reilly & Associates is committed to using paper with the highest recycled content available consistent with high quality.

ISBN: 1-56592-484-3

For Kristen
A 2D book for a 3D lady

Table of Contents

Preface

Who Are You?

This book is intended for Java developers who want to produce stunning graphics. The latest version of the Java platform, version 2, includes a set of classes that make it easy to produce professional-looking graphics. These classes are known as Java 2D or the 2D Application Programming Interface (2D API).

I don't assume that you know anything about computer graphics, which is an extensive field. I'll explain the concepts of Java 2D's features as well as the classes and methods you need to take advantage of them.

To get the most out of this book, however, you should be comfortable programming in Java. You should also have at least a rudimentary knowledge of the Abstract Windowing Toolkit (AWT).

About This Book

This book covers a lot of ground. It presents the essentials of several complex fields—computer graphics, signal processing, typesetting, and color handling—in a compact form. I concentrate on what you need to know to use the features in the 2D API. Although you'll get a good conceptual background in computer graphics, this is a very practical book: it includes a working example for almost every concept.

Java 2D was designed so that simple operations are simple and complex operations are feasible. This book is designed the same way. I explain the simple way to do things first, then follow up with the full details. For example, two chapters are devoted to drawing text with the 2D API. The first chapter explains how to draw strings and perform other mainstream operations. If you really need fine control over each letter shape, however, you can go ahead and read the second chapter.

Here's a description of each chapter in this book:

Chapter 1, *Introduction*, talks about Java 2D's role in the larger scheme of things, its origins, and related technology. It also includes an example that demonstrates some of the power of the 2D API.

Chapter 2, *The Big Picture*, presents a bird's-eye view of the 2D API. You should definitely read this chapter so that you have a conceptual framework to hold the information that's in the rest of the book.

Chapter 3, *Geometry*, describes how shapes are represented in the 2D API.

Chapter 4, *Painting and Stroking*, shows how the 2D API can be used to produce dotted lines, lines of different thicknesses, and shapes that are filled with solid colors, color gradients, and textures.

Chapter 5, *Rendering*, talks about four aspects of drawing that can be applied to shapes, text, or images: geometric transformation, compositing, clipping, and rendering hints.

Chapter 6, *Text*, introduces text operations in the 2D API. You'll learn how to work with fonts, draw text, and measure text.

Chapter 7, *Advanced Text Layout*, delves into the more arcane aspects of text, including carets, highlighting, hit testing, and the manipulation and measurement of individual character shapes.

Chapter 8, *Color*, discusses the difficulties involved in representing color and how the 2D API deals with color.

Chapter 9, *Images*, talks about how to draw and use images with the 2D API.

Chapter 10, *Image Processing*, covers 2D's ability to digitally manipulate images using standard signal processing techniques.

Chapter 11, *Image Guts*, is devoted to the innards of 2D's image classes. It covers color models and image data storage schemes.

Chapter 12, *Devices*, covers the 2D classes that provide information about the graphics hardware of a particular system.

Chapter 13, *Printing*, describes the 2D API's new printing capabilities.

Chapter 14, *Animation and Performance*, explores some of the speed issues involved in 2D applications.

This book contains an eight-page full-color insert with 32 figures. These figures are referenced throughout the text with a prefix of C, as in Figure C-1.

About the Examples

Versions

This book describes the 2D API in the Java 2 platform. The Java 2 platform used to be known as the Java Development Kit (JDK) 1.2. In this book I use the terms "Java 2" and "JDK 1.2" more or less interchangeably. The examples were tested with an early access release of JDK 1.2.2 (build K, March 1999).

About paint()

Some of the examples in this book are assumed to be inside the `paint()` method of a `Component`. These examples make use of a `Graphics2D` object, named `g2`. In Java 2, however, `Component`'s `paint()` method is passed a `Graphics` object. You must cast this object to a `Graphics2D` as follows:

```
public void paint(Graphics g) {
  Graphics2D g2 = (Graphics2D)g;
  // Shake your funky groove thang...
}
```

File Naming

This book assumes you are comfortable programming in Java. The source code for examples in this book should be saved in files based on the class name. For example, consider the following code:

```
import java.awt.*;
import java.awt.event.*;
import java.awt.geom.*;

public class Transformers
    extends Component {

  // ...

}
```

This file describes the `Transformers` class; therefore, you should save it in a file named *Transformers.java*.

Variable Naming

The examples in this book are presented in my own coding style, which is an amalgam of conventions from a grab-bag of platforms.

I follow standard Java coding practices with respect to capitalization. All member variables of a class are prefixed with a small m, like so:

```
private float mTheta;
```

This makes it easy to distinguish between member variables and local variables. Static members are prefixed with a small s, like this:

```
private static int sID = 0;
```

Array types are always written with the square brackets immediately following the array type. This keeps all the type information for a variable in one place:

```
private float[] mPoints;
```

As for local variables, a `Graphics` object is always called g. Likewise, a `Graphics2D` is always called g2.

Downloading

All of the examples in this book can be downloaded from *ftp://ftp.oreilly.com/pub/ examples/java/2d*.

Font Conventions

`Constant width` is used for:

- Class names and method names
- Source code
- Objects and packages
- Example command-line sessions. The input you type is shown in boldface.

Italic is used for:

- Paths and filenames
- New terms where they are defined
- Internet addresses, such as domain names and URLs

Boldface is used for the names of interface buttons.

Request for Comments

If you find typos, inaccuracies, or bugs, please let us know. You can reach O'Reilly by mail, telephone, fax, or email:

O'Reilly & Associates, Inc.
101 Morris Street
Sebastopol, CA 95472
(800) 998-9938 (in the U.S. or Canada)
(707) 829-0515 (international or local)
(707) 829-0104 (fax)
bookquestions@oreilly.com

Please let us know what we can do to make the book more helpful to you. We take your comments seriously, and will do whatever we can to make this book as useful as it can be.

Acknowledgments

I'd like to thank my family for their love and support. Everyone helped in a different way. Kristen reviewed almost all of this book and helped me say things frontwards instead of backwards. Daphne helped me take breaks by asking me to juggle. Luke encouraged me to back up my files frequently by deleting some of them one day. The cats, Asher and Basteet—well, they didn't help at all, but I love them anyhow.

Mike Loukides once again proved himself to be a great editor: he helped me when I needed help and left me alone otherwise. Thanks also to Val Quercia for helping me learn the ins and outs of working at O'Reilly.

I had outstanding technical support from several sources. Eduardo Martinez, at Ductus, provided me with clear and detailed explanations of 2D's rendering pipeline, particularly the ClearView Rasterizer that forms a part of the 2D implementation. The 2D team at Sun was also very helpful: Jim Graham, Jerry Evans, Parry Kejriwal, Thanh Nguyen, and Jeannette Hung patiently and thoroughly answered my questions. Thanks to Jeannette Hung, in particular, for getting me an early access copy of post-beta JDK 1.2—that really helped me finish this book. I'd also like to thank Bill Day for the opportunity to coauthor a column in *JavaWorld*.

This book was blessed with an outstanding group of technical reviewers. Eric Brower, Matt Diamond, Doug Felt, Dave Geoghegan, Jim Graham, Jeannette Hung, Marc Loy, and John Raley reviewed some or all of this manuscript and provided excellent, detailed feedback. Thank you all for the hard work you put into reviewing this book.

I learned a lot of interesting things from people on the 2D email list, as well. Thanks especially to Richard Blanchard for pointing out that Swing components print much better with double buffering turned off. My `ComponentPrintable` class, in Chapter 13, owes a lot to you. Thanks also to Pete Cockerell for many interesting explanations and example applications.

1

Introduction

This chapter describes Java 2D's roots, contributors, related technologies, and capabilities. I'll also explain how you can obtain a Graphics2D object in your application, and then I'll present a useful class that will be used throughout the book. Finally, the chapter concludes with a "teaser" example that shows off some of Java 2D's features.

What Is Java 2D?

The Java 2D Application Programming Interface (the 2D API) is a set of classes that can be used to create high quality graphics. It includes features like geometric transformation, antialiasing, alpha compositing, image processing, and bidirectional text layout, just to name a few. Don't worry if you don't know what some of these features are—I'll explain them all.

Java 2D is part of the core classes of the Java 2 platform (formerly JDK 1.2). The 2D API introduces new classes in the following packages:

- java.awt
- java.awt.image

In addition, the 2D API encompasses six entirely new packages:

- java.awt.color
- java.awt.font
- java.awt.geom
- java.awt.print

- `java.awt.image.renderable`
- `com.sun.image.codec.jpeg`

All of these packages are part of the core Java 2 platform, except `com.sun.image.code.jpeg`. This means that, except for the JPEG package, you can rely on the 2D API in all implementations of the Java 2 platform.

This book covers all of the new packages, with the exception of `java.awt.image.renderable`. This package serves as a bridge to the Java Advanced Imaging API (JAI), which is outside the scope of this book.

What Can Java 2D Do?

Java 2D is designed to do anything you want it to do (with computer graphics, at least). Prior to Java 2D, AWT's graphics toolkit had some serious limitations:

- All lines were drawn with a single-pixel thickness.
- Only a handful of fonts were available.
- AWT didn't offer much control over drawing. For example, you couldn't manipulate the individual shapes of characters.
- If you wanted to rotate or scale anything, you had to do it yourself.
- If you wanted special fills, like gradients or patterns, you had to make them yourself.
- Image support was rudimentary.
- Control of transparency was awkward.

The 2D API remedies these shortcomings and does a lot more, too. To appreciate what the 2D API can offer, you need to see it in action. Java 2 includes a sample program that demonstrates many of the features of the API. To run it, navigate to the *demo/jfc/Java2D* directory in the JDK installation directory. Then run the `Java2Demo` class. For example:

```
C:> cd \jdk1.2\demo\jfc\Java2D
C:> java Java2Demo
```

You should see a window that looks like Figure 1-1. Each of the tabs across the top displays a set of 2D's features. Spend some time with this application. Then come back and read about all the things 2D can do, including:

shapes

Arbitrary geometric shapes can be represented by combinations of straight lines and curves. The 2D API also provides a useful toolbox of standard shapes, like rectangles, arcs, and ellipses. See Chapter 3, *Geometry*, for details.

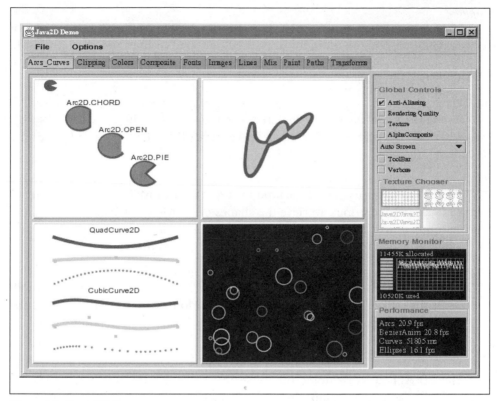

Figure 1-1. Sun's 2D demo

stroking

Lines and shape outlines can be drawn as a solid or dotted line of any width—a process called *stroking*. You can define any dotted-line pattern and specify how shape corners and line ends should be drawn. Chapter 4, *Painting and Stroking*, has all the details.

filling

Shapes can be filled using a solid color, a pattern, a color gradient, or anything else you can imagine. See Chapter 4 for more information.

transformations

Everything that's drawn in the 2D API can be stretched, squished, and rotated. This applies to shapes, text, and images. You tell 2D what transformation you want and it takes care of everything. For more information, see Chapter 5, *Rendering*.

alpha compositing

Compositing is the process of adding new elements to an existing drawing. The 2D API gives you considerable flexibility by using the Porter-Duff compositing rules, which are described in Chapter 5.

clipping

> *Clipping* is the process of limiting the extent of drawing operations. For example, drawing in a window is normally clipped to the window's bounds. In the 2D API, however, you can use any shape for clipping. This process is described in Chapter 5.

antialiasing

> *Antialiasing* is a technique that reduces jagged edges in drawings. It's fully described in Chapter 5. The 2D API takes care of the details of producing antialiased drawing.

text

> The 2D API can use any TrueType or Type 1 font installed on your system.[*] You can render strings, retrieve the shapes of individual strings or letters, and manipulate text in the same ways that shapes are manipulated. Drawing text is fully covered in Chapter 6, *Text*, and Chapter 7, *Advanced Text Layout*.

color

> It's hard to show colors correctly. The 2D API includes classes and methods that support representing colors in ways that don't depend on any particular hardware or viewing conditions. Chapter 8, *Color*, discusses these issues in detail.

images

> The 2D API supports doing the same neat stuff with images that you can do with shapes and text. Specifically, you can transform images, use clipping shapes, and use alpha compositing with images. Java 2 also includes a set of classes for loading and saving images in the JPEG format. Chapter 9, *Images*, has the scoop on drawing images. Chapter 11, *Image Guts*, describes how image data is stored and interpreted.

image processing

> The 2D API also includes a set of classes for processing images. Image processing is used to highlight certain aspects of pictures, to achieve aesthetic effects, or to clean up messy scans. For full coverage of the 2D API's image processing capabilities, see Chapter 10, *Image Processing*.

printing

> Finally, Java developers have a decent way to print. The Printing API is part of the 2D API and provides a compact, clean solution to the problem of producing output on a printer. This API is covered in Chapter 13, *Printing*.

---

[*] TrueType is a font standard originally developed at Apple and now widespread in the MacOS and Windows platforms. Type 1 fonts are based on Adobe's PostScript language. Both standards have their merits. See *http://www.truetype.demon.co.uk/* for a fascinating description of both formats.

Relatives

The Abstract Windowing Toolkit (AWT) that comes with JDK 1.0 and 1.1 is a large set of classes that encapsulate windows, controls, fonts, images, and drawing. However, the AWT lacks a number of important features, as users of more mature graphics toolkits were quick to point out. Instead of applying a quick fix, the engineers at Sun created the largest, most powerful graphics toolkit yet, the Java Foundation Classes (JFC). JFC is included with Java 2. The 2D API is part of JFC. It is a "core" API, which means that it is present in every implementation of Java 2. It cannot run in older versions of the JDK, however.

To understand how 2D fits into the larger scheme of things, it's helpful to examine how it evolved from AWT. Conceptually, AWT can be split into two pieces: a user interface (UI) toolkit and a drawing toolkit. Between JDK 1.1 and Java 2 (JDK 1.2), these two pieces evolved considerably. The UI toolkit became Swing, and the drawing toolkit became the 2D API.

In this section, I'll explain how Java 2D relates to some other APIs and buzzwords:

Java Foundation Classes (JFC)
> Java 2D is one part of JFC. The other parts are AWT, Swing, the Accessibility API, and the Drag and Drop API. See *http://java.sun.com/products/jfc/* for details.

AWT
> In Java 2, you can use the 2D API to draw on AWT components. AWT is described in books such as John Zukowski's *Java AWT Reference* (published by O'Reilly & Associates, Inc.).

Swing
> As with AWT components in Java 2, you can use 2D to draw on Swing components.* You may want to use 2D to develop your own components or your own look and feel. For more on Swing, see *Java Swing*, by Robert Eckstein, Marc Loy, and Dave Wood (O'Reilly). Online information is also available at *http://java.sun.com/products/jfc/tsc/*.

Java Media APIs
> The Java Media APIs are designed to provide Java multimedia capabilities. The 2D API is part of the Java Media APIs. Other APIs in this collection include the 3D API, the Sound API, and the Advanced Imaging API. The Java Media APIs are described at *http://java.sun.com/products/jfc/tsc/*.

---

* This is only true if you're using Swing in Java 2. Although it is possible to use Swing in JDK 1.1, the 2D API runs only in Java 2 (JDK 1.2).

Java 3D
> Although the 2D and 3D APIs aren't tightly integrated, you can use 2D to create textures for 3D. You can read more about the 3D API at *http://java.sun.com/products/java-media/3D/*.

Java Advanced Imaging API (JAI)
> Of all the JFC and Media APIs, JAI is the most closely related to 2D because it builds on the image handling classes in 2D. JAI offers sophisticated image processing and handling features. For heavy-duty processing of large images, check out JAI, which is described at *http://java.sun.com/products/java-media/jai/*.

Genesis

The Java people at Sun have a crazy ambition to redefine all of computing. Each new version of the Java platform includes vastly expanded capabilities. Between the JDK itself and the extension APIs, Sun seems intent on making Java able to do anything you could possibly want to do with a computer. In order to create the 2D API, the good people at Sun conspired with several industry partners, including the following four companies.

Adobe

Sun's most important partner for the 2D API was Adobe Systems, Inc. These are the people who developed the PostScript language as well as an impressive lineup of graphics and text applications, including Framemaker, Acrobat, Illustrator, and others. Adobe helped Sun design the 2D API. If you're familiar with PostScript, you'll probably see echoes of it in the classes and methods of the 2D API. Adobe's web site is at *http://www.adobe.com/*.

Ductus

A small company called Ductus provided a key piece of the 2D API's implementation, called a *rasterizer*. The rasterizer handles the task of representing idealized mathematical shapes on output devices with pixels, like monitors and printers. You can read more about Ductus at their web site, *http://www.ductus.com/*.

Kodak

Another important partner was Eastman Kodak (*http://www.kodak.com/*). Sun worked closely with Kodak to develop the imaging and color management classes in the 2D API. Some of the implementation of these classes is based on technology licensed from Kodak. Just as Adobe helped design the graphics part of the

2D API, Kodak helped with the design and implementation of the imaging and color management portions of the 2D API.

Taligent

It's a funny industry we work in: Taligent, one of Sun's partners in the 2D API, no longer exists. Formerly an IBM subsidiary, Taligent has now been reabsorbed into the mother ship. During Taligent's independent existence, however, Sun licensed two technologies from them for use in the 2D API: bidirectional text layout and constructive area geometry.

Where Do I Get a Graphics2D?

Shapes, text, and images are all ultimately drawn by a Graphics2D object. But where does the Graphics2D come from? As usual, there's more than one way to do it.

Drawing on Components

Every Component that AWT shows on the screen has a paint() method. The system passes a Graphics to this method. In JDK 1.1 and earlier, you could draw on Components by overriding the paint() method and using the Graphics to draw things.

It works exactly the same way in Java 2, except that it's a Graphics2D that is passed to paint(). To take advantage of all the spiffy 2D features, you'll have to perform a cast in your paint() method, like this:

```
public void paint(Graphics g) {
   Graphics2D g2 = (Graphics2D)g;
   // Now we can do cool 2D stuff.
}
```

Note that your component may not necessarily be drawn on the screen. The Graphics2D that gets passed to paint() might actually represent a printer or any other output device.

Swing components work almost the same way. Strictly speaking, however, you should implement the paintComponent() method instead of paint(). Swing uses the paint() method to draw child components. Swing's implementation of paint() calls paintComponent() to draw the component itself. You may be able to get away with implementing paint() instead of paintComponent(), but then don't be surprised if the component is not drawn correctly.

Drawing on Images

You can use a `Graphics` or `Graphics2D` to draw on images, as well. If you have an `Image` that you have created yourself, you can get a corresponding `Graphics2D` by calling `createGraphics()`, as follows:

```
public void drawOnImage(Image i) {
  Graphics g = i.getGraphics();
  // Now draw on the image using g.
}
```

This works only for any `Image` you've created yourself, not for an `Image` loaded from a file.

If you have a `BufferedImage` (Java 2D's new image class), you can obtain a `Graphics2D` as follows:

```
public void drawOnBufferedImage(BufferedImage bi) {
  Graphics2D g2 = bi.createGraphics();
  // Now draw on the image using g2.
}
```

I'll talk more about these techniques in Chapter 9, *Images*.

ApplicationFrame

Many of the examples in this book assume that you have a `Graphics2D` object to work with. This section contains a simple test window that makes it easy to use a `Graphics2D`. The window, `ApplicationFrame`, appears centered on your screen and goes away when you close it. You can test `Graphics2D` features easily by subclassing `ApplicationFrame` and overriding the `paint()` method.

```
import java.awt.*;
import java.awt.event.*;

public class ApplicationFrame
    extends Frame {
  public ApplicationFrame() { this("ApplicationFrame v1.0"); }

  public ApplicationFrame(String title) {
    super(title);
    createUI();
  }

  protected void createUI() {
    setSize(500, 400);
    center();

    addWindowListener(new WindowAdapter() {
```

```
        public void windowClosing(WindowEvent e) {
          dispose();
          System.exit(0);
        }
      });
  }

  public void center() {
    Dimension screenSize = Toolkit.getDefaultToolkit().getScreenSize();
    Dimension frameSize = getSize();
    int x = (screenSize.width - frameSize.width) / 2;
    int y = (screenSize.height - frameSize.height) / 2;
    setLocation(x, y);
  }
}
```

Remember that the programming examples in this book are available online. See the Preface for details.

File Formats

There are many, many ways to store graphics information in a file. In this section I'll briefly describe two formats, GIF and JPEG. These formats are common currencies of the Internet—any web browser that shows images knows how to show GIF and JPEG images. Similarly, the JDK can load and display GIF or JPEG images.

For more detailed information on these formats, or on other popular graphics file formats, see the *Encyclopedia of Graphics File Formats*, by James D. Murray and William vanRyper (O'Reilly).

GIF

GIF stands for *Graphics Interchange Format*. GIF images can have 2 to 256 colors and are compressed before being stored. The compression algorithm is lossless, which means that the original picture will be restored verbatim when the image is decompressed and displayed.

There are actually two common flavors of this format, GIF87a and GIF89a. GIF89a offers the option of designating one of the image colors as transparent. Applications that know how to show GIF89a images correctly will allow the background to show through the transparent areas of the image. You've probably seen these "transparent GIFs" in web pages.

GIF89a also supports simple animations, which you've probably seen in web pages. These are called *animated GIFs*; they've been supported in Java since JDK 1.1. For more information on animated GIFs, see *GIF Animation Studio* by Richard Koman (published by Songline Studios, Inc.).

JPEG

JPEG stands for *Joint Photographic Experts Group*. Unlike some other file formats, it was designed specifically for photographic images. JPEG images support more colors than GIF images, up to 24 bits per pixel. JPEG images are compressed before being stored using a *lossy* compression algorithm. This means that when the image is loaded and displayed, it will not be exactly the same as the original image. The 2D API includes support for reading and writing JPEG files in the `com.sun.image.codec.jpeg` package, which is covered in Chapter 9.

Utilities

There are many utilities that convert images between different file formats. Here are five freeware or shareware solutions:

GNU Image Manipulation Program (GIMP) (Unix, freeware)
> Much of the functionality of Adobe Photoshop is included in this freeware application. See *http://www.gimp.org/*.

ImageMagick (Unix, freeware)
> This free application lets you convert from one file format to another, change the size of an image, and perform other basic manipulations. See *http://www.wizards.dupont.com/cristy/ImageMagick.html*.

xv (Unix, shareware)
> This shareware application performs a variety of image manipulation functions. The full source code is available. See *http://www.trilon.com/xv/xv.html*.

GraphicConverter (MacOS, shareware)
> This versatile tool handles most common graphics file formats with a clean interface and lots of useful features. See *http://www.lemkesoft.de/*.

LView Pro (Windows, shareware)
> This is a Windows program, similar to GraphicConverter for the Mac. It handles a variety of file formats and offers some editing features. See *http://www.lview.com/*.

If you're more serious about images and image processing, you should get a real tool like Adobe's Photoshop (*http://www.adobe.com/*) or Live Picture from the company of the same name (*http://www.livepicture.com/*).

Hello, 2D!

This chapter ends with a bang—an example that demonstrates the power of the 2D API. You probably won't understand much of the code at this point, but rest assured that it all will become clear as you work through the rest of the book.

In general terms, this is what the example does:

- The example draws a background of colored circles.

- Then the example draws an image. The image is broken into small pieces, and each piece is drawn partially transparent, allowing the circles to show through. The image is Raphael's self-portrait, taken from the Virtual Uffizi at *http://www.arca.net/uffizi/*.

- Finally, the example draws some text on a color-gradient–filled background. Then the text is drawn a second time, rotated 90°.

The results are shown in Figure C-1 (in the color insert). This is a less than 200 lines of code (with lots of comments). It's a small subset of what can be accomplished with the 2D API.

Note that this example depends on the `ApplicationFrame` class presented earlier in this chapter. If you haven't entered and compiled `ApplicationFrame`, do it now.*

```java
import java.awt.*;
import java.awt.event.*;
import java.awt.font.*;
import java.awt.geom.*;
import java.awt.image.BufferedImage;
import java.io.*;
import java.util.Random;

import com.sun.image.codec.jpeg.*;

public class ShowOff
    extends Component {
  public static void main(String[] args) {
    try {
      // The image is loaded either from this
      //    default filename or the first command-
      //    line argument.
      // The second command-line argument specifies
      //    what string will be displayed. The third
      //    specifies at what point in the string the
      //    background color will change.
      String filename = "Raphael.jpg";
      String message = "Java2D";
      int split = 4;
      if (args.length > 0) filename = args[0];
      if (args.length > 1) message = args[1];
      if (args.length > 2) split = Integer.parseInt(args[2]);
```

---

* Like all the other examples in this book, ShowOff is available online. See the Preface for details.

```
      ApplicationFrame f = new ApplicationFrame("ShowOff v1.0");
      f.setLayout(new BorderLayout());
      ShowOff showOff = new ShowOff(filename, message, split);
      f.add(showOff, BorderLayout.CENTER);
      f.setSize(f.getPreferredSize());
      f.center();
      f.setResizable(false);
      f.setVisible(true);
    }
    catch (Exception e) {
      System.out.println(e);
      System.exit(0);
    }
  }

  private BufferedImage mImage;
  private Font mFont;
  private String mMessage;
  private int mSplit;
  private TextLayout mLayout;

  public ShowOff(String filename, String message, int split)
      throws IOException, ImageFormatException {
    // Get the specified image.
    InputStream in = getClass().getResourceAsStream(filename);
    JPEGImageDecoder decoder = JPEGCodec.createJPEGDecoder(in);
    mImage = decoder.decodeAsBufferedImage();
    in.close();
    // Create a font.
    mFont = new Font("Serif", Font.PLAIN, 116);
    // Save the message and split.
    mMessage = message;
    mSplit = split;
    // Set our size to match the image's size.
    setSize((int)mImage.getWidth(), (int)mImage.getHeight());
  }

  public void paint(Graphics g) {
    Graphics2D g2 = (Graphics2D)g;

    // Turn on antialiasing.
    g2.setRenderingHint(RenderingHints.KEY_ANTIALIASING,
        RenderingHints.VALUE_ANTIALIAS_ON);

    drawBackground(g2);
    drawImageMosaic(g2);
    drawText(g2);
  }
```

```
protected void drawBackground(Graphics2D g2) {
  // Draw circles of different colors.
  int side = 45;
  int width = getSize().width;
  int height = getSize().height;
  Color[] colors = { Color.yellow, Color.cyan, Color.orange,
      Color.pink, Color.magenta, Color.lightGray };
  for (int y = 0; y < height; y += side) {
    for (int x = 0; x < width; x += side) {
      Ellipse2D ellipse = new Ellipse2D.Float(x, y, side, side);
      int index = (x + y) / side % colors.length;
      g2.setPaint(colors[index]);
      g2.fill(ellipse);
    }
  }
}

protected void drawImageMosaic(Graphics2D g2) {
  // Break the image up into tiles. Draw each
  //   tile with its own transparency, allowing
  //   the background to show through to varying
  //   degrees.
  int side = 36;
  int width = mImage.getWidth();
  int height = mImage.getHeight();
  for (int y = 0; y < height; y += side) {
    for (int x = 0; x < width; x += side) {
      // Calculate an appropriate transparency value.
      float xBias = (float)x / (float)width;
      float yBias = (float)y / (float)height;
      float alpha = 1.0f - Math.abs(xBias - yBias);
      g2.setComposite(AlphaComposite.getInstance(
          AlphaComposite.SRC_OVER, alpha));
      // Draw the subimage.
      int w = Math.min(side, width - x);
      int h = Math.min(side, height - y);
      BufferedImage tile = mImage.getSubimage(x, y, w, h);
      g2.drawImage(tile, x, y, null);
    }
  }
  // Reset the composite.
  g2.setComposite(AlphaComposite.getInstance(AlphaComposite.SRC_OVER));
}

protected void drawText(Graphics2D g2) {
  // Find the bounds of the entire string.
  FontRenderContext frc = g2.getFontRenderContext();
  mLayout = new TextLayout(mMessage, mFont, frc);
  // Find the dimensions of this component.
```

```
    int width = getSize().width;
    int height = getSize().height;
    // Place the first full string, horizontally centered,
    //   at the bottom of the component.
    Rectangle2D bounds = mLayout.getBounds();
    double x = (width - bounds.getWidth()) / 2;
    double y = height - bounds.getHeight();
    drawString(g2, x, y, 0);
    // Now draw a second version, anchored to the right side
    //   of the component and rotated by -PI / 2.
    drawString(g2, width - bounds.getHeight(), y, -Math.PI / 2);
}

protected void drawString(Graphics2D g2,
      double x, double y, double theta) {
    // Transform to the requested location.
    g2.translate(x, y);
    // Rotate by the requested angle.
    g2.rotate(theta);
    // Draw the first part of the string.
    String first = mMessage.substring(0, mSplit);
    float width = drawBoxedString(g2, first, Color.white, Color.red, 0);
    // Draw the second part of the string.
    String second = mMessage.substring(mSplit);
    drawBoxedString(g2, second, Color.blue, Color.white, width);
    // Undo the transformations.
    g2.rotate(-theta);
    g2.translate(-x, -y);
}

protected float drawBoxedString(Graphics2D g2,
      String s, Color c1, Color c2, double x) {
    // Calculate the width of the string.
    FontRenderContext frc = g2.getFontRenderContext();
    TextLayout subLayout = new TextLayout(s, mFont, frc);
    float advance = subLayout.getAdvance();
    // Fill the background rectangle with a gradient.
    GradientPaint gradient = new GradientPaint((float)x, 0, c1,
        (float)(x + advance), 0, c2);
    g2.setPaint(gradient);
    Rectangle2D bounds = mLayout.getBounds();
    Rectangle2D back = new Rectangle2D.Double(x, 0,
        advance, bounds.getHeight());
    g2.fill(back);
    // Draw the string over the gradient rectangle.
    g2.setPaint(Color.white);
    g2.setFont(mFont);
    g2.drawString(s, (float)x, (float)-bounds.getY());
    return advance;
```

```
    }
  }
```

To run this example, do the following:

```
C:> java ShowOff
```

You can change the image used, the string that is displayed, and the point at which the string background changes from red to blue. In the following command, the image *Daphne & Luke.jpg* will be used. The string displayed will be "DaphneLuke," with the background color transition occurring between "Daphne" and "Luke."

```
C:> java ShowOff "Daphne & Luke.jpg" DaphneLuke 6
```

How does it work? Internally, the `ShowOff` example is divided into eight pieces:

1. The `main()` method handles setting up a frame window to contain a `ShowOff`, which is a `Component` subclass.

2. `ShowOff`'s constructor loads the image file, creates a font that will be used later, and sets the size of the component to match the size of the image. Image loading will be covered in Chapter 9. Fonts are explained in Chapter 6.

3. The `paint()` method draws the picture you see in Figure 1-1. It does this using three helper methods: `drawBackground()`, `drawImageMosaic()`, and `drawText()`.

4. The `drawBackground()` method draws circles of different colors across the area of the component. Chapter 3 contains information on creating shapes, and Chapter 4 describes different ways they can be drawn.

5. The `drawImageMosaic()` method divides up the image into square tiles and draws each tile with a calculated amount of transparency. See Chapter 5 for a description of transparency and compositing rules.

6. The `drawText()` method takes care of drawing the text ("Java2D" by default). Most of this process involves measuring the text so that it is correctly positioned. The text is drawn twice, once on the bottom of the component, and once, rotated, going up the right side of the component. (Rotation and other transformations are covered in Chapter 5.) This method uses two helper methods, `drawString()` and `drawBoxedString()`.

7. The `drawString()` method splits up the text into two pieces. The first piece is drawn on top of a color gradient running from white to red. The second piece is drawn on top of a color gradient running from blue to white.

8. The `drawBoxedString()` method handles drawing a string and a background rectangle with a color gradient. Color gradients are described in Chapter 4, while text is covered in Chapter 6.

2

The Big Picture

The Graphics2D class is the cornerstone of Java 2D. But what is it, exactly? And how does it work? In this chapter, I'll lay the groundwork for the rest of the book by covering the fundamental topics of the 2D API. I'll talk about the Graphics2D class, compositing, and coordinate spaces.

Graphics2D

Rendering is the process of taking a collection of shapes, text, and images and figuring out what colors the pixels should be on a screen or printer. Shapes, text, and images are called *graphics primitives*; screens and printers are called *output devices*. If I wanted to be pompous, I'd tell you that rendering is the process of displaying graphics primitives on output devices. A *rendering engine* performs this work; in the 2D API, the Graphics2D class is the rendering engine. Figure 2-1 shows this process at a high level. The 2D rendering engine takes care of the details of underlying devices and can accurately reproduce the geometry and color of a drawing, regardless of the device that displays it.

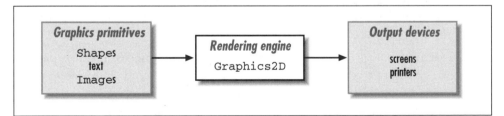

Figure 2-1. Rendering, the short story

Apart from being a rendering engine, an instance of `Graphics2D` also represents a *drawing surface*, which is simply some collection of pixels, each of which holds a color. It might be the inside of a window or a page in a printer, or even an offscreen image. Each time you draw something new, the new element is added to the existing drawing represented by the `Graphics2D`.

The Rendering Pipeline

`Graphics2D` uses its internal state to decide exactly how graphics primitives are converted to pixel colors. For example, part of `Graphics2D`'s internal state is a `java.awt.Paint` object, which describes the colors that should be used to fill shapes. Whenever you ask `Graphics2D` to fill a shape, it uses its current `Paint` to fill the shape.

`Graphics2D`'s internal state is comprised of seven elements:

paint

> The current paint determines what colors will be used to fill a shape. This also affects shape outlines and text, since stroked outlines and character shapes are both filled.

stroke

> `Graphics2D` uses the current stroke for shapes that are passed to its `draw()` method. The stroke determines how the outline of the shape is drawn. The resulting shape (the stroked outline) is then filled.

font

> Text is rendered by creating a shape that represents the characters to be drawn. The current font determines what shapes are created for a given set of characters. The resulting shape is then filled.

transformation

> All primitives are geometrically transformed before they are rendered. This means that they may be moved, rotated, and stretched. `Graphics2D`'s transformation converts primitives from User Space to Device Space. By default, `Graphics2D` creates a transformation that maps 72 User coordinates to one inch on the output device.

compositing rule

> A compositing rule is used to determine how the colors of a primitive should be combined with existing colors on the `Graphics2D`'s drawing surface.

clipping shape

> All rendering operations are limited to the interior of the clipping shape. No pixels outside of this shape will be modified. By default, the clipping shape is `null`, which means that the drawing is limited only by the drawing surface.

rendering hints

> There are different techniques that can be used to render graphics primitives. *Rendering hints* tell a Graphics2D which techniques you want to use.

The current paint and stroke elements apply only to shapes; these are covered in Chapter 4, *Painting and Stroking*. I'll talk about fonts and text in Chapter 6, *Text*. The remaining four parts of Graphics2D's state are discussed in Chapter 5, *Rendering*.

Graphics primitives pass through the rendering engine in a series of operations, called the *rendering pipeline*.* Figure 2-2 shows how the Graphics2D's seven elements of internal state are used in the rendering pipeline. The figure shows Graphics2D's four basic operations:

- You can fill a shape by passing it to the fill() method. In the 2D API, shapes are represented by implementations of the java.awt.Shape interface.

- You can draw the outline of a shape by calling draw().

- Text is rendered by calling one of Graphics2D's drawString() methods.

- You can draw an image by passing a java.awt.Image to one of the drawImage() methods.

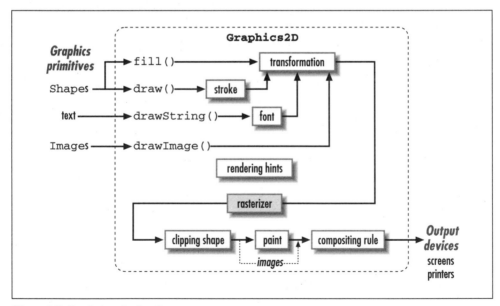

Figure 2-2. Rendering, in detail

---

* The actual implementation of the rendering engine may combine or compress different parts of the pipeline. Conceptually, however, it's useful to think of a series of distinct operations.

Let's walk through the pipeline. It can be described in five steps, where the first step depends heavily on which primitive is being rendered.

1. Determine the shape to be rendered. This is different for each of the rendering operations. For shapes that will be filled, the shape is simply transformed using the `Graphics2D`'s current transformation. For shapes whose outlines are drawn using `draw()`, the current stroke is used to turn the outline into a shape. Then the stroked outline is transformed, just like any other filled shape. Text is displayed by translating characters to shapes using the current font. The resulting shapes are transformed, just like any other filled shape. For images, the outline of the image is transformed using the current transformation.

   As you can see, the rendering engine knows only how to fill shapes and draw images. Although drawing shape outlines and drawing text appear to be distinct operations, they are really special cases of filling shapes.

2. *Rasterize* the shape. Rasterizing is the process of converting an ideal shape to a set of pixel coverage values. I'll explain more about this later. In the case of images, it's the outline of the image that is rasterized. *Rendering hints* are used to control the behavior of the rasterization.

3. Clip the results using the current clipping shape.

4. Determine the colors to be used. For a filled shape, use the current paint object to determine what colors should be used to fill the shape. For an image, the colors are taken from the image itself.

5. Combine the colors with the existing drawing using the current compositing rule.

All About Alpha

Rendering is an approximation. When you ask to have an ideal shape filled, the rendering engine figures out how the pixels of an output device should be colored to best approximate the shape. For example, suppose the rendering engine is asked to fill a shape with some color. There's a fast way to do it, and then there's a good way to do it.

Aliasing and Antialiasing

The fast method is to color the pixels whose centers fall within the shape. Using this algorithm, pixels are either fully colored or left unchanged. Figure 2-3 shows an example of this technique with a single letter shown on some device with very large pixels. The ideal outline of the shape is also shown. The filled shape exhibits unattractive *jaggies,* or ragged edges. Images produced using this algorithm are said to be *aliased.*

Figure 2-3. Aliased rendering

The better method for filling a shape involves a little more work. The basic idea is to calculate the intersection of the shape with each pixel of the output device. Pixels are colored in proportion to the amount they are covered by the shape. This reduces the jaggies that are symptomatic of aliased rendering. Not surprisingly, this technique is called *antialiasing.* Figure 2-4 shows the same shape as Figure 2-3, but rendered with antialiasing. The pixels on the edge aren't just black or white; they're varying shades of gray.

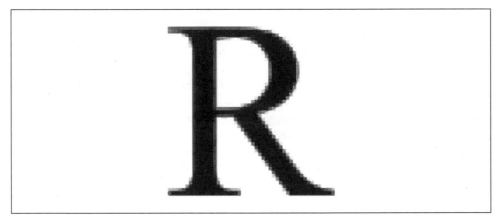

Figure 2-4. Antialiased rendering

Fortunately, the 2D API takes care of all the details for you. You just need to specify whether you want antialiasing, using *rendering hints.*

The Rasterizer

Inside the rendering pipeline, a *rasterizer* takes ideal shapes and produces coverage values for each pixel. The coverage values represent how much of each pixel is covered by the shape. These coverage values are called *alpha values*. Each pixel has its own alpha value. The collection of all alpha values in an image is sometimes called the *alpha channel*.

A pixel, then, is defined by a color and an alpha value. Intuitively, the alpha value indicates the transparency of the pixel. You can even think of the alpha value as part of the pixel's color. As you'll find out, colors are sometimes defined with an associated alpha value. In this context, the alpha value indicates the transparency of the color itself.

Alpha values typically range from 0.0, for no coverage, to 1.0, which represents full coverage. In Figure 2-3, the rasterizer did not use antialiasing and produced either 0.0 or 1.0 for the alpha values. In Figure 2-4, antialiasing was used and the rasterizer produced a range of alpha values from 0.0 on the outside of the shape to 1.0 in the interior of the shape. Figure 2-5 shows the alpha values for each pixel in the upper left corner of the same shape. The grid lines and the ideal shape are superimposed for clarity. You can tell that the rasterizer used antialiasing because there is a range of values between 0.0 and 1.0.

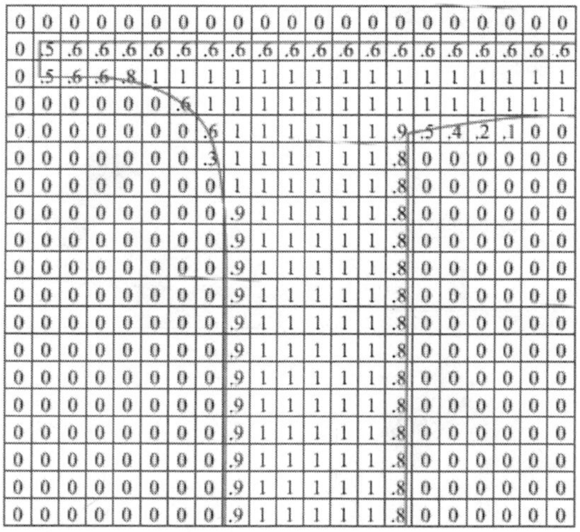

Figure 2-5. The rasterizer produces an alpha value for every pixel

The rasterizer produces alpha values from ideal shapes, but that's only part of the story. Rendering is the process of determining the color for pixels. A technique called *compositing* is used to decide how to translate alpha values into color information.

Compositing

Once the rasterizer has generated alpha values for an ideal shape, there are several ways to use them to modify the drawing surface of a Graphics2D. A *compositing rule* determines how the colors of a new graphics primitive are combined with the existing colors on a drawing surface, as shown in Figure 2-6.

In Figure 2-6, the alpha values are used to blend colors between the background color, white, and the color that is used to fill the shape, black. This is probably the most intuitive compositing rule, but there are other possibilities. Conceptually, at least, the rasterizer produces a set of alpha values for the new shape that is the same size as the drawing surface on which the shape will be rendered. Then this set of alpha values and the desired color of the new shape are combined, pixel by pixel, with the drawing surface. The equation that is used to combine these values is the compositing rule.

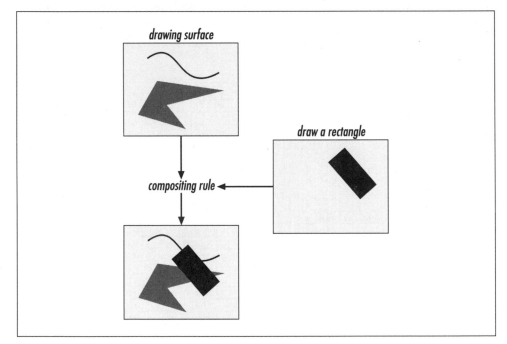

Figure 2-6. Adding to a drawing surface

For example, you might place the new shape behind the other elements on the drawing surface. The 2D API's compositing rules are covered in Chapter 5.

Coordinate Space

Java 2D objects live in a plane defined by Cartesian coordinates. This plane is called User Coordinate Space, or just *User Space*. When objects are drawn on a screen or a printer, User Space coordinates are transformed into *Device Space* coordinates. Device Space corresponds to a particular monitor or printer—usually, one unit in Device Space corresponds to one pixel of a device. By default, User Space and Device Space are aligned, with the x and y axes oriented as shown in Figure 2-7. The x axis increases from left to right, and the y axis increases from top to bottom. The origin is placed at the upper left corner of the drawing surface. This applies for any device, where left, right, top, and bottom are defined in terms of the device itself—the sides of a monitor, for example, or the orientation of a sheet of paper in a printer. Note that the y axis is aligned so that it increases as you go down—this may be the opposite of what you were expecting.

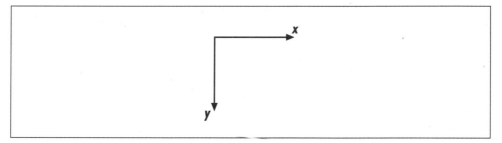

Figure 2-7. Device Space coordinate system

Although User Space and Device Space are aligned by default, some scaling must take place to ensure that objects are drawn the same size, regardless of the output device. Device Space is determined by the resolution of a particular device. A monitor, for example, typically has about 72 pixels per inch, while a laser printer generally has 300 or 600 pixels per inch (or DPI, dots per inch).

User Space is converted to Device Space when objects are drawn. A *transformation* is used to convert from one system to the other. The default transformation converts 72 User Space coordinates into 1 physical inch. Let's say, for example, that you create a rectangle that is 144 User Space coordinates wide and 72 User Space coordinates high. The default transformation into Device Space for a monitor will map User Space directly to Device Space. Since monitors have (more or less) 72 pixels per inch, the rectangle will be 2 inches wide and 1 inch high. If you draw the same rectangle on a 300 DPI printer, the default transformation will convert the rectangle into a 600 by 300 pixel rectangle. The end result will still be a rectangle that is 2 inches wide and 1 inch high.

In general, you don't ever have to worry about the details of a particular device. Your applications live in User Space. As long as you remember that User Space, by default, has 72 coordinates per inch, Java 2D will ensure that everything is the right size on your output devices.

3

Geometry

Java 2D allows you to represent any shape as a combination of straight and curved line segments. This chapter describes the Java 2D classes that represent geometric shapes. You'll learn about the following topics:

- classes that represent points

- the two central interfaces for geometric shapes: `Shape` and `PathIterator`

- 2D's toolbox of shapes in the `java.awt.geom` package

- 2D's support for combining shapes with each other

Points

The `java.awt.geom.Point2D` class encapsulates a single point (an *x* and a *y*) in User Space. It is the most basic of the Java 2D classes and is used throughout the API. Note that a point is not the same as a pixel. A pixel is a tiny square (ideally) on a screen or printer that contains some color. A point, by contrast, has no area, so it can't be rendered. Points are used to build rectangles or other shapes that have area and can be rendered.

`Point2D` demonstrates an inheritance pattern that is used throughout `java.awt. geom`. In particular, `Point2D` is an abstract class with inner child classes that provide concrete implementations. Figure 3-1 shows `Point2D`'s family tree. It's a pattern that you'll see again and again in the `java.awt.geom` package.

`Point2D` represents a point in User Space, but it doesn't specify how the point's coordinates are stored. The subclasses provide different levels of precision for storing the coordinates of the point. The original `java.awt.Point`, which dates back to JDK 1.0, stores the coordinates as integers. Java 2D provides `Point2D. Float` and `Point2D.Double` for higher precision.

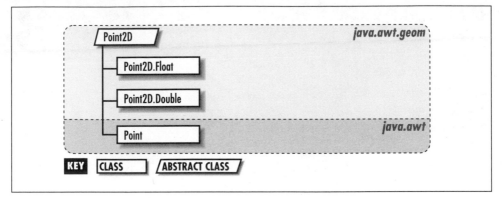

Figure 3-1. Point2D family of classes

Find Your Inner Child

What's an inner child class?

An inner class, introduced to the Java language in JDK 1.1, is a class that is defined inside another class. For example, a class called `Painter` might have an inner class called `Raphael`. The full name of that inner class is `Painter.Raphael`.

A *child class* is a class that extends another class. In the AWT, for example, classes like `Button` and `Canvas` extend the `Component` class.

An *inner child class* combines both of these techniques: it is a class that is defined inside its own superclass. Inner child classes are a recurring theme in the `java.awt.geom` package. The `Point2D` class, for example, has two inner child classes, called `Point2D.Double` and `Point2D.Float`.

For more information on inner classes, see *Java in a Nutshell,* by David Flanagan (O'Reilly), or *Exploring Java,* by Pat Niemeyer and Josh Peck (O'Reilly).

You can either set a point's location or find out where it is:

public abstract void setLocation(double x, double y)
> This method sets the position of the point. Although it accepts `double` values, be aware that the underlying implementation may not store the coordinates as `double` values.

public abstract void setLocation(Point2D p)
> This method sets the position of the point using the coordinates of another `Point2D`.

public abstract double getX()

>   This method returns the x (horizontal) coordinate of the point as a `double`.

public abstract double getY()

>   This method returns the y (vertical) coordinate of the point as a `double`.

`Point2D` also includes a handy method for calculating the distance between two points:

public double distance(double PX, double PY)

>   Use this method to calculate the distance between this `Point2D` and the point specified by `PX` and `PY`.

public double distance(Point2D pt)

>   This method calculates the distance between this `Point2D` and `pt`.

The inner child class `Point2D.Double` has two constructors:

public Point2D.Double()

>   This constructor creates a `Point2D.Double` at the coordinates 0, 0.

public Point2D.Double(double x, double y)

>   This constructor creates a `Point2D.Double` at the given coordinates.

`Point2D.Float` has a similar pair of constructors, based around `floats` instead of `doubles`:

public Point2D.Float()
public Point2D.Float(float x, float y)

Furthermore, `Point2D.Float` provides an additional `setLocation()` method that accepts `floats` instead of `doubles`:

public void setLocation(float x, float y)

>   This method sets the location of the point using the given coordinates.

Why use `floats` instead of `doubles`? If you have special concerns about the speed of your application or interfacing with an existing body of code, you might want to use `Point2D.Float`. Otherwise, I suggest using `Point2D.Double`, since it provides the highest level of precision.

Shapes and Paths

As you saw in Chapter 2, *The Big Picture*, the `Graphics2D` class is the rendering engine for the Java 2D API. Two of its basic operations are filling shapes and drawing their outlines. But `Graphics2D` doesn't know much about geometry, as the song says. In fact, `Graphics2D` only knows how to draw one thing: a `java.awt.Shape`. The `Shape` interface represents a geometric shape, something that has an outline and an interior. With `Graphics2D`, you can draw the border of the shape using `draw()`, and you can fill the inside of a shape using `fill()`.

The `java.awt.geom` package is a toolbox of useful classes that implement the `Shape` interface. There are classes that represent ellipses, arcs, rectangles, and lines. First, I'll talk about the `Shape` interface, and then briefly discuss the `java.awt.geom` package.

If You're an Old Dog

You probably remember that the `Graphics` class had methods for drawing and filling simple shapes: `drawRect()`, `drawOval()`, `drawArc()`, `fillRect()`, `fillOval()`, `fillArc()`, etc. Because `Graphics2D` is a subclass of `Graphics`, you can still call these methods to render shapes. In some cases, it's easier to call one of these methods, because you can render a shape in a single step.

On the other hand, these methods use only integer coordinates, and they don't allow you to reuse shapes. Furthermore, the most complex shape that `Graphics` supports is a polygon defined with straight line segments. The `Shape` interface also supports curved line segments and multiple sub-shapes, as you'll see later.

---

java.awt.Shape

The `java.awt.Shape` interface is one of the common currencies of the 2D API. It contains four groups of methods: `getBounds()`, `contains()`, `intersects()`, and `getPathIterator()`.

The `getBounds()` methods return rectangles that completely enclose a `Shape`:

public abstract Rectangle getBounds()
> This method returns a `java.awt.Rectangle` that completely encloses the `Shape`. `Rectangle` stores its coordinates as integers.

public abstract Rectangle2D getBounds2D()
> This method returns a `java.awt.geom.Rectangle2D` that completely encloses the `Shape`. `Rectangle2D` returns its coordinates as `doubles`. This method provides a higher precision bounding box than `getBounds()`; you should use it unless you have a specific reason to work with integer coordinates.

WARNING   The initial release of Java 2 (formerly JDK 1.2) contains a bug in `Arc2D`'s implementation of `getBounds2D()`. The returned rectangle is the right size but in the wrong place. This bug is fixed in JDK 1.2.1.

Figure 3-2 shows the bounds rectangles of a few shapes.

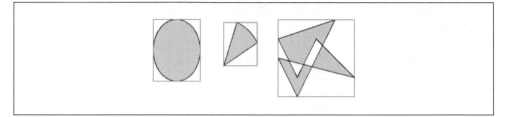

Figure 3-2. Bounds rectangles

A Shape has an interior and an exterior. You can see if a point or rectangle is inside the Shape using the contains() methods:

public abstract boolean contains(double x, double y)
public abstract boolean contains(Point2D p)
> These methods return true if the Shape contains the given point. This can actually be pretty complicated, as you can see from the right side of Figure 3-2. I'll explain how the interior of a shape is determined later in this chapter.

public abstract boolean contains(double x, double y, double w, double h)
public abstract boolean contains(Rectangle2D r)
> These methods return true if the given rectangle is completely in the interior of the Shape.

A related set of methods tests to see if any part of a rectangle intersects the interior of the Shape:

public abstract boolean intersects(double x, double y, double w, double h)
public abstract boolean intersects(Rectangle2D r)
> These methods return true if any part of the given rectangle is in the interior of the Shape.

Finally, a Shape can describe its own outline, using the getPathIterator() methods. These methods return a PathIterator, which I'll talk about later in this chapter. For now, just think of it as an object that describes a geometric outline.

The getPathIterator() methods accept a transform object that can be used to move, rotate, or otherwise modify the PathIterator that is returned. I'll cover transformations in detail in Chapter 5, *Rendering*.

public abstract PathIterator getPathIterator(AffineTransform at)
> This method returns a PathIterator representing the Shape's outline, transformed by the given AffineTransform. You can pass null for this parameter if you don't wish to transform the outline.

public abstract PathIterator getPathIterator(AffineTransform at, double flatness)

> This method returns a flattened `PathIterator` representing the `Shape`'s outline, transformed by the given transform. A flattened path contains only straight line segments. The `flatness` parameter is the maximum allowed distance from the original path to the flattened version of the path. You'll probably never have to call this method yourself. (See the sidebar.)

Flattened Shapes

A *flattened path* is a path whose curved line segments have been approximated by multiple straight line segments. Your `Graphics2D` implementation may not be able to draw or fill shapes with curved line segments, so a flattened path may be used to render shapes that have curved line segments. In fact, the 2D API includes a class, `java.awt.geom.FlatteningPathIterator`, that does the work of flattening a path. Normally, path flattening happens behind the scenes, and you won't ever have to worry about the details.

All the geometric classes in Java 2D implement the `Shape` interface, as illustrated in Figure 3-3. Directly or indirectly, every geometric class in Java 2D implements the `Shape` interface. This means that they can all be passed to `Graphics2D`'s `draw()` and `paint()` methods.

java.awt.geom.PathIterator

A `Shape`'s border is represented by something called a *path*. A path is simply a series of instructions, like a set of directions for getting from one place to another. The instructions describe each *segment*, or piece, of the path. You could describe the outline of a square with a set of instructions like this:

1. Move to 0, 0.

2. Draw a line to 72, 0.

3. Draw a line to 72, 72.

4. Draw a line to 0, 72.

5. Draw a line back to 0, 0.

In Java 2D, the segments of a path are encapsulated by the `java.awt.geom.PathIterator` interface. You can get an object that describes the outline of a `Shape` by calling the `Shape`'s `getPathIterator()` method.

`PathIterator` allows you to walk through the segments of a path. A `PathIterator` is designed to work like a `java.util.Enumeration`. When you first

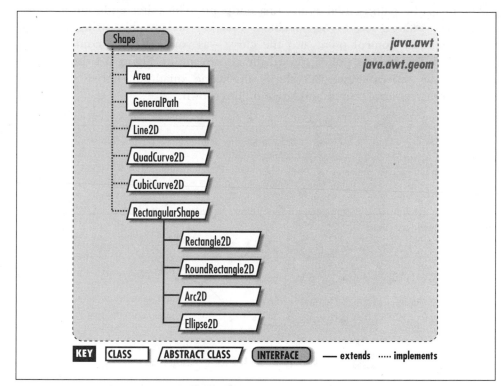

Figure 3-3. The Shape interface and its progeny

obtain a `PathIterator`, it is positioned at the beginning of the path, and you can move through the different segments of the path until you reach the end of the path. Note that `PathIterator` is read-only: it describes a path but doesn't let you change it.

Path segments

The `PathIterator` interface defines constants representing the five possible segment types:

public static final int SEG_MOVETO
　This segment type is used to update the location of the path without drawing anything.

public static final int SEG_LINETO
　This segment type is a straight line, drawn from the last point in the path.

public static final int SEG_QUADTO
　This segment type is a curved line that is represented by a quadratic (second-order) equation. The segment is fully described by two endpoints and a *control point*, which determines the curve's tangents at its endpoints. The previous

point in the path is used as the first endpoint. The other endpoint and the control point need to be specified. Imagine an invisible string running between the control point and the curve—as you move the control point around, the curve is pulled toward the control point. Figure 3-4 shows a few quadratic curves. Figure 3-5 shows the same quadratic curves with the endpoints, control points, and tangent lines shown.

Figure 3-4. Quadratic curves

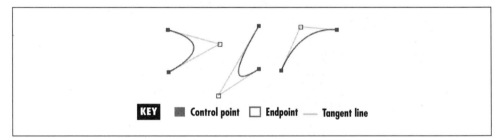

Figure 3-5. Endpoints, control points, and tangent lines of quadratic curves

public static final int SEG_CUBICTO

This segment type represents a Bézier cubic curve. A cubic curve is basically a quadratic curve with an additional control point; mathematically, it is described by a third-order equation and can be specified with two endpoints and two control points. Each control point determines the tangent of the curve at one of the endpoints. Figure 3-6 shows a few cubic curves, and Figure 3-7 shows the endpoints, control points, and tangent lines of the same curves.

Figure 3-6. Cubic curves

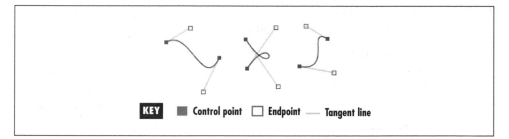

Figure 3-7. Endpoints, control points, and tangent lines of cubic curves

public static final int SEG_CLOSE

> This type of segment draws a line back to the end of the last SEG_MOVETO. A path may be composed of several different subpaths. The beginning of each subpath is marked with a SEG_MOVETO, so the effect of SEG_CLOSE is to close the last subpath. This segment type is only useful if you want to draw a straight line back to the subpath's origin. If you want to draw a curved line to close the subpath, you'll have to explicitly create a SEG_QUADTO or SEG_CUBICTO segment.

You can examine the PathIterator's current segment using one of the currentSegment() methods:

public abstract int currentSegment(float[] coords)

> This method returns information about the path's current segment. The segment type is returned by the method, and any relevant coordinates are returned in the supplied array. The array should have six elements. SEG_LINETO and SEG_MOVETO segments return a coordinate pair, which is simply the next point in the path. A SEG_QUADTO segment returns two pairs of coordinates; one of these is the next point in the path, while the other is the control point for a quadratic curve. A SEG_CUBICTO segment returns three points. One is the next point in the path, and the other two are the control points for the cubic curve. A SEG_CLOSE segment returns no points. If you try to call this method when you've moved past the end of the path (see next() and isDone() below), you'll get a java.util.NoSuchElementException.

public abstract int currentSegment(double[] coords)

> This method is the same as above, except that it returns coordinates as double values in the supplied array.

PathIterator also includes methods for advancing through the path and testing if the end of the path has been reached:

public abstract void next()

> This method moves the PathIterator forward by one path segment. If you're already at the end of the path, this method does nothing.

public abstract boolean isDone()

 If there are no more segments in this path, this method returns `true`.

The following class includes a static method that prints out the segments of the outline of any `Shape`. It includes a sample `main()` method that prints out the path segments of a rectangle (the `Rectangle` class will be explained later).

```java
import java.awt.*;
import java.awt.geom.*;

public class DescribePath {
  public static void describePath(Shape s) {
    PathIterator pi = s.getPathIterator(null);

    while (pi.isDone() == false) {
      describeCurrentSegment(pi);
      pi.next();
    }
  }

  public static void describeCurrentSegment(PathIterator pi) {
    double[] coordinates = new double[6];
    int type = pi.currentSegment(coordinates);
    switch(type) {
      case PathIterator.SEG_MOVETO:
        System.out.println("move to " +
            coordinates[0] + ", " + coordinates[1]);
        break;
      case PathIterator.SEG_LINETO:
        System.out.println("line to " +
            coordinates[0] + ", " + coordinates[1]);
        break;
      case PathIterator.SEG_QUADTO:
        System.out.println("quadratic to " +
            coordinates[0] + ", " + coordinates[1] + ", " +
            coordinates[2] + ", " + coordinates[3]);
        break;
      case PathIterator.SEG_CUBICTO:
        System.out.println("cubic to " +
            coordinates[0] + ", " + coordinates[1] + ", " +
            coordinates[2] + ", " + coordinates[3] + ", " +
            coordinates[4] + ", " + coordinates[5]);
        break;
      case PathIterator.SEG_CLOSE:
        System.out.println("close");
        break;
      default:
        break;
    }
```

```
    }

    public static void main(String[] args) {
      describePath(new Rectangle2D.Double(0, 0, 72, 72));
    }
  }
```

If you compile and execute `DescribePath`, you'll get the following output:

```
move to 0, 0
line to 72, 0
line to 72, 72
line to 0, 72
line to 0, 0
close
```

What's on the inside?

The `PathIterator` interface defines one more method, `getWindingRule()`. A *winding rule* determines what part of a shape is defined as the interior, and consequently what part of the shape will be filled by a call to `fill()`. Although this is obvious for simple shapes like ellipses and rectangles, it's more ambiguous for complicated shapes with intersecting sides. Consider, for example, the shape shown in Figure 3-8.

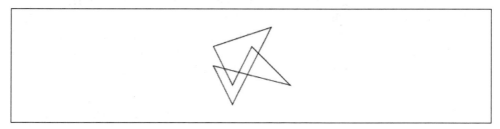

Figure 3-8. A peculiar shape

What is the interior of this shape? The `PathIterator` interface supports two winding rules, represented by constants:

public static final int WIND_EVEN_ODD

This constant represents the *even-odd* winding rule. To see how this winding rule works, draw a line through the entire shape. Each time the line crosses the shape's border, increment a counter. When the counter is even, the line is outside the shape. When the counter is odd, the line is in the interior of the shape. Figure 3-9 shows the shape of Figure 3-8 as filled using the even-odd winding rule. A line has been drawn through the shape to show how the even-odd rule works. The line's intersections with the shape's border are tallied. As you can see, the line is in the interior of the shape when the intersection count is odd. This tells you about only the interior of the shape at points on the test line—to determine the entire interior of the shape, you'd have to draw a lot of lines through the entire shape and apply the same formula to each.

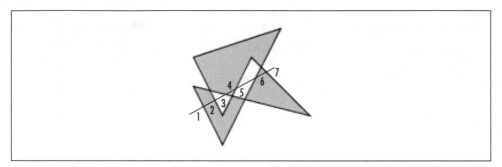

Figure 3-9. Even-odd winding rule

public static final int WIND_NON_ZERO

This constant represents the *non-zero* winding rule. As with the even-odd winding rule, this rule works by drawing a line through the entire shape. Again, the edge crossings are tallied. This time, however, it matters which way the edge is drawn. As the line crosses each edge, a +1 is counted for edges drawn from left to right and a -1 is counted for edges drawn from right to left. Portions of the line where the accumulated count is not zero are considered the interior of the shape. Figure 3-10 shows the shape filled with the non-zero winding rule. It also shows the edge count as the line makes its way through the shape. Curiously, the direction in which you draw the line doesn't make a difference.[*]

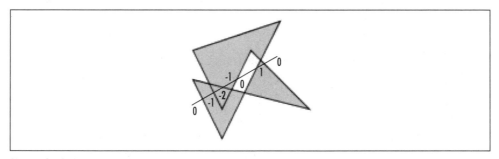

Figure 3-10. Non-zero winding rule

---

[*] You could draw the shape's outline in the reverse direction, but it wouldn't make any difference in how the shape was filled. It would just reverse the sign of the edge count. In the figure above, the edge count tallies would be 0, 1, 2, 1, 0, -1, and 0. Since the zero-ness of the tally is the only thing that matters, this reversal of polarity makes no difference.

To find out the winding rule of a `PathIterator`, use `getWindingRule()`:

public abstract int getWindingRule()
> This method returns the winding rule for this path. It will be either `WIND_EVEN_ODD` or `WIND_NON_ZERO`.

Remember, `PathIterators` are read-only. You can find out the path's winding rule but you can't change it.

NOTE   There is a third winding rule, called *nonexterior*, but it's not supported by Java 2D. It is possible to create shapes with intersecting sides that are not completely filled by either the even-odd or the non-zero rule but are completely filled using the nonexterior rule. If you need the behavior of the nonexterior rule, you may have to break your complex shapes into simpler pieces and use `WIND_NON_ZERO`.

GeneralPath

Lurking behind the `Shape` interface, there's a handy toolbox of shapes in the `java.awt.geom` package—rectangles, ellipses, and so on. I'll discuss these soon. If you want to draw pentagons, decagons, stars, or something completely different, you'll have to describe the path yourself using a `java.awt.geom.GeneralPath`. This class implements the `Shape` interface and allows you to build a path, segment by segment.

public GeneralPath()
> This constructor creates a `GeneralPath` with the default winding rule, `WIND_NON_ZERO`. (Note that `GeneralPath` defines its own winding rule constants, which have the same names as the `PathIterator` winding rule constants.)

public GeneralPath(int rule)
> This constructor creates a `GeneralPath` with the given winding rule, which should be either `GeneralPath.WIND_EVEN_ODD` or `GeneralPath.WIND_NON_ZERO`.

public GeneralPath(int rule, int initialCapacity)
> This advanced constructor allows you to specify the `GeneralPath`'s initial coordinate capacity. You should use this constructor only if you are concerned about performance. The `GeneralPath` stores coordinates internally in an array. When you add more coordinates than the array can hold, a larger array must be allocated, which takes time. If you are concerned about performance and have an idea how many coordinates your `GeneralPath` will contain, you should use this constructor to set the initial capacity of the `GeneralPath`. The other constructors use a default of ten coordinates for the initial capacity.

The initial capacity is a count of coordinates, not of segments. Segments representing moves and lines use two coordinates (one point) each. Quadratic curve segments use four coordinates, representing one endpoint and one control point. Likewise, cubic curve segments use six coordinates, representing the endpoint and two control points. A closing segment has no coordinates associated with it. Thus, a path with one move, two lines, one cubic curve, and one close would use a total of twelve coordinates (six points).

To add segments to the `GeneralPath`, use one of the following methods. There is a method for each of the five segment types.

public void moveTo(float x, float y)
This method moves the current point of the path without drawing anything.

public void lineTo(float x, float y)
This method appends a line segment to the current path. The line is drawn from the current path point to the point specified by `x` and `y`.

public void quadTo(float x1, float y1, float x2, float y2)
This method appends a quadratic curve segment to the path. The control point of the curve is given by `x1` and `y1`, and the endpoint of the curve is `x2` and `y2`.

public void curveTo(float x1, float y1, float x2, float y2, float x3, float y3)
This method adds a cubic curve to the path, using `x3` and `y3` as the endpoint of the curve. The other coordinates are used as the control points of the curve.

public void closePath()
This method closes the current path (or subpath). It's equivalent to drawing a line back to the end of the last move segment. If you'd rather close your path with a curve, you'll have to use a quadratic or cubic curve segment instead.

You can add an entire path to the end of your `GeneralPath` with one of the `append()` methods:

public void append(PathIterator pi, boolean connect)
This method adds the supplied `PathIterator` to this `GeneralPath`. The winding rule of the given path is ignored. If `connect` is `true`, a leading move segment in the given path will be changed to a line segment when it is added to this `PathIterator`.

public void append(Shape s, boolean connect)
This method appends the given shape's path to this `PathIterator`.

The following code creates a `GeneralPath` and draws it:

```
GeneralPath path = new GeneralPath(GeneralPath.WIND_EVEN_ODD);
path.moveTo(50, 50);
```

```
path.lineTo(70, 44);
path.curveTo(100, 10, 140, 80, 160, 80);
path.lineTo(190, 40);
path.lineTo(200, 56);
path.quadTo(100, 150, 70, 60);
path.closePath();
g2.draw(path);
```

Lines and Curves

The 2D API includes shape classes that represent straight and curved line segments. These classes all implement the Shape interface, so they can be rendered and manipulated like any other Shape. Although you could create a single straight or curved line segment yourself using GeneralPath, it's easier to use these canned shape classes. It's interesting that these classes are Shapes, even though they represent the basic segment types that make up a Shape's path.

Line2D

The java.awt.geom.Line2D class represents a line whose coordinates can be retrieved as doubles. Like Point2D, Line2D is abstract. Subclasses can store coordinates in any way they wish. Figure 3-11 shows the hierarchy.

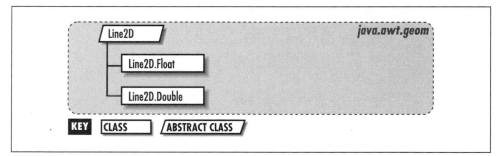

Figure 3-11. Line2D family of classes

Line2D includes several setLine() methods you can use to set a line's endpoints:

public abstract void setLine(double x1, double x2, double y1, double y2)
> This method sets the endpoints of the line to x1, y1, and x2, y2.

public void setLine(Point2D p1, Point2D p2)
> This method sets the endpoints of the line to p1 and p2.

public void setLine(Line2D l)
> This method sets the endpoints of the line to be the same as the endpoints of the given line.

Here are the constructors for the `Line2D.Float` class. Two of them allow you to specify the endpoints of the line, which saves you the trouble of calling `setLine()`.

public Line2D.Float()
  This constructor creates a line whose endpoints are 0, 0 and 0, 0.

public Line2D.Float(float X1, float Y1, float X2, float Y2)
  This constructor creates a line whose endpoints are x1, y1 and x2, y2.

public Line2D.Float(Point2D p1, Point2D p2)
  This constructor creates a line whose endpoints are p1 and p2.

The `Line2D.Double` class has a corresponding set of constructors:

public Line2D.Double()
public Line2D.Double(double X1, double Y1, double X2, double Y2)
public Line2D.Double(Point2D p1, Point2D p2)

The following example shows how to create lines and draw them using different colors. (You'll need to have entered the `ApplicationFrame` class, from Chapter 1, *Introduction,* to run this example.)

```
import java.awt.*;
import java.awt.geom.*;

public class StringArt {
  public static void main(String[] args) {
    Frame f = new ApplicationFrame("StringArt v1.0") {
      private int mNumberOfLines = 25;
      private Color[] mColors = { Color.red, Color.green, Color.blue };

      public void paint(Graphics g) {
        Graphics2D g2 = (Graphics2D)g;

        Dimension d = getSize();
        for (int i = 0; i < mNumberOfLines; i++) {
          double ratio = (double)i / (double)mNumberOfLines;
          Line2D line = new Line2D.Double(0, ratio * d.height,
              ratio * d.width, d.height);
          g2.setPaint(mColors[i % mColors.length]);
          g2.draw(line);
        }
      }
    };
    f.setSize(200, 200);
    f.setVisible(true);
  }
}
```

The example above simply generates a series of lines, using the `Line2D.Double` constructor, and renders them with a call to `draw()`. Figure 3-12 shows how the example looks when it's run.*

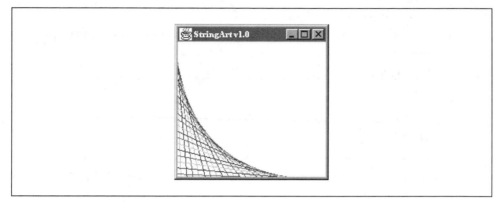

Figure 3-12. Drawing lines

QuadCurve2D

The `java.awt.geom.QuadCurve2D` class represents a quadratic curve segment. As with `Point2D` and `Line2D`, it is an abstract class—child classes decide how coordinates are stored.

You can set the shape of the curve by specifying two endpoints and a control point. `QuadCurve2D` provides a handful of overloaded versions of `setCurve()`:

public abstract void setCurve(double x1, double y1, double ctrlx, double ctrly, double x2, double y2)

This method sets the endpoints of the curve to `x1`, `y1` and `x2`, `y2`. The control point is set to `ctrlx`, `ctrly`.

public void setCurve(Point2D p1, Point2D cp, Point2D p2)

This method sets the endpoints of the curve to `p1` and `p2`. The control point is given by `cp`.

public void setCurve(double[] coords, int offset)

This method sets the quadratic curve using the coordinates supplied in the given array. The endpoints are defined by `coords[offset]`, `coords[offset + 1]`, and `coords[offset + 4]`, `coords[offset + 5]`, while the control point is given by `coords[offset + 2]`, `coords[offset + 3]`.

---

* Sharp-eyed readers will notice that the lines are drawn to the very edges of the frame window and hidden by the frame's borders. To draw only in the interior of the window, you could retrieve the insets of the window using the `getInsets()` method in `Frame`. Then, use the insets to modify the starting and ending points of the lines.

public void setCurve(Point2D[] pts, int offset)

> This method sets the quadratic curve using the points supplied in the given array. The endpoints are `pts[offset]` and `pts[offset + 2]`, while the control point is `pts[offset + 1]`.

public void setCurve(QuadCurve2D c)

> This method sets the curve to have the same endpoints and control point as the supplied curve.

The inner subclass, `QuadCurve2D.Float`, provides two constructors:

public QuadCurve2D.Float()

> This constructor creates a `QuadCurve2D.Float` whose endpoints and control point are all 0, 0.

public QuadCurve2D.Float(float x1, float y1, float ctrlx, float ctrly, float x2, float y2)

> This constructor creates a `QuadCurve2D.Float` using the specified endpoints and control point.

And, of course, `QuadCurve2D.Double` has a corresponding pair of constructors:

public QuadCurve2D.Double()
public QuadCurve2D.Double(double x1, double y1, double ctrlx, double ctrly, double x2,
> *double y2)*

CubicCurve2D

`java.awt.CubicCurve2D` is just like `QuadCurve2D`, except with a second control point. There are similar methods for setting the shape of the curve:

public abstract void setCurve(double x1, double y1, double ctrlx1, double ctrly1,
> *double ctrlx2, double ctrly2, double x2, double y2)*

> This method sets the endpoints of the curve to `x1`, `y1` and `x2`, `y2`. The control points are set to `ctrlx1`, `ctrly1` and `ctrlx2`, `ctrly2`.

public void setCurve(Point2D p1, Point2D cp1, Point2D cp2, Point2D p2)

> This method sets the endpoints of the curve to `p1` and `p2`. The control points are given by `cp1` and `cp2`.

public void setCurve(double[] coords, int offset)

> This method sets the quadratic curve using the coordinates supplied in the given array. The endpoints are defined by `coords[offset]`, `coords[offset + 1]`, and `coords[offset + 6]`, `coords[offset + 7]`, while the control points are given by `coords[offset + 2]`, `coords[offset + 3]` and `coords[offset + 4]`, `coords[offset + 5]`.

public void setCurve(Point2D[] pts, int offset)

This method sets the quadratic curve using the points supplied in the given array. The endpoints are `pts[offset]` and `pts[offset + 3]`, while the control points are `pts[offset + 1]` and `pts[offset + 2]`.

public void setCurve(CubicCurve2D c)

This method sets the curve to have the same endpoints and control points as the supplied curve.

And `CubicCurve2D.Float` provides the following constructors:

public CubicCurve2D.Float()

This constructor creates a `CubicCurve2D.Float` whose endpoints and control points are all 0, 0.

public CubicCurve2D.Float(float x1, float y1, float ctrlx1, float ctrly1, float ctrlx2, float ctrly2, float x2, float y2)

This constructor creates a `CubicCurve2D.Float` using the specified endpoints and control points.

Again, the `CubicCurve2D.Double` inner class has a corresponding pair of constructors:

public CubicCurve2D.Double()
public CubicCurve2D.Double(double x1, double y1, double ctrlx1, double ctrly1, double ctrlx2, double ctrly2, double x2, double y2)

An Interactive Example

This section contains an application, `DragKing`, that draws a line, a quadratic curve, and a cubic curve. It draws small squares to represent the endpoints and control points of each line segment. The tangent lines are also drawn for the curved line segments. Figure 3-13 shows this example in action. The cool part about this example is that you can use the mouse to drag the endpoints and controls points around.

Let's take a look at the details. `DragKing` keeps track of the endpoints and control points using a member variable, `mPoints`, that is an array of points. In its `paint()` method, `DragKing` converts these points to a `CubicCurve2D`, a `QuadCurve2D`, and a `Line2D`. Then each shape is drawn with a call to `Graphics2D`'s `draw()` method:

```
CubicCurve2D c = new CubicCurve2D.Float();
c.setCurve(mPoints, 0);
g2.setPaint(Color.black);
g2.draw(c);
// ...
QuadCurve2D q = new QuadCurve2D.Float();
q.setCurve(mPoints, 4);
```

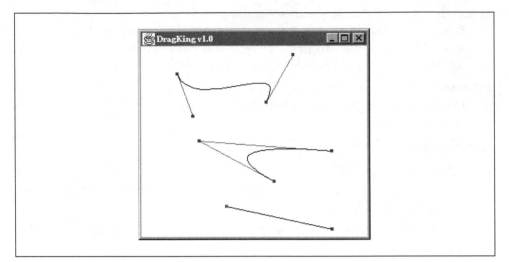

Figure 3-13. The DragKing application

```
// ...
g2.draw(q);
// ...
Line2D l = new Line2D.Float();
l.setLine(mPoints[7], mPoints[8]);
// ...
g2.draw(l);
```

A simple method, `getControlPoint()`, makes a square that represents the control points and the endpoints. This shape is used both for drawing the points and for seeing if the user has clicked on a point with the mouse:

```
protected Shape getControlPoint(Point2D p) {
    // Create a small square around the given point.
    int side = 4;
    return new Rectangle2D.Double(
        p.getX() - side / 2, p.getY() - side / 2,
        side, side);
}
```

Finally, `DragKing` listens for mouse events. Whenever the mouse button is pressed, `DragKing` checks to see if any of its points have been selected:

```
public void mousePressed(MouseEvent me) {
    mSelectedPoint = null;
    for (int i = 0; i < mPoints.length; i++) {
        Shape s = getControlPoint(mPoints[i]);
        if (s.contains(me.getPoint())) {
            mSelectedPoint = mPoints[i];
            break;
        }
```

```
    }
    repaint();
  }
```

If a point is selected, its position can be changed by dragging it around:

```
public void mouseDragged(MouseEvent me) {
  if (mSelectedPoint != null) {
    mSelectedPoint.setLocation(me.getPoint());
    repaint();
  }
}
```

Here's the complete code:

```
import java.awt.*;
import java.awt.event.*;
import java.awt.geom.*;

public class DragKing
    extends ApplicationFrame
    implements MouseListener, MouseMotionListener {
  public static void main(String[] args) {
    new DragKing();
  }

  protected Point2D[] mPoints;
  protected Point2D mSelectedPoint;

  public DragKing() {
    super("DragKing v1.0");
    setSize(300, 300);
    center();

    mPoints = new Point2D[9];
    // Cubic curve.
    mPoints[0] = new Point2D.Double(50, 75);
    mPoints[1] = new Point2D.Double(100, 100);
    mPoints[2] = new Point2D.Double(200, 50);
    mPoints[3] = new Point2D.Double(250, 75);
    // Quad curve.
    mPoints[4] = new Point2D.Double(50, 175);
    mPoints[5] = new Point2D.Double(150, 150);
    mPoints[6] = new Point2D.Double(250, 175);
    // Line.
    mPoints[7] = new Point2D.Double(50, 275);
    mPoints[8] = new Point2D.Double(250, 275);

    mSelectedPoint = null;

    // Listen for mouse events.
```

```
    addMouseListener(this);
    addMouseMotionListener(this);

    setVisible(true);
  }

  public void paint(Graphics g) {
    Graphics2D g2 = (Graphics2D)g;

    // Draw the tangents.
    Line2D tangent1 = new Line2D.Double(mPoints[0], mPoints[1]);
    Line2D tangent2 = new Line2D.Double(mPoints[2], mPoints[3]);
    g2.setPaint(Color.gray);
    g2.draw(tangent1);
    g2.draw(tangent2);
    // Draw the cubic curve.
    CubicCurve2D c = new CubicCurve2D.Float();
    c.setCurve(mPoints, 0);
    g2.setPaint(Color.black);
    g2.draw(c);

    // Draw the tangents.
    tangent1 = new Line2D.Double(mPoints[4], mPoints[5]);
    tangent2 = new Line2D.Double(mPoints[5], mPoints[6]);
    g2.setPaint(Color.gray);
    g2.draw(tangent1);
    g2.draw(tangent2);
    // Draw the quadratic curve.
    QuadCurve2D q = new QuadCurve2D.Float();
    q.setCurve(mPoints, 4);
    g2.setPaint(Color.black);
    g2.draw(q);

    // Draw the line.
    Line2D l = new Line2D.Float();
    l.setLine(mPoints[7], mPoints[8]);
    g2.setPaint(Color.black);
    g2.draw(l);

    for (int i = 0; i < mPoints.length; i++) {
      // If the point is selected, use the selected color.
      if (mPoints[i] == mSelectedPoint)
        g2.setPaint(Color.red);
      else
        g2.setPaint(Color.blue);
      // Draw the point.
      g2.fill(getControlPoint(mPoints[i]));
    }
  }
```

```
      protected Shape getControlPoint(Point2D p) {
        // Create a small square around the given point.
        int side = 4;
        return new Rectangle2D.Double(
            p.getX() - side / 2, p.getY() - side / 2,
            side, side);
      }

      public void mouseClicked(MouseEvent me) {}
      public void mousePressed(MouseEvent me) {
        mSelectedPoint = null;
        for (int i = 0; i < mPoints.length; i++) {
          Shape s = getControlPoint(mPoints[i]);
          if (s.contains(me.getPoint())) {
            mSelectedPoint = mPoints[i];
            break;
          }
        }
        repaint();
      }
      public void mouseReleased(MouseEvent me) {}
      public void mouseMoved(MouseEvent me) {}
      public void mouseDragged(MouseEvent me) {
        if (mSelectedPoint != null) {
          mSelectedPoint.setLocation(me.getPoint());
          repaint();
        }
      }

      public void mouseEntered(MouseEvent me) {}
      public void mouseExited(MouseEvent me) {}
    }
```

Rectangles

RectangularShape

As Figure 3-3 shows, java.awt.geom.RectangularShape is an important class. It's the abstract parent class of the rectangle, rounded rectangle, arc, and ellipse classes in java.awt.geom. It implements the methods of Shape and adds a few of its own.

First, a RectangularShape returns information about its location and size:

public abstract double getX()
    This method returns the horizontal location of the left side of the rectangle.

public abstract double getY()
> This method returns the vertical location of the top side of the rectangle.

public abstract double getWidth()
> This method returns the width of the rectangle.

public abstract double getHeight()
> This method returns the height of the rectangle.

public double getMinX()
> This method returns the smallest x coordinate of the rectangle.

public double getMaxX()
> This method returns the largest x coordinate of the rectangle.

public double getMinY()
> This method returns the smallest y coordinate of the rectangle.

public double getMaxY()
> This method returns the largest y coordinate of the rectangle.

Two methods are provided to examine the center point of the rectangle:

public double getCenterX()
public double getCenterY()

A rectangular shape is empty if its width and height are 0. The `isEmpty()` method returns `true` in this case:

public abstract boolean isEmpty()

Finally, `RectangularShape` includes three methods for setting the bounds of the shape:

public abstract void setFrame(double x, double y, double w, double h)
> This method sets the location of the rectangle to x, y, and its width and height to w and h.

public abstract void setFrame(Point2D loc, Dimension2D size)
> This method sets the location of the rectangle to loc, and its width and height to the given dimensions.*

public abstract void setFrame(Rectangle2D r)
> This method sets the bounds of the rectangle to be the same as in the supplied rectangle.

---

* `java.awt.geom.Dimension2D` is the double precision version of the `java.awt.Dimension` class. It has `getWidth()` and `getHeight()` methods that return `double`s. In Java 2, `java.awt.Dimension` is its only concrete subclass. Wherever you need a `Dimension2D`, you can simply pass a `Dimension` instance.

You can also define the bounds of the RectangularShape by specifying two endpoints of a diagonal. In other words, you can specify the locations of two opposing corners:

public abstract void setFrameFromDiagonal(double x1, double y1, double x2, double y2)
public abstract void setFrameFromDiagonal(Point2D p1, Point2D p2)

Finally, you can set the bounds of the rectangle by specifying the center point and one of the corners:

public abstract void setFrameFromCenter(double centerX, double centerY, double cornerX,
    double cornerY)
public abstract void setFrameFromCenter(Point2D p1, Point2D p2)

Rectangle2D

Like the Point2D class, java.awt.geom.Rectangle2D is abstract. Two inner subclasses, Rectangle2D.Double and Rectangle2D.Float, provide concrete representations.

Because so much functionality is already in Rectangle2D's parent class, RectangularShape, there are only a few new methods defined in Rectangle2D. First, you can set a Rectangle2D's position and size using setRect():

public abstract void setRect(double x, double y, double w, double h)
public void setRect(Rectangle2D r)
> These methods work just like the setFrame() methods with the same argument types.

Two methods are provided to test if a line intersects a rectangle:

public boolean intersectsLine(double x1, double y1, double x2, double y2)
> If the line described by x1, y1, x2, and y2 intersects this Rectangle2D, this method returns true.

public boolean intersectsLine(Line2D l)
> If the line represented by l intersects this Rectangle2D, this method returns true.

Two other methods will tell where a point is, with respect to a rectangle. Rectangle2D includes some constants that describe the position of a point outside a rectangle. A combination of constants is returned as appropriate.

public abstract int outcode(double x, double y)
public int outcode(Point2D p)
> These methods return some combination of OUT_TOP, OUT_BOTTOM, OUT_LEFT, and OUT_RIGHT, indicating where the given point lies with respect to this Rectangle2D. For points inside the rectangle, this method returns 0.

Figure 3-14 shows the return values of outcode() in the regions around a rectangle.

OUT_TOP	OUT_LEFT	OUT_TOP	OUT_TOP	OUT_RIGHT
	OUT_LEFT		OUT_RIGHT	
OUT_BOTTOM	OUT_LEFT	OUT_BOTTOM	OUT_BOTTOM	OUT_RIGHT

Figure 3-14. Return values of Rectangle2D's outcode() method

The Old Rectangle

But wait a minute. Didn't JDK 1.0 have a Rectangle class? It did indeed: java. awt.Rectangle still exists in Java 2, for backwards compatibility, but it is now a subclass of Rectangle2D. Just as Rectangle2D.Double stores a rectangle's coordinates using doubles, java.awt.Rectangle stores its coordinates as integers. The complete Rectangle2D family is shown in Figure 3-15.

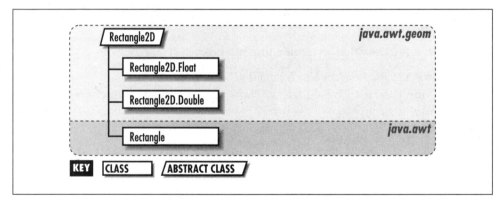

Figure 3-15. Rectangle2D family of classes

RoundRectangle2D

A *round rectangle* is a rectangle with curved corners, represented by instances of java.awt.geom.RoundRectangle2D. Figure 3-16 shows a RoundRectangle2D's outline.

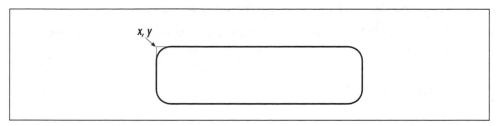

Figure 3-16. A RoundRectangle2D in the wild

Interestingly, a round rectangle's location is outside its outline. (Remember, you can retrieve the location using the getX() and getY() methods of RectangularShape.)

Round rectangles are specified with a location, a width, a height, and the height and width of the curved corners. Figure 3-17 shows the arc width and arc height on a RoundRectangle2D.

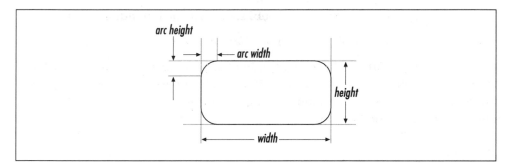

Figure 3-17. RoundRectangle2D parameters

To set the location, size, and corner arcs of a RoundRectangle2D, use the following method:

public abstract void setRoundRect(double x, double y, double w, double h, double arcWidth, double arcHeight)
This method sets the location of this round rectangle to x and y. The width and height are provided by w and h, and the corner arc lengths are arcWidth and arcHeight.

Like the other geometry classes, RoundRectangle2D is abstract. Two concrete subclasses are provided. RoundRectangle2D.Float uses floats to store its coordinates. One of its constructors allows you to completely specify the rounded rectangle:

public RoundRectangle2D.Float(float x, float y, float w, float h, float arcw, float arch)
This constructor creates a RoundRectangle2D.Float using the specified location, width, height, arc width, and arc height.

`RoundRectangle2D.Double` has a corresponding constructor:

public RoundRectangle2D.Double(double x, double y, double w, double h, double arcw,
    double arch)

Ellipses and Arcs

Ellipse2D

An ellipse, like a rectangle, is fully defined by a location, a width, and a height. As with the other geometry classes, `java.awt.geom.Ellipse2D` is abstract. A concrete inner subclass, `Ellipse2D.Float`, stores its coordinates as `floats`:

public Ellipse2D.Float(float x, float y, float w, float h)
    This constructor creates an `Ellipse2D.Float` using the specified location, width, and height.

Another inner subclass, `Ellipse2D.Double`, offers a corresponding constructor:

public Ellipse2D.Double(double x, double y, double w, double h)

Note that `Ellipse2D` is a descendent of `RectangularShape`. While this may not seem very intuitive, it does mean that `Ellipse2D` inherits all of `Rectangular-Shape`'s methods. As with round rectangles, an ellipse's location (x and y) is outside the outline of the ellipse.

Arc2D

The 2D API includes `java.awt.geom.Arc2D` for drawing pieces of an ellipse. `Arc2D` defines three different kinds of arcs, as shown in Figure 3-18. These are represented by constants in the `Arc2D` class:

public static final int OPEN
    This constant represents an open arc. This simply defines a curved line that is a portion of an ellipse's outline.

public static final int PIE
    This constant represents an arc in the shape of a slice of pie. This outline is produced by drawing the curved arc as well as straight lines from the arc's endpoints to the center of the ellipse that defines the arc.

public static final int CHORD
    In this arc type, a straight line is drawn to connect the two endpoints of the arc.

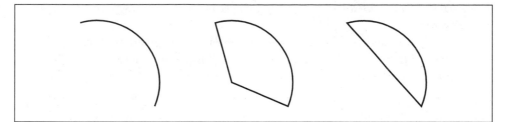

Figure 3-18. Arc flavors: from left to right, OPEN, PIE, and CHORD

Arc2D provides quite a few different ways to set the size and parameters of the arc:

public abstract void setArc(double x, double y, double w, double h, double angSt,
  double angExt, int closure)

This method sets the shape of the arc using the given parameters. The arc will be part of the ellipse defined by x, y, w, and h. x and y are the top left corner of the bounding box of the ellipse, while w and h are the width and height of the bounding box. The given angles determine the start angle and angular extent of the arc. Finally, the new arc has the type given by closure. Figure 3-19 shows the relationship of this method's parameters to the arc.

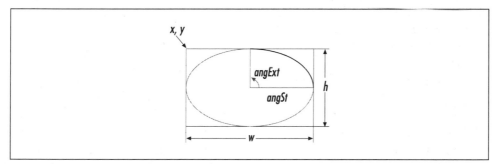

Figure 3-19. Arc2D parameters, with a starting angle of 0° and an extent of 90°

public void setArc(Point2D loc, Dimension2D size, double angSt, double angExt, int closure)

This method is the same as the previous method, except the supplied Point2D and Dimension2D are used to specify the location and size of the whole ellipse.

public void setArc(Rectangle2D rect, double angSt, double angExt, int closure)

This method is the same as the previous method, except the given rectangle gives the location and size of the arc's ellipse.

public void setArc(Arc2D a)

This method makes this arc have the same shape as the supplied Arc2D.

public void setArcByCenter(double x, double y, double radius, double angSt, double angExt, int closure)

> This method specifies an arc from a center point, given by x and y, and a radius. The angle start, angle extent, and closure parameters are the same as before. Note that this method will only produce arcs that are part of a circle.

Like the other geometry classes, Arc2D is abstract, with Arc2D.Float and Arc2D. Double as concrete subclasses. Arc2D.Float has four useful constructors:

public Arc2D.Float()

> This constructor creates a new OPEN arc.

public Arc2D.Float(int type)

> This constructor creates a new arc of the given type, which should be OPEN, PIE, or CHORD.

public Arc2D.Float(float x, float y, float w, float h, float start, float extent, int type)
public Arc2D.Float(Rectangle2D ellipseBounds, float start, float extent, int type)

> This constructor is the same as the previous constructor, but it uses the supplied rectangle as the ellipse's bounding box.

The other inner subclass, Arc2D.Double, has four corresponding constructors:

public Arc2D.Double()
public Arc2D.Double(int type)
public Arc2D.Double(double x, double y, double w, double h, double start, double extent, int type)
public Arc2D.Double(Rectangle2D ellipseBounds, float start, float extent, int type)

There are two things you need to know about arc angles:

1. They're measured in degrees. This might not seem like a big deal, but it's important. In Chapter 5, *Rendering*, you'll find out that rotational transformations are measured in radians. So every time you need an angle, make sure you know which units you're using.

2. Finally, the arc angles aren't really genuine angles. Instead, they're defined relative to the arc's ellipse, such that a 45° arc angle is always defined as the line from the center of the ellipse through a corner of the bounding box of the ellipse. Figure 3-20 shows an arc that goes from 0° to 45°, measured as arc angles. The figure also shows the true 45° angle. If the arc's ellipse is a circle, the two angles are equal.

Constructive Area Geometry

Constructive area geometry is a fancy name for combining shapes. Two or more shapes can be combined using different rules or *operations*, much the way numbers

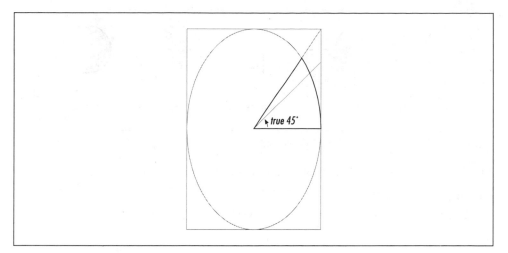

Figure 3-20. Skewing of arc angles

can be combined in an equation. The 2D API supports four different operations
for combining the areas of two shapes:

addition (union)

> The addition of two shapes is the area covered by one or both of the shapes.

intersection

> The intersection of two shapes is the area that is covered by both shapes
> simultaneously.

subtraction

> The result of subtracting one shape from another is the area covered by one
> that is not covered by the other.

exclusive or

> The exclusive or operator is the inverse of the intersection operator. In other
> words, the exclusive or of two shapes is the area that is covered by one or the
> other of the shapes. But it does not include the area covered by both.

It's hard to visualize these operators just by reading about them. Figure 3-21 shows
the result of applying these operators to two overlapping shapes.

In Java 2D, the `java.awt.geom.Area` class supports constructive area geometry.
This class offers two constructors:

public Area()

> This constructor creates an empty `Area`. You can accumulate area using the
> `add()` method, described below.

public Area(Shape g)

> This constructor creates an `Area` using the interior of the supplied `Shape`.

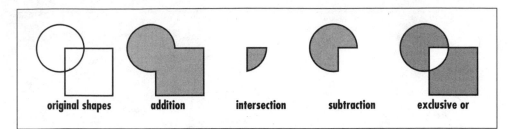

original shapes   addition   intersection   subtraction   exclusive or

Figure 3-21. Different ways of combining two shapes

The four area operators are implemented as `Area`'s methods:

public void add(Area rhs)
    Use this method to add the given area, `rhs`, to this `Area`.

public void intersect(Area rhs)
    This method modifies this `Area` to represent the intersection of its original shape and the supplied area.

public void subtract(Area rhs)
    Use this method to subtract the area represented by `rhs` from this `Area`.

public void exclusiveOr(Area rhs)
    This method modifies this `Area` so that it represents the exclusive or of its original shape and the given area.

`Area` itself implements the `Shape` interface. Once you've created an `Area` that you like, you can draw it, fill it, and manipulate it like any other `Shape`.

The following interactive example, `CombiningShapes`, demonstrates the four area operators. It displays two shapes and a combo box that allows you to choose which area operator will be used to combine the shapes. All of this is accomplished in two methods and one constructor. The `main()` method sets up a frame window to contain the example. `CombiningShapes`'s constructor creates the two shapes and a combo box that holds the area operator names. Finally, the `paint()` method combines the two shapes according to the selected operator and draws the result. Figure 3-22 shows how this example looks while it's running.

```
import java.awt.*;
import java.awt.event.*;
import java.awt.geom.*;

import javax.swing.*;

public class CombiningShapes
    extends JComponent {
  public static void main(String[] args) {
    ApplicationFrame f = new ApplicationFrame("CombiningShapes v1.0");
```

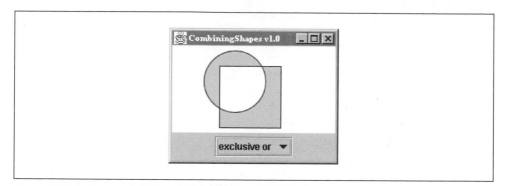

Figure 3-22. An interactive constructive area geometry example

```
    f.add(new CombiningShapes());
    f.setSize(220, 220);
    f.center();
    f.setVisible(true);
  }

  private Shape mShapeOne, mShapeTwo;
  private JComboBox mOptions;

  public CombiningShapes() {
    // Create the two shapes, a circle and a square.
    mShapeOne = new Ellipse2D.Double(40, 20, 80, 80);
    mShapeTwo = new Rectangle2D.Double(60, 40, 80, 80);
    setBackground(Color.white);
    setLayout(new BorderLayout());
    // Create a panel to hold the combo box.
    JPanel controls = new JPanel();
    // Create the combo box with the names of the area operators.
    mOptions = new JComboBox(
      new String[] { "outline", "add", "intersection",
          "subtract", "exclusive or" }
    );
    // Repaint ourselves when the selection changes.
    mOptions.addItemListener(new ItemListener() {
      public void itemStateChanged(ItemEvent ie) {
        repaint();
      }
    });
    controls.add(mOptions);
    add(controls, BorderLayout.SOUTH);
  }

  public void paintComponent(Graphics g) {
    Graphics2D g2 = (Graphics2D)g;
    g2.setRenderingHint(RenderingHints.KEY_ANTIALIASING,
```

```
                RenderingHints.VALUE_ANTIALIAS_ON);

        // Retrieve the selection option from the combo box.
        String option = (String)mOptions.getSelectedItem();
        if (option.equals("outline")) {
            // Just draw the outlines and return.
            g2.draw(mShapeOne);
            g2.draw(mShapeTwo);
            return;
        }
        // Create Areas from the shapes.
        Area areaOne = new Area(mShapeOne);
        Area areaTwo = new Area(mShapeTwo);
        // Combine the Areas according to the selected option.
        if (option.equals("add")) areaOne.add(areaTwo);
        else if (option.equals("intersection")) areaOne.intersect(areaTwo);
        else if (option.equals("subtract")) areaOne.subtract(areaTwo);
        else if (option.equals("exclusive or")) areaOne.exclusiveOr(areaTwo);

        // Fill the resulting Area.
        g2.setPaint(Color.orange);
        g2.fill(areaOne);
        // Draw the outline of the resulting Area.
        g2.setPaint(Color.black);
        g2.draw(areaOne);
    }
}
```

Painting and Stroking

In the last chapter, we saw how shapes are defined in the 2D API. But what can you do with shapes?

- *Painting* is the process of filling the interior of the shape with a color, color gradient, or texture.

- *Stroking* is the process of drawing the shape's outline. You can draw an outline using different line widths, line styles, and colors.

Painting and stroking are very closely related. Stroking, in fact, is just the process of creating a shape that represents an outline and filling it. You can draw outlines using any type of paint. Figure 4-1 shows some examples. On the left, a circle has been filled with a color gradient. In the middle, the same circle's outline is drawn with a thick line using a solid color. On the right, the circle's outline is drawn with the same thick line using the color gradient.

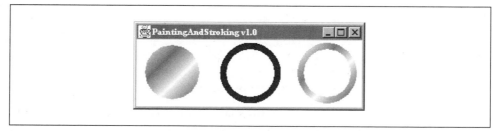

Figure 4-1. Examples of painting and stroking

The following class produces the window shown in Figure 4-1. It uses some unfamiliar methods and classes: setPaint(), setStroke(), GradientPaint, and BasicStroke. I'll explain these classes and methods, and more, in the rest of the chapter. For now, this example should show you some of the potential of painting and stroking:

```
import java.awt.*;
import java.awt.geom.*;

public class PaintingAndStroking
     extends ApplicationFrame {
  public static void main(String[] args) {
    PaintingAndStroking f = new PaintingAndStroking();
    f.setTitle("PaintingAndStroking v1.0");
    f.setSize(300, 150);
    f.center();
    f.setVisible(true);
  }

  public void paint(Graphics g) {
    Graphics2D g2 = (Graphics2D)g;
    double x = 15, y = 50, w = 70, h = 70;
    Ellipse2D e = new Ellipse2D.Double(x, y, w, h);
    GradientPaint gp = new GradientPaint(75, 75, Color.white,
         95, 95, Color.gray, true);
    // Fill with a gradient.
    g2.setPaint(gp);
    g2.fill(e);
    // Stroke with a solid color.
    e.setFrame(x + 100, y, w, h);
    g2.setPaint(Color.black);
    g2.setStroke(new BasicStroke(8));
    g2.draw(e);
    // Stroke with a gradient.
    e.setFrame(x + 200, y, w, h);
    g2.setPaint(gp);
    g2.draw(e);
  }
}
```

Painting

Filling the interior of a shape is a two-step process:

1. First, tell the Graphics2D how to fill shapes with a call to setPaint(). This method accepts any object that implements the java.awt.Paint interface. The Graphics2D stores the Paint away as part of its state. When it comes time to fill a shape, Graphics2D will use the Paint to determine what colors should be used to fill the shape. The 2D API comes with three kinds of

"canned" paints: solid colors, a linear color gradient, and a texture fill. You can add your own `Paint` implementations if you wish.

2. Now you can tell `Graphics2D` to fill a shape by passing it to `fill()`.

Paints are *immutable*, which means they can't be modified after they are created. The reason for this is to avoid funky behavior when rendering. Imagine, for example, if you wanted to fill a series of shapes with a solid color. First, you'd call `setPaint()` on the `Graphics2D`; then you would paint the shapes using `fill()`. But what if another part of your program changed the `Paint` that `Graphics2D` was using? The results might be quite bizarre. For this reason, objects that implement `Paint` should not allow themselves to be changed after they are created.

Figure 4-2 shows the three types of painting supported by the 2D API. The figure contains three shapes:

- The ellipse is filled with a solid color.

- The rounded rectangle is filled with a color gradient.

- The arc is filled with a texture, built from van Gogh's *Starry Night*.

Figure 4-2. Three shapes and three paints

Solid Colors

The `java.awt.Color` class implements the `Paint` interface. Thus, any `Color` may be used to fill the interior of a shape. The correct handling of color is a big can of worms—we'll cover it fully in Chapter 8, *Color*. In the meantime, let's take a quick look at `Color`. First, the `Color` class includes some useful colors as static member variables:

```
public static final Color white;
public static final Color lightGray;
public static final Color gray;
public static final Color darkGray;
public static final Color black;
public static final Color red;
public static final Color pink;
public static final Color orange;
public static final Color yellow;
public static final Color green;
```

```
public static final Color magenta;
public static final Color cyan;
public static final Color blue;
```

If you don't see a color you like, it's easy to create a new color by specifying red, green, and blue values. Colors created in this way are part of a default standard RGB color space called sRGB. We'll talk all about this concept in Chapter 8. You can create new colors using integers or floating point values:

public Color(int r, int g, int b)

This constructor creates a new `Color` using the specified values for red, green and blue. The values should range from 0 to 255, inclusive.

public Color(float r, float g, float b)

This constructor creates a new `Color` using the specified values for red, green and blue. The values should range from 0.0 to 1.0, inclusive.

In the following example, a pie-shaped arc is filled with the color blue.

```
import java.awt.*;
import java.awt.geom.*;

public class SolidPaint
    extends ApplicationFrame {
  public static void main(String[] args) {
    SolidPaint f = new SolidPaint();
    f.setTitle("SolidPaint v1.0");
    f.setSize(200, 200);
    f.center();
    f.setVisible(true);
  }

  public void paint(Graphics g) {
    Graphics2D g2 = (Graphics2D)g;
    Arc2D pie = new Arc2D.Float(0, 50, 150, 150, -30, 90, Arc2D.PIE);
    g2.setPaint(Color.blue);
    g2.fill(pie);
  }
}
```

You may remember that `setColor()`, defined in `Graphics`, could be used to affect the color of filled shapes. In the 2D API, it is now a convenience method; a call to `setColor(c)` on a `Graphics2D` is equivalent to calling `setPaint(c)`.

Swing's Color Chooser Dialog

If you want your users to be able to choose colors in your application, you're in luck. Swing has a ready-made dialog for this purpose. The name of the class is `javax.swing.JColorChooser`. You can use this dialog with one line of code, using the following static method:

public static Color showDialog(Component component, String title, Color initialColor)

This method displays a color chooser dialog. The supplied `Component` is used as the parent component of the dialog. The dialog will have the supplied title; its controls will be initialized to show the given `initialColor`.

The following example demonstrates the use of this dialog. You can invoke the color chooser by pressing the button. After you've made a selection, the background of the frame window changes to the selected color.

```java
import java.awt.*;
import java.awt.event.*;

import javax.swing.*;

public class RedTown
    extends JFrame {
  public static void main(String[] args) {
    new RedTown();
  }

  public RedTown() {
    super("RedTown v1.0");
    createUI();
    setVisible(true);
  }

  protected void createUI() {
    setSize(400, 400);
    setLocation(100, 100);
    getContentPane().setLayout(new GridBagLayout());
    JButton colorButton = new JButton("Choose a color...");
    getContentPane().add(colorButton);
    colorButton.addActionListener(new ActionListener() {
      public void actionPerformed(ActionEvent ae) {
        Color c = JColorChooser.showDialog(
            RedTown.this, "Choose a color...", getBackground());
        if (c != null) getContentPane().setBackground(c);
      }
    });

    addWindowListener(new WindowAdapter() {
      public void windowClosing(WindowEvent we) {
        System.exit(0);
      }
    });
  }
}
```

For more information about the color chooser dialog, see *Java Swing*, by Robert Eckstein, Marc Loy, and Dave Wood (O'Reilly).

GradientPaint

A *gradient* is a smooth transition from one color to another. In the late evening on a clear day, the sky has a gradient from dark blue at the horizon to black over-head. The 2D API provides an implementation of a simple color gradient, called `java.awt.GradientPaint`. This class defines a color gradient using two points and two colors. The gradient smoothly shifts from one color to the other as you move along the line that connects the two points, which I'll call the *gradient line*. The `GradientPaint` creates parallel bands of color, perpendicular to the gradient line. Figure 4-3 shows a gradient that runs from white to dark gray. The gradient line and its endpoints are also shown.

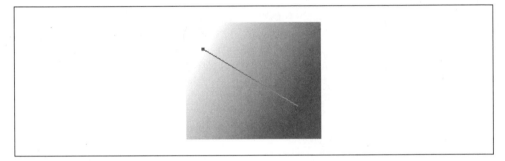

Figure 4-3. An acyclic linear gradient

`GradientPaints` may be *cyclic* or *acyclic*. In an acyclic `GradientPaint`, any points beyond the end of the gradient line are the same color as the endpoint of the line, as shown in Figure 4-3. In a cyclic `GradientPaint`, the colors continue to shift beyond the end of the gradient line, as though the gradient line segment were mirrored and replicated ad infinitum. Figure 4-4 shows what this looks like.

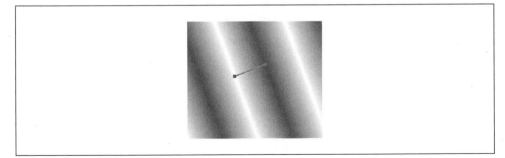

Figure 4-4. A cyclic linear gradient

NOTE   The appearance of a gradient depends on your screen settings. If your display uses fewer than 24 bits per pixel (bpp), for example, you may see bands of color in gradients, rather than a smooth transition from one color to another.

To create a `GradientPaint`, you simply need to supply two points and two `Color`s. By default, `GradientPaint`s are acyclic.

public GradientPaint(Point2D pt1, Color color1, Point2D pt2, Color color2)
public GradientPaint(float x1, float y1, Color color1, float x2, float y2, Color color2)
> These constructors create acyclic `GradientPaint`s. The gradient runs from `color1` at the first point to `color2` at the second point.

public GradientPaint(Point2D pt1, Color color1, Point2D pt2, Color color2, boolean cyclic)
public GradientPaint(float x1, float y1, Color color1, float x2, float y2, Color color2, boolean cyclic)
> These constructors create `GradientPaint`s that run from `color1` at the first point to `color2` at the second point. If the `cyclic` parameter is `true`, the gradient will be cyclic.

You can retrieve the parameters of the gradient paint with the following methods:

public Point2D getPoint1()
public Color getColor1()
public Point2D getPoint2()
public Color getColor2()
public boolean isCyclic()

The next example shows how to create a circle and fill it with a cyclic gradient:

```
import java.awt.*;
import java.awt.geom.*;

public class GradientPaintFill
    extends ApplicationFrame {
  public static void main(String[] args) {
    GradientPaintFill f = new GradientPaintFill();
    f.setTitle("GradientPaintFill v1.0");
    f.setSize(200, 200);
    f.center();
    f.setVisible(true);
  }

  public void paint(Graphics g) {
    Graphics2D g2 = (Graphics2D)g;
    Ellipse2D e = new Ellipse2D.Float(40, 40, 120, 120);
```

```
        GradientPaint gp = new GradientPaint(75, 75, Color.white,
            95, 95, Color.gray, true);
      g2.setPaint(gp);
      g2.fill(e);
   }
 }
```

TexturePaint

The third type of `Paint` is a *texture* fill. In the 2D API, a texture is created using an image that is repeated over and over, like a kitchen floor tile. The `java.awt.TexturePaint` class represents a texture. You can construct a `TexturePaint` with two pieces of information:

1. The image to be used should be supplied as a `BufferedImage`. I'll talk about images in detail in Chapter 9, *Images* For now, just think of a `BufferedImage` as a rectangular picture.

2. A `Rectangle2D` specifies how the image will be replicated to form the texture. I'll call this the *texture rectangle*.

The image is scaled to fit in the given rectangle. This rectangle is reproduced like a floor tile to build the texture. Figure 4-5 shows a `TexturePaint` and its texture rectangle. Note that the image is drawn to exactly fill the texture rectangle.

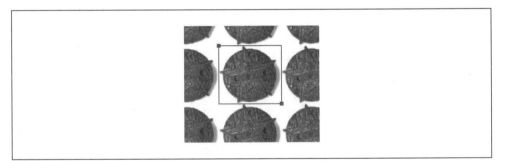

Figure 4-5. A texture fill

Figure 4-6 shows a `TexturePaint` built from the same image. In this case, however, the texture rectangle is smaller—and the image is scaled to fit.

Creating a `TexturePaint` is as simple as specifying an image and a rectangle:

public TexturePaint(BufferedImage txtr, Rectangle2D anchor)
    This constructor creates a `TexturedImage` that replicates the supplied image using the anchor rectangle.

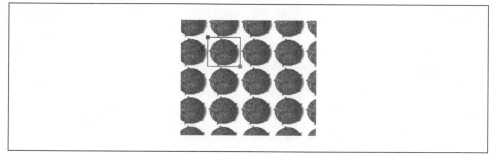

Figure 4-6. A texture with a small texture rectangle

You can retrieve the image and the rectangle of a `TexturePaint` with the following methods:

public BufferedImage getImage()
public Rectangle2D getAnchorRect()

The following example shows how to create a `TexturePaint` from a JPEG image file. The constructor takes care of these details, which I'll describe fully in Chapter 9. In the `paint()` method, the image is used to create a `TexturePaint`. Then the texture is used to fill a rounded rectangle.

```
import java.awt.*;
import java.awt.geom.*;
import java.awt.image.BufferedImage;
import java.io.*;

import com.sun.image.codec.jpeg.*;

public class TexturePaintFill
    extends ApplicationFrame {
  public static void main(String[] args) throws Exception {
    TexturePaintFill f = new TexturePaintFill("roa2.jpg");
    f.setTitle("TexturePaintFill v1.0");
    f.setSize(200, 200);
    f.center();
    f.setVisible(true);
  }

  private BufferedImage mImage;

  public TexturePaintFill(String filename)
      throws IOException, ImageFormatException {
    // Load the specified JPEG file.
    InputStream in = getClass().getResourceAsStream(filename);
    JPEGImageDecoder decoder = JPEGCodec.createJPEGDecoder(in);
    mImage = decoder.decodeAsBufferedImage();
```

```
    in.close();
  }

  public void paint(Graphics g) {
    Graphics2D g2 = (Graphics2D)g;
    // Create a round rectangle.
    RoundRectangle2D r =
        new RoundRectangle2D.Float(25, 35, 150, 150, 25, 25);
    // Create a texture rectangle the same size as the texture image.
    Rectangle2D tr = new Rectangle2D.Double(0, 0,
        mImage.getWidth(), mImage.getHeight());
    // Create the TexturePaint.
    TexturePaint tp = new TexturePaint(mImage, tr);
    // Now fill the round rectangle.
    g2.setPaint(tp);
    g2.fill(r);
  }
}
```

Under the Hood

How does the `Paint` interface really work? Every `Paint` object has an associated context, a `java.awt.PaintContext`, which knows what colors to put on a drawing surface. When `Graphics2D` needs to fill a shape, it asks its current `Paint` for the corresponding `PaintContext`. Then it uses the `PaintContext` to actually put color on the drawing surface.

The Transparency interface

`Paint` is a subinterface of `java.awt.Transparency`, an interface which describes an object's use of alpha. It describes three modes, represented by constants:

public static final int OPAQUE
> This constant represents objects whose pixels are all opaque (alpha is 1.0 everywhere).

public static final int BITMASK
> This constant represents objects whose pixels are either opaque or completely transparent (alpha is 1.0 or 0.0).

public static final int TRANSLUCENT
> This constant is used for objects whose pixels may have any values of alpha.

The `Transparency` interface has only one method:

public int getTransparency()
> This method returns the transparency mode, either OPAQUE, BITMASK, or TRANSLUCENT.

The `Transparency` interface is implemented by the `ColorModel` class, which is related to images and drawing surfaces (see Chapter 11, *Image Guts*).

The Paint interface

As I mentioned, `Transparency` is the parent interface of `Paint`. The `Paint` interface itself has only one method—it just knows how to generate a `PaintContext`:

public PaintContext createContext(ColorModel cm, Rectangle deviceBounds, Rectangle2D userBounds, AffineTransform xform, RenderingHints hints)
> This method is called to create a `PaintContext`. The `PaintContext` is encouraged to produce colors in the given color model (see Chapter 11). The `deviceBounds` rectangle indicates the bounds of the drawing surface, while `userBounds` indicates the bounds of the shape that is being filled. The supplied `AffineTransform` (see Chapter 5, *Rendering*) indicates the transformation currently in effect, while `hints` contains information that the `PaintContext` can use to modify its behavior. The `TexturePaint` context, for example, is responsive to the `KEY_INTERPOLATION` hint. See Chapter 5 for an explanation of rendering hints.

Simple `Paint` implementations can ignore a lot of the parameters that are passed to `createContext()`, as you'll see in an upcoming example.

The PaintContext interface

The `PaintContext` returned by `createContext()` knows how to actually generate the colors of the `Paint`. The `PaintContext` interface defines three methods:

public void dispose()
> This method is called when the `PaintContext` is no longer needed. If you've allocated any images or other large objects, you can free up their references in this method.

public ColorModel getColorModel()
> This method returns the color model that will be used for this context's output. This could be a different color model than the one suggested in the `createContext()` method, back in the `Paint` interface.

public Raster getRaster(int x, int y, int w, int h)
> This is the mother lode of the `PaintContext` interface. This method returns a `Raster` that contains the color data that should be used to fill a shape. (The `Raster` class is part of 2D's image classes. See Chapter 11.)

There's a lot of material here that I won't cover until later chapters. But to show you how simple a `Paint` can be, I'll present a custom implementation of the `Paint` interface.

A radial color gradient

The goal of this example is to create a round, or radial, gradient. This gradient defines a color at a point; the gradient blends into another color as a function of the distance from that point. The end result is a big, fuzzy spot. Figure C-2 shows a round rectangle that is filled with the radial gradient.

The implementation consists of two classes, RoundGradientPaint and RoundGradientContext. RoundGradientPaint doesn't do much except return a RoundGradientPaintContext from its createContext() method. Round-GradientPaint's constructor accepts a point and a color that describe the center of the gradient, a radius, and a background color. The gradient blends color from the center point to the background color over the length of the radius.

```
import java.awt.*;
import java.awt.geom.*;
import java.awt.image.ColorModel;

public class RoundGradientPaint
    implements Paint {
  protected Point2D mPoint;
  protected Point2D mRadius;
  protected Color mPointColor, mBackgroundColor;

  public RoundGradientPaint(double x, double y, Color pointColor,
      Point2D radius, Color backgroundColor) {
    if (radius.distance(0, 0) <= 0)
      throw new IllegalArgumentException("Radius must be greater than 0.");
    mPoint = new Point2D.Double(x, y);
    mPointColor = pointColor;
    mRadius = radius;
    mBackgroundColor = backgroundColor;
  }

  public PaintContext createContext(ColorModel cm,
      Rectangle deviceBounds, Rectangle2D userBounds,
      AffineTransform xform, RenderingHints hints) {
    Point2D transformedPoint = xform.transform(mPoint, null);
    Point2D transformedRadius = xform.deltaTransform(mRadius, null);
    return new RoundGradientContext(transformedPoint, mPointColor,
        transformedRadius, mBackgroundColor);
  }

  public int getTransparency() {
    int a1 = mPointColor.getAlpha();
    int a2 = mBackgroundColor.getAlpha();
    return (((a1 & a2) == 0xff) ? OPAQUE : TRANSLUCENT);
  }
}
```

The getTransparency() method, from the Transparency interface, returns either OPAQUE or TRANSLUCENT, depending on the colors that were passed to RoundGradientPaint's constructor. If both colors are fully opaque (alpha = 255), then the resulting RoundGradientPaint is also fully opaque. Otherwise, the pixels filled by the RoundGradientPaint will have variable transparency, indicated by the TRANSLUCENT value.

Instead of creating a RoundGradientPaint that uses two opaque colors, you could also achieve an interesting effect using a single color. Consider what would happen if you used new Color(255, 0, 0, 255) as the point color, and new Color(255, 0, 0, 0) as the background color. The gradient would fade from opaque red at the point to a completely transparent red in the background.

The implementation of RoundGradientContext is straightforward. The get-Raster() method iterates over each point in the requested rectangle, calculating the distance from the center point. It calculates a weighting factor, from 0.0 to 1.0, based on the ratio of this distance and the radius.

```
for (int j = 0; j < h; j++) {
  for (int i = 0; i < w; i++) {
    double distance = mPoint.distance(x + i, y + j);
    double radius = mRadius.distance(0, 0);
    double ratio = distance / radius;
    if (ratio > 1.0)
      ratio = 1.0;
```

Then it simply uses the weighting factor to linearly interpolate between the center color and the background color:

```
data[base + 0] = (int)(mC1.getRed() + ratio *
    (mC2.getRed() - mC1.getRed()));
data[base + 1] = (int)(mC1.getGreen() + ratio *
    (mC2.getGreen() - mC1.getGreen()));
data[base + 2] = (int)(mC1.getBlue() + ratio *
    (mC2.getBlue() - mC1.getBlue()));
data[base + 3] = (int)(mC1.getAlpha() + ratio *
    (mC2.getAlpha() - mC1.getAlpha()));
```

Here's the entire class:

```
import java.awt.*;
import java.awt.geom.*;
import java.awt.image.*;

public class RoundGradientContext
    implements PaintContext {
  protected Point2D mPoint;
  protected Point2D mRadius;
  protected Color mC1, mC2;
```

```
public RoundGradientContext(Point2D p, Color c1, Point2D r, Color c2) {
  mPoint = p;
  mC1 = c1;
  mRadius = r;
  mC2 = c2;
}

public void dispose() {}

public ColorModel getColorModel() { return ColorModel.getRGBdefault(); }

public Raster getRaster(int x, int y, int w, int h) {
  WritableRaster raster =
      getColorModel().createCompatibleWritableRaster(w, h);

  int[] data = new int[w * h * 4];
  for (int j = 0; j < h; j++) {
    for (int i = 0; i < w; i++) {
      double distance = mPoint.distance(x + i, y + j);
      double radius = mRadius.distance(0, 0);
      double ratio = distance / radius;
      if (ratio > 1.0)
        ratio = 1.0;

      int base = (j * w + i) * 4;
      data[base + 0] = (int)(mC1.getRed() + ratio *
          (mC2.getRed() - mC1.getRed()));
      data[base + 1] = (int)(mC1.getGreen() + ratio *
          (mC2.getGreen() - mC1.getGreen()));
      data[base + 2] = (int)(mC1.getBlue() + ratio *
          (mC2.getBlue() - mC1.getBlue()));
      data[base + 3] = (int)(mC1.getAlpha() + ratio *
          (mC2.getAlpha() - mC1.getAlpha()));
    }
  }
  raster.setPixels(0, 0, w, h, data);

  return raster;
}
}
```

And here's a simple class that demonstrates how you can use Round-
GradientPaint to fill a round rectangle:

```
import java.awt.*;
import java.awt.geom.*;

public class RoundGradientPaintFill
    extends ApplicationFrame {
```

```
    public static void main(String[] args) {
      RoundGradientPaintFill f = new RoundGradientPaintFill();
      f.setTitle("RoundGradientPaintFill v1.0");
      f.setSize(200, 200);
      f.center();
      f.setVisible(true);
    }

    public void paint(Graphics g) {
      Graphics2D g2 = (Graphics2D)g;
      RoundRectangle2D r = new RoundRectangle2D.Float(25, 35, 150, 150, 25,
         25);
      RoundGradientPaint rgp = new RoundGradientPaint(75, 75, Color.magenta,
         new Point2D.Double(0, 85), Color.blue);
      g2.setPaint(rgp);
      g2.fill(r);
    }
  }
```

When you run this example, you should see the window shown in Figure C-2.

Stroking

Stroking is the process of drawing the outline of a shape. Stroking is similar to painting:

1. First, tell the Graphics2D how you want the outline to be drawn by calling setStroke(). This method accepts any object that implements the java.awt.Stroke interface. The 2D API comes with a class, java.awt.BasicStroke, that implements common stroking options.

2. Use setPaint() to tell the Graphics2D how the outline itself should be drawn. Outlines, like the interior of shapes, can be drawn using a color, a gradient, a texture, or anything else that implements the Paint interface.

3. Draw the outline of the shape using Graphics2D's draw() method. The Graphics2D uses the Stroke from step 1 to determine what the outline looks like. The Paint from step 2 is used to actually render the outline.

Stroke

Graphics2D uses a Stroke to figure out what the outline of a particular shape looks like. When you ask Graphics2D to draw() a shape, it asks its Stroke what the outline of the shape should look like. Interestingly, Stroke returns the stroked outline as another shape:

public abstract Shape createStrokedShape(Shape p)
> This method returns a `Shape` that represents the stroked outline of the supplied shape.

This is the only method in `Stroke`. Usually, you won't call it yourself—a `Graphics2D` will call it on your behalf when you `draw()` a shape.

At first glance, it seems strange that the outline of a `Shape` is also a `Shape`. It may help to think of the outline of a `Shape` as an infinitesimally thin line—to actually draw the outline, you need to give it some area, which is the process of stroking. Once you have the stroked outline, you can fill it in to draw the original shape's outline. In fact, calling `draw()` on a `Graphics2D` is equivalent to the following code:

```
public void longwindedDraw(Graphics2D g2, Shape s) {
    Stroke stroke = g2.getStroke();
    Shape strokedOutline = stroke.createStrokedShape(s);
    g2.fill(strokedOutline);
}
```

BasicStroke

The 2D API comes with a `Stroke` implementation called `java.awt.BasicStroke`. This class supports solid and dashed lines of any width. `BasicStroke` also handles two details of drawing thick lines: end styles and join styles.

End styles

There are several ways to draw the end of a thick line. `BasicStroke` supports three styles, represented by constants. Figure 4-7 shows an example of each end style.

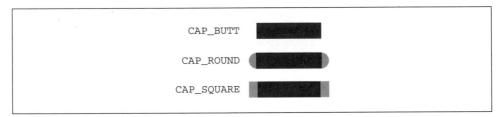

Figure 4-7. End styles

public static final int CAP_BUTT
> This end style adds no decoration to the end of line segments. Straight line segments stroked using this end style appear as rectangles.

public static final int CAP_ROUND

> This end style caps a line segment with a semicircle whose radius is half the line width.

public static final int CAP_SQUARE

> This end style extends the end of the line with a rectangle whose length is half the line width.

Note that these end styles apply to the ends of any line segment, straight or curved.

Join styles

BasicStroke offers three different ways to join line segments. Again, these join styles are represented by constants in BasicStroke. Figure 4-8 shows how the different join styles work. Figure 4-9 shows an example of each join style.

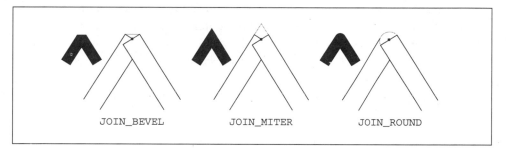

Figure 4-8. Join styles

Figure 4-9. Join styles in action: JOIN_BEVEL, JOIN_MITER, and JOIN_ROUND

public static final int JOIN_BEVEL

> Lines are joined by connecting the outer edges of their ends.

public static final int JOIN_MITER

> In this join style, the outer edges of lines are extended until they intersect. If the miter is longer than a supplied *miter limit*, however, the join will be rendered as a beveled join.

public static final int JOIN_ROUND

> Each line segment is ended with a semicircle, as in the CAP_ROUND end style. This creates a rounded effect at the intersection of line segments.

The miter limit used with JOIN_MITER does not correspond directly to the length of the miter. The algorithm depends on three quantities:

halfLength

> This is half of the line width.

miterLength

> The length of the miter is measured from the intersection of the two (unstroked) lines to the tip of the miter.

miterLimit

> This is the miter limit as specified in the BasicStroke constructor.

If miterLength is greater than (miterLimit * halfWidth), a beveled join will be used instead of a mitered join. Otherwise, a mitered join is used. The purpose of the miter limit is to prevent awkward-looking miter joins from being drawn. If two lines are nearly parallel, a mitered join will extend far beyond the actual intersection of the lines. Figure 4-10 illustrates this effect. In it, the same shape is stroked with a miter limit of 10.0 and 25.0.

Figure 4-10. Mitered joins can be unruly

Dashes

BasicStroke uses a *dash array* and a *dash phase* to stroke dashed lines. The dash array is an array of floats that represent the length of the solid and clear sections of the line. For example, an array consisting of { 12, 12 } would produce a line that was visible for 12 units and invisible for 12 units. The even elements of the array (starting at index 0) determine where the line is visible, while the odd elements determine where it's invisible. Figure 4-11 shows a GeneralPath stroked with two varieties of dotted lines. The shape on the left has been stroked with a solid line. In the middle, the shape has been stroked using a dash array of { 12, 12 }. The same shape is stroked again on the right, using a dash array of { 4, 4, 12, 4 }.

Figure 4-11. Stroking dashed lines

The end style is used on each dash in a dashed line. Figure 4-12 shows the same dashed line drawn using the CAP_BUTT, CAP_ROUND, and CAP_SQUARE end styles.

Figure 4-12. End styles apply to dashes, too

The *dash phase* acts as an offset into the dash pattern. Consider, for example, the dash array { 12, 12 }. When the dash phase is 0, lines stroked with this dash pattern will begin with 12 units of visible outline followed by 12 units that are invisible. Suppose, instead, that the dash phase is set to 8. Now, lines stroked with the dash pattern will begin with 4 units of visible line, followed by 12 units of invisible, followed by 12 of visible, and so forth. Figure 4-13 shows how this works for two straight lines.

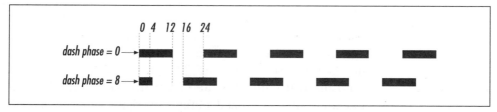

Figure 4-13. Same dashes, different dash phases

Constructors

Once you understand the end styles, join styles, and dashes, it's easy to create a `BasicStroke` that does exactly what you want it to do. Like `Paint` objects, `Strokes` cannot be changed after they have been constructed.

public BasicStroke()

This constructor creates a stroke object with all the default settings: a solid stroke with a line width of 1.0, an end style of CAP_SQUARE, a join style of JOIN_MITER, a miter limit of 10.0.

public BasicStroke(float width)

This constructor creates a stroke object with the supplied width. The other settings are set to their defaults, as described in the previous constructor.

public BasicStroke(float width, int cap, int join)

This constructor creates a solid stroke object with the given width, end style, and join style. If the join style is JOIN_MITER, the default miter limit of 10.0 is used.

public BasicStroke(float width, int cap, int join, float miterlimit)

This constructor is the same as the previous constructor, except that the given miter limit will be used if the join style is JOIN_MITER.

public BasicStroke(float width, int cap, int join, float miterlimit, float[] dash, float dash_phase)

This constructor creates a dashed stroke object. The supplied dash array and phase are used to determine the dashing pattern.

The following example creates a square and strokes it:

```
Rectangle2D r = new Rectangle2D.Double(50, 50, 100, 100);
Stroke stroke = new BasicStroke(8,
    BasicStroke.CAP_BUTT, BasicStroke.JOIN_BEVEL, 0,
    new float[] { 12, 12 }, 0);
g2.setStroke(stroke);
g2.draw(r);
```

Overlap

What happens if you both stroke and paint a shape? Interestingly, the results depend on whether you stroke or paint first. A shape's outline actually overlaps its interior, as shown in Figure 4-14. The shape's real outline, strictly speaking, is an infinitesimally thin line, shown black in the figure. The process of stroking creates an outline shape around the real outline. Some of the stroked outline extends outside the shape, and some of the stroked outline overlaps with the shape's interior.

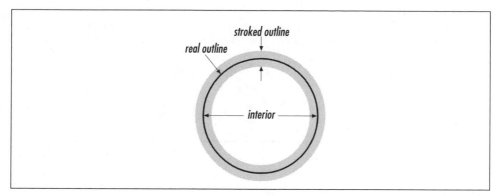

Figure 4-14. The stroked outline and interior of a circle

If you're using opaque colors, then you'll get different results depending on the order in which you do things. If you use partially transparent colors, then you'll be able to observe the overlap of stroked outlines and filled interiors in your results. The following shows how this happens in practice. First, it strokes the outline and fills the interior of a circle using a partially transparent color:

```
Color smokey = new Color(128, 128, 128, 128);
g2.setPaint(smokey);
g2.fill(e);
g2.draw(e);
```

Then, in a different location, it strokes the circle's outline using a solid black color and fills the interior using a solid gray:

```
g2.setPaint(Color.black);
g2.draw(e);
g2.setPaint(Color.gray);
g2.fill(e);
```

Finally, it fills the circle with gray and then strokes the outline with black:

```
g2.setPaint(Color.gray);
g2.fill(e);
g2.setPaint(Color.black);
g2.draw(e);
```

The results of this example are shown in Figure 4-15.

Here's the source code:

```
import java.awt.*;
import java.awt.geom.*;

public class Overlap
    extends ApplicationFrame {
  public static void main(String[] args) {
```

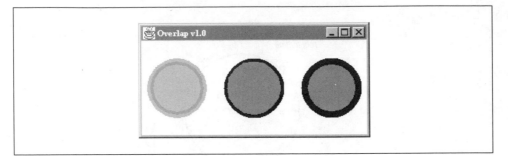

Figure 4-15. Stroking and painting overlap

```
    Overlap f = new Overlap();
    f.setTitle("Overlap v1.0");
    f.setSize(300, 150);
    f.center();
    f.setVisible(true);
}

public void paint(Graphics g) {
  Graphics2D g2 = (Graphics2D)g;
  double x = 15, y = 50, w = 70, h = 70;
  Ellipse2D e = new Ellipse2D.Double(x, y, w, h);
  g2.setStroke(new BasicStroke(8));
  // Stroke and paint.
  Color smokey = new Color(128, 128, 128, 128);
  g2.setPaint(smokey);
  g2.fill(e);
  g2.draw(e);
  // Stroke, then paint.
  e.setFrame(x + 100, y, w, h);
  g2.setPaint(Color.black);
  g2.draw(e);
  g2.setPaint(Color.gray);
  g2.fill(e);
  // Paint, then stroke.
  e.setFrame(x + 200, y, w, h);
  g2.setPaint(Color.gray);
  g2.fill(e);
  g2.setPaint(Color.black);
  g2.draw(e);
 }
}
```

5

In this chapter:
- *Transforming*
- *Compositing*
- *Clipping*
- *Rendering Hints*

Rendering

One of the strengths of the 2D API is that shapes, text, and images can be manipulated in many of the same ways. In this chapter, I'll talk about the four parts of the rendering pipeline that apply to every graphics object:

transforming

> Any graphics object can be transformed as it is rendered. A transformation can include translation, rotation, scaling, or shearing, or a combination of all four.

compositing

> The process of putting pieces of a picture together is called compositing. The 2D API supports a handful of compositing rules and allows pieces of a picture to be partly or fully transparent.

clipping

> Sometimes you don't want to draw outside a certain area, as though you were drawing only the part of a picture that's visible through a door frame. This operation is called clipping. The 2D API allows you to specify any Shape as a clipping path.

rendering hints

> Antialiasing is a technique that is used to smooth out the rough edges ("jaggies") of a picture. The 2D rendering engine supports antialiasing and other speed and quality tradeoffs through a mechanism called *rendering hints*.

Transforming

A single class, `java.awt.geom.AffineTransform`, represents transformations in the 2D API. An *affine* transformation is one in which parallel lines are still parallel after being transformed. Affine transformations are based on matrix math, but you don't have to know anything about the math to use the `AffineTransform` class.

`Graphics2D` has an internal `AffineTransform` that it applies to graphics objects as they are rendered. You can set or modify this transformation with the following methods in the `Graphics2D` class:

public abstract void setTransform(AffineTransform Tx)
> This method sets the current transformation of this `Graphics2D`.

public abstract void transform(AffineTransform Tx)
> Use this method to modify this `Graphics2D`'s current transformation with the supplied `AffineTransform`.

`Graphics2D` also includes convenience methods for performing simple transformations on User Space. These are described in a later section.

In general, it's a good idea to modify the existing transformation rather than replacing it. If you're drawing inside a `Component`, the `Graphics2D` that is passed to the `Component`'s `paint()` method is already set up with a default transformation that places the origin at the upper left corner of the `Component`'s drawing surface. If you replace this transformation using `setTransform()`, you may not get the results you expected. Instead, use `transform()` to modify the current transformation.

A single instance of `AffineTransform` can represent more than one transformation. A translation and a rotation, for example, can be combined to form a single `AffineTransform`. I'll talk more about this later.

You can construct a new `AffineTransform` as follows:

public AffineTransform()
> This constructor creates a new `AffineTransform`. Initially, this object represents an *identity transformation*. An identity transformation has no effect whatsoever—points and shapes that are processed by it remain the same.

Once you have an `AffineTransform`, you can make it do interesting things by combining the four fundamental transformations: translation, rotation, scaling, and shearing.

There are two basic ways to transform graphics elements. You can modify the transformation in a `Graphics2D` and let the `Graphics2D` worry about the details. The other approach is to transform everything yourself and then render it. Which approach you choose depends on your needs.

If you don't want to modify the transformation contained in the `Graphics2D`, you can perform the transformations yourself. `AffineTransform` contains useful methods for transforming points and shapes. Here are three useful methods:

public Point2D transform(Point2D ptSrc, Point2D ptDst)

> This method transforms `ptSrc` and stores the result in `ptDst`. `ptDst` may be `null` or equal to `ptSrc`. The transformed point is returned.

public Shape createTransformedShape(Shape pSrc)

> This method transforms the given `Shape` and returns the result as another `Shape`.

public Point2D deltaTransform(Point2D ptSrc, Point2D ptDst)

> Use this method to transform a vector ("delta") represented by a point. This method applies every aspect of the `AffineTransform` except for the translation component. As usual, `ptDst` can be `null` or the same as `ptSrc`. The transformed point is returned. The `RoundGradientPaint` example in Chapter 4 uses this method.

Translation

One of the fundamental types of transformation is *translation*. Translation is simply the process of moving, or translating, the coordinate space so that its origin is in a new place. Figure 5-1 shows the effects of a translation on a set of coordinate axes and a rectangle. The original shapes have been translated to the right.

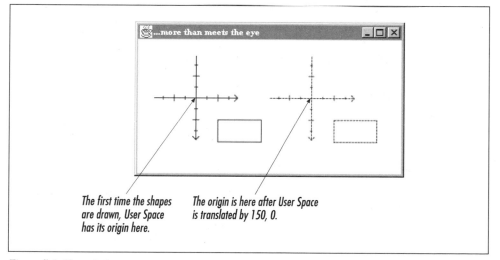

Figure 5-1. Translation

There are several methods in `AffineTransform` that relate to translation. You can either add a translation to an existing transformation or create a new, translational `AffineTransform`:

public void translate(double tx, double ty)

> This method adds a translational transformation of `tx` and `ty` to this `AffineTransform`. The translation is added to the end of the `Affine-Transform`'s transformations.

public void setToTranslation(double tx, double ty)

> This method sets this `AffineTransform` to represent a translation by `tx` and `ty`. Any previous transformations contained in this `AffineTransform` are lost.

public static AffineTransform getTranslateInstance(double tx, double ty)

> This factory method creates a new `AffineTransform` and initializes it to represent a translation using the given offsets. It is equivalent to creating a new `AffineTransform` and calling `setToTranslation(tx, ty)`.

The following abstract class, `Transformers`, draws a set of coordinate axes and a simple rectangle. Then it applies a transformation and draws the axes and the shape again using dotted lines.

Later, I'll use subclasses of `Transformers` to demonstrate different kinds of transformations. The coordinate axes and the rectangle are both represented by `Shape` member variables. They are initialized in `getAxes()` and `getShape()` methods. In the `paint()` method, the shapes are drawn twice. The first time looks like this:*

```
g2.draw(mAxes);
g2.draw(mShape);
```

Before the second rendering, the `Graphics2D` is transformed, using the abstract `getTransform()` method. Subclasses will define this method to supply an appropriate transformation:

```
g2.transform(getTransform());
```

Then the shapes are drawn again, after a dotted line `Stroke` has been created:

```
g2.draw(mAxes);
g2.draw(mShape);
```

Remember, I'm not actually transforming the shapes. What really happens is that the entire User Space of the `Graphics2D` is transformed before the shapes are rendered the second time.

The `getFrame()` method is a handy utility method that creates an enclosing `Frame` for the `Transformers` object. Here's the example:

---

* Before the shapes are drawn the first time, User Space is translated by calling `g2.transform(75, 75)`. This simply moves the origin of User Space so that the axes will be fully visible the first time they are drawn.

```java
import java.awt.*;
import java.awt.geom.*;

public abstract class Transformers
    extends Component {
  Shape mAxes, mShape;
  int mLength = 54, mArrowLength = 4, mTickSize = 4;

  public Transformers() {
    mAxes = createAxes();
    mShape = createShape();
  }

  protected Shape createAxes() {
    GeneralPath path = new GeneralPath();

    // Axes.
    path.moveTo(-mLength, 0);
    path.lineTo(mLength, 0);
    path.moveTo(0, -mLength);
    path.lineTo(0, mLength);
    // Arrows.
    path.moveTo(mLength - mArrowLength, -mArrowLength);
    path.lineTo(mLength, 0);
    path.lineTo(mLength - mArrowLength, mArrowLength);
    path.moveTo(-mArrowLength, mLength - mArrowLength);
    path.lineTo(0, mLength);
    path.lineTo(mArrowLength, mLength - mArrowLength);
    // Half-centimeter tick marks
    float cm = 72 / 2.54f;
    float lengthCentimeter = mLength / cm;
    for (float i = 0.5f; i < lengthCentimeter; i += 1.0f) {
      float tick = i * cm;
      path.moveTo( tick, -mTickSize / 2);
      path.lineTo( tick,  mTickSize / 2);
      path.moveTo(-tick, -mTickSize / 2);
      path.lineTo(-tick,  mTickSize / 2);
      path.moveTo(-mTickSize / 2,  tick);
      path.lineTo( mTickSize / 2,  tick);
      path.moveTo(-mTickSize / 2, -tick);
      path.lineTo( mTickSize / 2, -tick);
    }
    // Full-centimeter tick marks
    for (float i = 1.0f; i < lengthCentimeter; i += 1.0f) {
      float tick = i * cm;
      path.moveTo( tick, -mTickSize);
      path.lineTo( tick,  mTickSize);
      path.moveTo(-tick, -mTickSize);
      path.lineTo(-tick,  mTickSize);
```

```
      path.moveTo(-mTickSize,  tick);
      path.lineTo( mTickSize,  tick);
      path.moveTo(-mTickSize, -tick);
      path.lineTo( mTickSize, -tick);
    }
    return path;
  }

  protected Shape createShape() {
    float cm = 72 / 2.54f;
    return new Rectangle2D.Float(cm, cm, 2 * cm, cm);
  }

  public void paint(Graphics g) {
    Graphics2D g2 = (Graphics2D)g;

    // Use antialiasing.
    g2.setRenderingHint(RenderingHints.KEY_ANTIALIASING,
        RenderingHints.VALUE_ANTIALIAS_ON);

    // Move the origin to 75, 75.
    AffineTransform at = AffineTransform.getTranslateInstance(75, 75);
    g2.transform(at);

    // Draw the shapes in their original locations.
    g2.setPaint(Color.black);
    g2.draw(mAxes);
    g2.draw(mShape);

    // Transform the Graphics2D.
    g2.transform(getTransform());

    // Draw the shapes in their new locations, but dashed.
    Stroke stroke = new BasicStroke(1,
        BasicStroke.CAP_BUTT, BasicStroke.JOIN_BEVEL, 0,
        new float[] { 3, 1 }, 0);
    g2.setStroke(stroke);
    g2.draw(mAxes);
    g2.draw(mShape);
  }

  public abstract AffineTransform getTransform();

  public Frame getFrame() {
    ApplicationFrame f = new ApplicationFrame("...more than meets the eye");
    f.setLayout(new BorderLayout());
    f.add(this, BorderLayout.CENTER);
    f.setSize(350,200);
    f.center();
```

```
        return f;
    }
}
```

The following simple subclass demonstrates how translation works. The axes and rectangle are drawn. Then they are translated and drawn again using a dotted line. The results of this example are shown in Figure 5-1.

```
import java.awt.*;
import java.awt.geom.AffineTransform;

public class TransformersTranslation
    extends Transformers {
  public static void main(String[] args) {
    Transformers t = new TransformersTranslation();
    Frame f = t.getFrame();
    f.setVisible(true);
  }

  public AffineTransform getTransform() {
    return AffineTransform.getTranslateInstance(150, 0);
  }
}
```

Rotation

Another fundamental transformation is *rotation*. Figure 5-2 shows a rotation of -π/ 6 radians. As before, the original and transformed shapes are shown. The transformed shapes are shown with dotted lines.

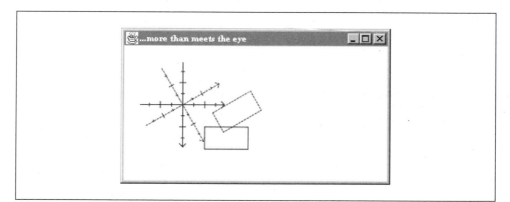

Figure 5-2. Rotation

Rotation can be performed around any point. In the rotation above, the transformation is a rotation about the origin. A rotation around any other point is a *translated rotation.* Figure 5-3 shows a rotation of $-\pi/6$ around the bottom right corner of the rectangle.

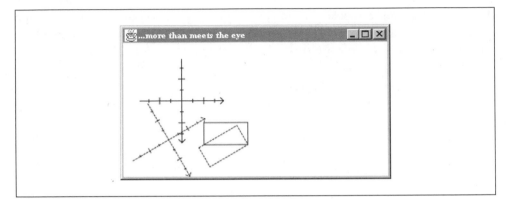

Figure 5-3. Rotation around a point other than the origin

`AffineTransform` offers a handful of useful methods for working with rotations and translated rotations:

public void rotate(double theta)
> This method adds a rotational transformation to this `AffineTransform`. The given angle is measured in radians. The rotation is performed around the origin.

public void rotate(double theta, double x, double y)
> This method adds a translated rotational transformation to this `Affine-Transform`. The rotation will be performed around the given point.

public void setToRotation(double theta)
> This method sets this `AffineTransform` to represent a rotation of `theta` radians.

public void setToRotation(double theta, double x, double y)
> This method sets this `AffineTransform` to a translated rotation.

public static AffineTransform getRotateInstance(double theta)
> This factory method creates a new `AffineTransform` and initializes it to represent a rotation using the supplied angle.

public static AffineTransform getRotateInstance(double theta, double x, double y)
> This factory method creates a new `AffineTransform` and initializes it to represent a translated rotation using the supplied angle and point.

To produce Figure 5-2, create another `Transformers` subclass as follows:

```
import java.awt.*;
import java.awt.geom.AffineTransform;
```

Angle Units

You may be wondering why `AffineTransfrom` uses angle measurements in radians, while `Arc2D`, in another part of 2D, uses degrees. It's not an oversight; there's just no graceful way to make `Arc2D` and `AffineTransform` use the same angular units.

Back in the old days before Java 2 (i.e., way back in 1997), before there was an `AffineTransform` class, `Graphics` had methods for drawing and filling arcs. These methods expect degrees, so it would create a strange inconsistency to use radians with `Arc2D`.

On the other hand, it doesn't make much sense to require degree measurements in the `AffineTransform` class. `AffineTransform` makes use of trigonometric methods in the `java.lang.Math` class, which all deal in radians.

Even though it is inconsistent to use degrees for `Arc2D` and radians for `AffineTransform`, the inconsistency wasn't introduced in 2D. It has its roots in JDK 1.0, which used radians for trigonometric methods and degrees for `drawArc()` and `fillArc()` in the `Graphics` class.

```
public class TransformersRotation
    extends Transformers {
  public static void main(String[] args) {
    Transformers t = new TransformersRotation();
    Frame f = t.getFrame();
    f.setVisible(true);
  }

  public AffineTransform getTransform() {
    return AffineTransform.getRotateInstance(-Math.PI / 6);
  }
}
```

To produce the translated rotation shown in Figure 5-3, use this class instead:

```
import java.awt.*;
import java.awt.geom.AffineTransform;

public class TransformersTranslatedRotation
    extends Transformers {
  public static void main(String[] args) {
    Transformers t = new TransformersTranslatedRotation();
    Frame f = t.getFrame();
    f.setVisible(true);
  }
```

```
public AffineTransform getTransform() {
  float cm = 72 / 2.54f;
  return AffineTransform.getRotateInstance(-Math.PI / 6, 3 * cm, 2 * cm);
  }
}
```

Scaling

Scaling is the operation of making things bigger or smaller. You might choose to scale a shape to make it 300% of its original width and height, as shown in Figure 5-4. There are three interesting side effects to scaling:

- Even the line thicknesses are scaled; the lines on the expanded axes and rectangle are thicker than their unscaled counterparts. If you don't want to change the line widths, don't modify the transformation of the Graphics2D. Instead, transform the shapes themselves, using AffineTransform's createTransformedShape(), and render the outlines of the transformed shapes.

- Another interesting detail is that scaling, like rotation, changes the location of every point except the origin. Notice, for instance, how the corners of the rectangle have moved as a result of the scaling transformation.

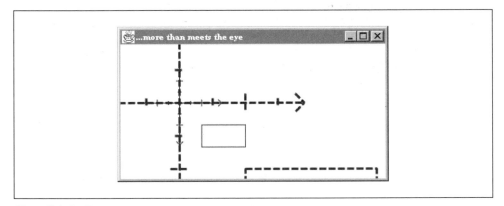

Figure 5-4. Scaling

- If you pass negative scaling values, you can switch the directions of the axes. For example, scaling by -1, 1 will flip the direction of the x axis.

Guess what? AffineTransform has a set of methods that deal with scaling, too:

public void scale(double sx, double sy)
   This method adds a scaling transformation of sx and sy to this Affine-Transform. The translation is added to the end of the AffineTransform's

translations. The given scale factors should be expressed as the ratio of the new size to the old size; for example, scale(1, 1) has no effect, and scale (.5, .5) will reduce both axes by 50%. You may scale down in one axis and up in the other if you wish.

public void setToScale(double sx, double sy)
This method sets this AffineTransform to represent a scaling transformation using sx and sy. Any previous transformations contained in this AffineTransform are lost.

public static AffineTransform getScaleInstance(double sx, double sy)
This factory method creates a new AffineTransform and initializes it to represent a scaling transformation using the given values. It is equivalent to creating a new AffineTransform and calling setToScale(sx, sy).

You can extend Transformers to perform scaling by creating a subclass as follows:

```
import java.awt.*;
import java.awt.geom.AffineTransform;

public class TransformersScale
    extends Transformers {
  public static void main(String[] args) {
    Transformers t = new TransformersScale();
    Frame f = t.getFrame();
    f.setVisible(true);
  }

  public AffineTransform getTransform() {
    return AffineTransform.getScaleInstance(3, 3);
  }
}
```

Shearing

The last fundamental transformation is *shearing*, in which coordinate space is stretched parallel to one axis or to both axes. To understand this, think of a big stack of paper. Suppose you drew a picture on the side of the stack with a marker. Shearing (in one dimension) is the effect of smooshing the stack to one side or the other, so that the stack looks like a parallelogram instead of a rectangle, and the picture you drew is no longer aligned.

Shearing is specified in terms of two values, shx and shy, which represent the amount to shear along the x and y axes, respectively. Any point (x, y) is transformed to a new point (x + (shx)y, y + (shy)x). Figure 5-5 shows the effect of shearing with shx = -.5 and shy = 0. (To make the figure easier to see, a translation was applied before the shearing.)

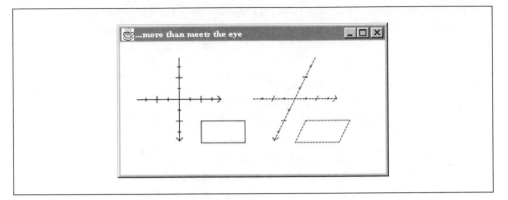

Figure 5-5. Translating and shearing along the x axis

The following methods are used to work with shearing in `AffineTransform`:

public void shear(double shx, double shy)

> This method adds a shearing transformation of `shx` and `shy` to this `AffineTransform`. If `shx` and `shy` are 0, this method has no effect.

public void setToShear(double shx, double shy)

> This method sets this `AffineTransform` to represent a shearing transformation using `shx` and `shy`. Any previous transformations contained in this `AffineTransform` are discarded.

public static AffineTransform getShearInstance(double shx, double shy)

> This factory method creates a new `AffineTransform` and initializes it to represent a shearing transformation using the given values. It is equivalent to creating a new `AffineTransform` and calling `setToShear(shx, shy)`.

The following `Transformers` subclass produces Figure 5-5:

```
import java.awt.*;
import java.awt.geom.AffineTransform;

public class TransformersShear
    extends Transformers {
  public static void main(String[] args) {
    Transformers t = new TransformersShear();
    Frame f = t.getFrame();
    f.setVisible(true);
  }

  public AffineTransform getTransform() {
    AffineTransform at = AffineTransform.getTranslateInstance(150, 0);
    at.shear(-.5, 0);
    return at;
  }
}
```

Compound Transformations

You've already seen one way to create compound transformations. Calling `translate()`, `rotate()`, `scale()`, or `shear()` on an `AffineTransform` will add a new transformation to whatever transformation was previously there. In the following example, the effects of a translation and a rotation are combined:

```java
import java.awt.*;
import java.awt.geom.AffineTransform;

public class TransformersTransrotate
    extends Transformers {
  public static void main(String[] args) {
    Transformers t = new TransformersTransrotate();
    Frame f = t.getFrame();
    f.setVisible(true);
  }

  public AffineTransform getTransform() {
    AffineTransform at = new AffineTransform();
    at.setToTranslation(100, 0);
    at.rotate(Math.PI / 6);
    return at;
  }
}
```

Note that the order of the transformations counts. The following example combines the same translation and rotation, but the rotation is applied first:

```java
import java.awt.*;
import java.awt.geom.AffineTransform;

public class TransformersRotranslate
    extends Transformers {
  public static void main(String[] args) {
    Transformers t = new TransformersRotranslate();
    Frame f = t.getFrame();
    f.setVisible(true);
  }

  public AffineTransform getTransform() {
    AffineTransform at = new AffineTransform();
    at.setToRotation(Math.PI / 6);
    at.translate(100, 0);
    return at;
  }
}
```

Figure 5-6 shows the effects of these two compound transformations. On the top, the translation is applied before the rotation. First, the origin moves to the right.

Then, User Space is rotated. On the bottom, the rotation is applied first. When the translation is applied, the origin actually moves down and right, along the x axis of the rotated space.

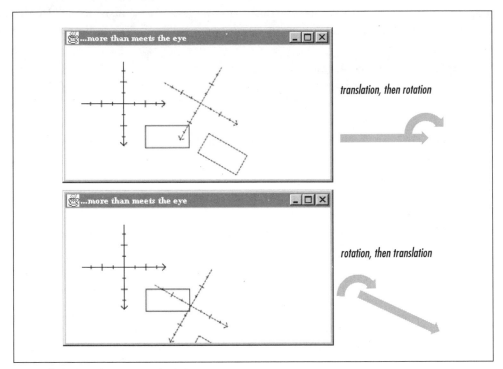

Figure 5-6. Transformation order is important

You can also combine two AffineTransform objects using the concatenate() and preConcatenate() methods:

public void concatenate(AffineTransform Tx)

> This method adds the transformation represented by Tx to this AffineTransform. This is the intuitive way to concatenate two transformations. For example, if this AffineTransform represents a translation, and concatenate() is called with a rotational transformation, this instance is modified to represent a translation followed by a rotation.

public void preConcatenate(AffineTransform Tx)

> This method is just like concatenate(), except the given transformation is performed before the transformation represented by this AffineTransform. Under normal circumstances, you probably won't want to use this method.

Inverting

An *inverse transformation* transforms shapes and points back to their original locations. For example, the inverse of a translation of 100, 50 is a translation of -100, -50. Not all transformations are invertible. `AffineTransform` includes the following method for calculating an inverse transformation, if it is possible:

public AffineTransform createInverse() throws NoninvertibleTransformException
> This method returns the inverse transformation of this `AffineTransform`. If this `AffineTransform` cannot be inverted, a `NoninvertibleTransform-Exception` is thrown.

Convenience Methods in Graphics2D

If you just want to perform one of the fundamental transformations on User Space, `Graphics2D` has a set of handy methods that will save you the trouble of creating your own `AffineTransform`:

public abstract void translate(double tx, double ty)
> This method concatenates a translation of `tx` and `ty` to the `Graphics2D`'s current transformation.

public abstract void rotate(double theta)
> Use this method to concatenate a rotation of `theta` radians to the `Graphics2D`'s current transformation. The rotation is applied at 0, 0.

public abstract void rotate(double theta, double x, double y)
> This is the same as the previous method, except the rotation is applied at `x`, `y`.

public abstract void scale(double sx, double sy)
> This method concatenates a scaling transformation to the current transformation.

public abstract void shear(double shx, double shy)
> This method concatenates a shearing transformation to the current transformation.

Compositing

Compositing is the process of putting two pictures together. In the 2D API, compositing occurs every time you draw a shape or an image. As I explained in Chapter 2, *The Big Picture*, an instance of `Graphics2D` represents a drawing surface. Each time you draw a shape, some text, or an image, the new element is added to the drawing surface. Conceptually, it happens in distinct steps:

1. The rasterizer takes the ideal shape and produces a set of alpha values from it. You can think of this as a grid of pixels, where each pixel has an alpha value.

Essentially, this is an image as large as the drawing surface. I'll call this new image the *source*; the drawing surface is the *destination*.

2. The colors in the source are determined, using either the current `Paint` of the `Graphics2D` or the colors of an image.

3. The source and the destination are combined to form the new destination (drawing surface). This is done at the pixel level. The color and alpha of each pixel is determined by combining the colors and alpha values from the corresponding pixels in the source and destination. A *compositing rule* specifies exactly how the color and alpha values are used.

For example, consider what happens when a black shape is rendered on a white canvas using the default *source over destination* compositing rule. The rasterizer converts the ideal shape to an array of alpha values. Source pixels that lie entirely outside the shape have an alpha of 0.0. This is interpreted as complete transparency; for these pixels, the color of the destination is not changed. Likewise, the source pixels on the interior of the shape have an alpha of 1.0. For these pixels, the destination will take on the color of the source. In this case, the shape is being filled with a solid color, black. The pixels that lie along the edges of the shape have alpha values ranging from 0.0 to 1.0 (assuming antialiasing is used). These pixels will be colored using a combination of the pixel colors from the source and destination. If a black shape is being rendered on a white drawing surface, then the border pixels will be colored with combinations of black and white—different shades of gray. The actual color used in a pixel is determined by the alpha value of the source pixel. A pixel with an alpha value of 0.9, for example, would end up being a very dark gray.

Most of the time, the source over destination rule is all you need. It's the most intuitive compositing rule—anything you render is placed "on top" of the drawing surface. If you render something that is partially transparent, the drawing surface will "show through." If you need something more exotic, keep reading to find out about the other compositing rules supported by Java 2D.

The Porter-Duff Rules

The source over destination rule makes sense, intuitively, but it is not the only compositing rule in the world. Thomas Porter and Tom Duff developed a definitive list of rules for compositing based on the colors and alpha of a source and a destination.* This type of compositing, unsurprisingly, is called *alpha compositing*.

---

* Porter and Duff's findings were published in an article entitled "Compositing Digital Images" in the 1984 SIGGRAPH proceedings.

Porter and Duff defined twelve compositing rules, of which eight are supported in the 2D API. These are shown in Table 5-1.*

The alpha values from the source and destination are denoted by α_s and α_d, respectively. The color and alpha of each destination pixel are determined by the following formulas:

$$newColor = \alpha_s \cdot f_s \cdot c_s + \alpha_d \cdot f_d \cdot c_d$$

$$newAlpha = f_s \cdot \alpha_s + f_d \cdot \alpha_d$$

In the formulas, c_s and c_d are the source and destination color, respectively, and f_s and f_d are the fractions of source and destination as given in Table 5-1.

The names correspond to constants in the `AlphaComposite` class, which is described in the next section. The intuitive source over destination rule that I just described is represented by `SrcOver`.

Table 5-1. Compositing Rules in the 2D API

Name	Fraction of Source Color	Fraction of Destination Color	Description
SrcOver	1	$1 - \alpha_s$	Places the source on top of the destination (source over destination)
DstOver	$1 - \alpha_d$	1	Places the source behind the destination
Clear	0	0	Clears the destination under the source
Src	1	0	Overwrites the destination with the source, regardless of alpha
SrcIn	α_d	0	Replaces the destination with the source, based on the destination's alpha
DstIn	0	α_s	Shows the part of the destination inside the source
SrcOut	$1 - \alpha_d$	0	Shows the part of the source outside of the destination
DstOut	0	$1 - \alpha_s$	Shows the part of the destination outside of the source

Figure 5-7 shows some simple examples of each of these rules using two rectangles filled with solid colors. In each picture, the light gray rectangle is an opaque part of a transparent drawing surface. The dark gray rectangle is rendered on this drawing surface using the named compositing rule. These figures should give you some idea of how the different compositing rules work, but remember they're very simple. More complex alpha values in the source or destination could make the

---

* Sun picked the most useful Porter-Duff compositing rules and implemented them in the 2D API. If you need one of the other four rules, you can always write your own `Composite` implementation.

results hard to visualize. Furthermore, the compositing rules are shown in their "pure" form. As you'll see, you can specify an additional alpha value for the compositing rules, which makes things more complicated still.

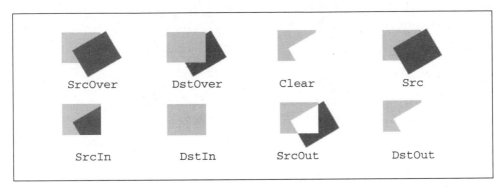

Figure 5-7. Compositing rules illustrated

AlphaComposite

The rendering engine, Graphics2D, keeps a compositing rule as part of its state. Compositing rules are represented by objects that implement the java.awt. Composite interface. To tell a Graphics2D which compositing rule to use, call its setComposite() method.

The 2D API includes one concrete implementation of the Composite interface, java.awt.AlphaComposite. This class implements the eight compositing rules described in Table 5-1. It defines constants representing each of the rules. The names of these constants are shown in the table. To tell a Graphics2D instance to use the clear rule, for example, do this:

```
g2.setComposite(AlphaComposite.Clear);
```

But Wait, There's More

AlphaComposite allows you to monkey around with alpha values even beyond the Porter-Duff rules. Specifically, it's possible to obtain an AlphaComposite that reduces the alpha values of graphics objects as they are rendered:

public static AlphaComposite getInstance(int rule, float alpha)

This method returns an AlphaComposite that embodies the supplied rule. The rule should be one of SRC_OVER, DST_OVER, CLEAR, SRC, SRC_IN, DST_ IN, SRC_OUT, or DST_OUT. These constants are also defined in the AlphaComposite class—they correspond to the similarly named Alpha-Composite constants shown in Table 5-1. The alpha values of rendered primitives are adjusted by multiplying them by the supplied parameter, which should be in the range from 0.0 to 1.0. For example, using an Alpha-Composite with an alpha of .5 will cause everything to be rendered at half its normal opacity.

Figure 5-8 shows how the additional alpha parameter affects the eight compositing rules. The light gray rectangle is opaque against a transparent drawing surface, just as in Figure 5-7. A dark gray rectangle is then rendered using a specific compositing rule and an additional alpha parameter of 0.8.

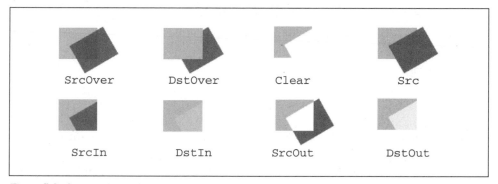

Figure 5-8. Compositing rules with an alpha parameter of 0.8

The following example shows how to use an AlphaComposite instance with the additional alpha parameter. First, a red rectangle is drawn, using the default compositing rule. Then an AlphaComposite with an alpha multiplier of 0.4 is used to render some blue text. The parts of the text that are over the rectangle are a shade of purple. The parts of the text outside the rectangle are a pale blue color. This is because the blue of the source (the text) is combined with the white background. Figure C-3 shows this example in action.

```
import java.awt.*;
import java.awt.geom.*;

public class TransparentText {
  public static void main(String[] args) {
    ApplicationFrame f = new ApplicationFrame("TransparentText v1.0") {
      private int mNumberOfLines = 25;
      private Color[] mColors = { Color.red, Color.green, Color.blue };

      public void paint(Graphics g) {
        Graphics2D g2 = (Graphics2D)g;

        // Set the rendering quality.
        g2.setRenderingHint(RenderingHints.KEY_ANTIALIASING,
          RenderingHints.VALUE_ANTIALIAS_ON);
        // Paint a red rectangle.
```

```
        Rectangle2D r = new Rectangle2D.Double(50, 50, 150, 100);
        g2.setPaint(Color.red);
        g2.fill(r);
        // Set a composite with transparency.
        Composite c = AlphaComposite.getInstance(AlphaComposite.SRC_OVER,
            .4f);
        g2.setComposite(c);
        // Draw some blue text.
        g2.setPaint(Color.blue);
        g2.setFont(new Font("Times New Roman", Font.PLAIN, 72));
        g2.drawString("Composite", 25, 130);
      }
    };
    f.setSize(400, 200);
    f.center();
    f.setVisible(true);
  }
}
```

The results of some of the Porter-Duff compositing rules are often confusing, even for very simple operations like rendering two rectangles. One of the complicating factors is that the results may vary based on whether you do your rendering in an offscreen image or directly on the screen. The reason for this has to do with the alpha values of the drawing surface. Drawing surfaces that are on the screen always have an alpha value of 1.0 everywhere. The pixels of an offscreen drawing surface, however, can take on any alpha value.

For example, suppose a red rectangle is rendered on the drawing surface using the SrcOver rule. Then a blue rectangle is rendered overlapping the red rectangle using the SrcOut rule.

When the rendering is done directly to the screen, the drawing surface has an alpha of 1.0 everywhere. When the red rectangle is rendered, the pixels in the rectangle are colored red without affecting the alpha of the drawing surface. When the blue rectangle is rendered using the SrcOut rule, neither the source color nor the destination color is used. (Look back at Table 5-1: it shows that none of the destination color is used, by definition, and that $1 - \alpha_d$ of the source color is used. But $\alpha_d = 1.0$ everywhere for this onscreen drawing surface, so none of the source color is used either.) The net result is that the area of the blue rectangle is cleared of either color, which sets it to black. Figure C-4 shows how this looks.

The results are quite different when this same rendering sequence is performed on an offscreen image, as shown in Figure C-5. Assume that the offscreen drawing surface has been filled with a color such that all of its pixels' alpha values are 0.0. When the red rectangle is rendered, the pixels underneath the rectangle are changed to red with an alpha of 1.0. The rest of the drawing surface remains transparent (alpha is 0.0 everywhere else). When the blue rectangle is rendered, some pixels overlap the red rectangle and some don't. The ones that do not overlap are rendered blue, because the alpha of the destination is 0.0 there and all of the source color is used. In the region of overlap with the red rectangle, the alpha of the drawing surface is 1.0. None of the source color and none of the destination color is used; the area of overlap is cleared, which includes setting the alpha to 0.0. When the offscreen drawing surface is rendered on-screen, the area of overlap is transparent, allowing the background color of the on-screen window to show through.

XOR, a Maverick

The 2D API supports one more compositing rule, but not in an obvious way. Before the 2D API existed, the `Graphics` class supported two simple compositing rules through two methods, `setPaintMode()` and `setXORMode()`. `Graphics2D` is a subclass of `Graphics` and inherits these methods and their functionality:

public abstract void setPaintMode()

> In this mode, `Graphics` overwrites pixels of the drawing surface with what-ever graphics primitive is being rendered. In a `Graphics2D`, this method is equivalent to `setComposite(AlphaComposite.SrcOver)`.

public abstract void setXORMode(Color cl)

> This method installs a special compositing rule. The color of pixels on the drawing surface is determined by combining the colors in the source and destination and the XOR color passed to this method: $c_d = c_s \oplus c_x \oplus c_{d0}$, where c_d is the new color of the destination pixel, c_s is the color of the source pixel, c_x is the color passed to `setXORMode()`, c_{d0} is the original color of the destination pixel, and $\oplus$ is the XOR operator.[*] This compositing rule is not one of the Porter-Duff alpha compositing rules, as alpha is not used in the calculation.

The reason XOR mode is interesting is that it makes rendering easily reversible. If you perform the exact same operation twice in XOR mode, the drawing surface is unchanged.

XOR is a bitwise binary operation, which makes it hard to understand visually. In the following example, an overlapping red and blue rectangle are drawn. Both rectangles are rendered using XOR mode with white as the XOR color.

```
import java.awt.*;
import java.awt.geom.*;
```

---

[*] The XOR calculation is performed on the pixel's samples, not color values. This means that the results depend on how the drawing surface represents colors. In the examples that follow, I assume that colors are represented by 8-bit red, green, and blue values.

```
public class XORRectangles {
  public static void main(String[] args) {
    ApplicationFrame f = new ApplicationFrame("XORRectangles v1.0") {
      private int mNumberOfLines = 25;
      private Color[] mColors = { Color.red, Color.green, Color.blue };

      public void paint(Graphics g) {
        Graphics2D g2 = (Graphics2D)g;

        // Set XOR mode, using white as the XOR color.
        g2.setXORMode(Color.white);
        // Paint a red rectangle.
        Rectangle2D r = new Rectangle2D.Double(50, 50, 150, 100);
        g2.setPaint(Color.red);
        g2.fill(r);
        // Shift the coordinate space.
        g2.transform(AffineTransform.getTranslateInstance(25, 25));
        // Draw a blue rectangle.
        g2.setPaint(Color.blue);
        g2.fill(r);
      }
    };
    f.setSize(300, 200);
    f.center();
    f.setVisible(true);
  }
}
```

Figure C-6 shows the results. When the red rectangle is rendered, it comes out red because the XOR color (white) cancels out the white color of the background, as shown in Figure 5-9. The same thing happens for the blue rectangle in the parts that don't overlap the red rectangle. The background (destination) color and the XOR color cancel out, and the rectangle appears blue. In the region where the two rectangles overlap, it's a little more interesting. Figure 5-10 shows the bitwise math. The end result is that the region of overlap appears green! It's even less predictable if the XOR color and the background color are not the same.

	red	green	blue
c_s (red)	11111111	00000000	00000000
$\oplus$ c_x (white)	11111111	11111111	11111111
$\oplus$ c_{d0} (white)	11111111	11111111	11111111
$=$ c_d (red)	11111111	00000000	00000000

Figure 5-9. Adding red to a white background using XOR

	red	green	blue
c$_s$ (blue)	00000000	00000000	11111111
⊕ c$_x$ (white)	11111111	11111111	11111111
⊕ cd0 (red)	11111111	00000000	00000000
= c$_d$ (green)	00000000	11111111	00000000

Figure 5-10. XOR mode with blue, white, and red

An interesting property of XOR is that two identical operations cancel each other out. In the previous example, if you draw the blue rectangle again in XOR mode, it will seem to disappear and you'll be left with a red rectangle on a white background.

XOR mode cannot be used with antialiasing. When XOR mode is enabled, any rendering done by the Graphics2D will not be antialiased.

Clipping

Clipping is a technique that limits the extent of a drawing. The effect is similar to drawing a picture on a sheet of paper and then cutting out part of the picture with scissors. Graphics2D can clip drawings using any Shape. In fact, Graphics2D maintains a clipping shape as part of its state. Figure 5-11 shows a simple drawing in three states: unclipped, clipped to a triangle, and clipped to a circle.

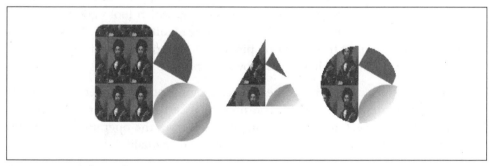

Figure 5-11. Clipping

Graphics2D has methods that manage the current clipping shape, including:

public abstract void clip(Shape s)
> This method clips rendering to the specified shape. The intersection of the supplied shape and the current clipping shape becomes the new clipping shape.

public abstract Shape getClip()

> Use this method to retrieve the `Graphics2D` 's current clipping shape. This is useful if you want to restore this shape again later.

public abstract void setClip(Shape clip)

> This method sets the current clipping shape for this `Graphics2D`. Unlike `clip()`, which only modifies the current clipping shape, this method completely replaces it. This is useful for restoring a clipping shape you've previously retrieved with a call to `getClip()`.

There's quite a bit of power here: you can clip rendering using any `Shape`, including complicated shapes with multiple subpaths. You can even use shapes of text strings for clipping. (Chapter 7, *Advanced Text Layout*, describes how to obtain a `Shape` representing some text.)

The following example shows how to set the clipping shape to a circle:

```
Ellipse2D e = new Ellipse2D.Float(-50, -50, 100, 100);
g2.clip(e);
```

Rendering Hints

The 2D API allows you to control the quality of its rendering through the use of *rendering hints*. They are called hints because they don't directly control the rendering engine; they merely suggest your preferences. The rendering engine can follow the hints or ignore them as it wishes. Rendering hints are encapsulated by the `java.awt.RenderingHints` class.

The rendering engine, `Graphics2D`, usually knows more than one way of doing things. If it's drawing a shape, it can use antialiasing, which looks good, or it can draw the shape with aliasing, which is fast. Similar tradeoffs of quality for speed are available in other parts of the rendering pipeline. Rendering hints give you a set of knobs that you can fiddle with to adjust how `Graphics2D` performs.

Rendering hints are used in one other place: image processing. (See Chapter 10, *Image Processing*, for the full story.) The image processing operators all accept a `RenderingHints` object in their constructors. This gives the operator suggestions about whether to give preference to processing speed or quality.

Rendering hints are specified using a key and value scheme. You tell `Graphics2D` that you want a certain key, like `KEY_ANTIALIASING`, to have a certain value, such as `VALUE_ANTIALIAS_ON`. The `Graphics2D` will then use antialiasing in its rendering, if it can. Keys are represented by constants in the `RenderingHints` class, which are all instances of `RenderingHints.Key`. The values are also represented by constants in the `RenderingHints` class. The keys and values are shown in Table 5-2.

Table 5-2. Rendering Hints, Keys, and Values

Key	Possible Values
KEY_ANTIALIASING	VALUE_ANTIALIAS_ON
	VALUE_ANTIALIAS_OFF
	VALUE_ANTIALIAS_DEFAULT
KEY_RENDERING	VALUE_RENDER_QUALITY
	VALUE_RENDER_SPEED
	VALUE_RENDER_DEFAULT
KEY_DITHERING	VALUE_DITHER_DISABLE
	VALUE_DITHER_ENABLE
	VALUE_DITHER_DEFAULT
KEY_COLOR_RENDERING	VALUE_COLOR_RENDER_QUALITY
	VALUE_COLOR_RENDER_SPEED
	VALUE_COLOR_RENDER_DEFAULT
KEY_FRACTIONALMETRICS	VALUE_FRACTIONALMETRICS_ON
	VALUE_FRACTIONALMETRICS_OFF
	VALUE_FRACTIONALMETRICS_DEFAULT
KEY_TEXT_ANTIALIASING	VALUE_TEXT_ANTIALIAS_ON
	VALUE_TEXT_ANTIALIAS_OFF
	VALUE_TEXT_ANTIALIAS_DEFAULT
KEY_INTERPOLATION	VALUE_INTERPOLATION_BICUBIC
	VALUE_INTERPOLATION_BILINEAR
	VALUE_INTERPOLATION_NEAREST_NEIGHBOR
KEY_ALPHA_INTERPOLATION	VALUE_ALPHA_INTERPOLATION_QUALITY
	VALUE_ALPHA_INTERPOLATION_SPEED
	VALUE_ALPHA_INTERPOLATION_DEFAULT

The meaning of cach hint is given below:

antialiasing (KEY_ANTIALIASING)

Antialiasing is explained in Chapter 2, *The Big Picture*. This hint controls whether antialiasing will be used to render shapes and text. (You can control text antialiasing separately, if you wish. See the KEY_TEXT_ANTIALIASING hint.)

rendering (KEY_RENDERING)

This hint tells the Graphics2D whether you'd rather have it run as fast as it can or do the best job that it can.

dithering (KEY_DITHERING)

Some displays have limits on how many colors they can display. Dithering is the process of computing approximate colors when the display can't render all the colors that are needed. This hint controls whether dithering is used to approximate colors on such displays.

color rendering (KEY_COLOR_RENDERING)

This hint controls whether colors are corrected for a given display using a device profile. See Chapter 8, *Color*, for more information on device color profiles.

fractional text metrics (KEY_FRACTIONALMETRICS)

Use this hint to control whether floating point or integer font measurements will be used. Historically, the JDK has used integer metrics, but the 2D API now supports floating point font metrics that allow for more precise text positioning. See Chapter 6, *Text*, for more information about text metrics.

text antialiasing (KEY_TEXT_ANTIALIASING)

This hint allows you to control the antialiasing of text separately from the antialiasing of other shapes. Text antialiasing may significantly slow down your application, so you might want to turn this hint off while leaving the KEY_ ANTIALIASING hint on. If you want text antialiasing to be under the control of the KEY_ANTIALIASING hint, just leave the KEY_TEXT_ANTIALIASING with the VALUE_TEXT_ANTIALIAS_DEFAULT value.

image interpolation (KEY_INTERPOLATION)

This hint is used by both Graphics2D and the image processing classes. It controls which algorithm is used to transform images. The VALUE_ INTERPOLATION_NEAREST_NEIGHBOR algorithm is fast but has low quality. VALUE_INTERPOLATION_BILINEAR provides higher quality at a lower speed. VALUE_INTERPOLATION_BICUBIC would provide even better quality, but it is not yet supported in the 2D API. See the "Geometric Transformations" section in Chapter 10 for a full explanation of the nearest neighbor and bilinear algorithms.

alpha interpolation (KEY_ALPHA_INTERPOLATION)

This hint controls how alpha values are calculated when shapes, text, or images are rendered using partially transparent colors or compositing rules with fractional alpha values. You can opt for quality or speed. In the initial release of Java 2 (JDK 1.2), however, the value of this hint has no effect: the rendering engine only implements one way of calculating alpha values.

There are two ways to pass rendering hints to Graphics2D. First, you can pass a single key and value pair using the setRenderingHint() method. Second, you can create a RenderingHints object that contains as many key and value pairs as you'd like. Then you can pass the whole object to Graphics2D using the setRenderingHints() (plural) method.

public abstract void setRenderingHint(RenderingHints.Key hintKey, Object hintValue)

Use this method to set a single rendering hint key to the specified value. To ask for antialiasing, for example, you would do the following:

```
public void paint(Graphics g) {
    Graphics2D g2 = (Graphics2D)g;
    g2.setRenderingHint(RenderingHints.KEY_ANTIALIASING,
        RenderingHints.VALUE_ANTIALIAS_ON);
    // ...
```

public abstract void setRenderingHints(Map hints)

This method sets rendering hints *en masse* in the Graphics2D using the keys and values in the given Map.* You can pass an instance of RenderingHints or any other class that implements the Map interface, including java.util. Hashtable. The new hints will replace all of the hints that are currently set in the Graphics2D. The following example shows how you can create a RenderingHints object and pass it to a Graphics2D:

```
public void paint(Graphics g) {
    Graphics2D g2 = (Graphics2D)g;
    RenderingHints hints = new RenderingHints(
        RenderingHints.KEY_ANTIALIASING,
        RenderingHints.VALUE_ANTIALIAS_ON);
    hints.add(RenderingHints.KEY_RENDERING,
        RenderingHints.VALUE_RENDER_ON);
    g2.setRenderingHints(hints);
    // ...
```

Graphics2D includes several other methods for managing rendering hints:

public abstract Object getRenderingHint(RenderingHints.Key hintKey)

This method returns the current value of a particular hint in this Graphics2D.

public abstract RenderingHints getRenderingHints()

This method returns the entire set of hints that are defined for this Graphics2D.

public abstract void addRenderingHints(Map hints)

Use this method to supplement, rather than to replace, the current set of hints in this Graphics2D. Only the hints defined in the given Map are modified. Other hints currently defined in this Graphics2D are left alone. In contrast, setRenderingHints() replaces the current selection of hints.

---

* The java.util.Map interface is part of the Collections API, a new part of the Java 2 platform.

6

In this chapter:
- *Overview*
- *Drawing Text*
- *Fonts*
- *Font Metrics*

Text

The 2D API has sophisticated text rendering capabilities, ranging from simple methods for rendering character strings to entire classes for text layout and editing. In this chapter, I'll begin by introducing the concepts and terminology of text rendering. Then I'll talk about how to render text in the 2D API, how to choose and manipulate fonts, and how to determine the dimensions of rendered text. Chapter 7, *Advanced Text Layout*, contains information about the 2D API's more powerful text features.

Overview

In Java, text is expressed as a series of Unicode characters. Unicode is a standardized list of characters matched up with 16-bit character codes. The Unicode standard includes character codes for the characters that are used in most of the world's written languages. For more information, visit *http://www.unicode.org/*. Java uses 16-bit Unicode characters in its `char` type. `Strings`, furthermore, are an array of Unicode characters.

Rendering text is the task of finding shapes that correspond to characters and rendering the shapes on a drawing surface. In the 2D API, this is the job of `Graphics2D`, the rendering engine.

Fonts and Glyphs

The shapes that represent characters are called *glyphs*. Frequently there is a one-to-one correspondence between characters and glyphs, but not all the time. For example, the characters "f" and "i" each have a corresponding glyph. But sometimes, for aesthetic reasons, "f" and "i" together are represented by a single glyph, called a *ligature*. An example of a ligature is shown in Figure 6-1. Notice how the dot on the "i" has been combined with the ball on the "f" to create an efficient representation of the two characters.

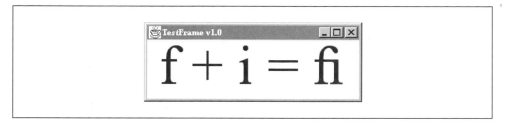

Figure 6-1. A ligature is a single glyph representing two or more characters

Furthermore, different glyphs may be used for a single character depending on the character's context. This is true in Arabic writing, where the same character can have different shapes depending on whether it's at the beginning, middle, or end of a word. You'll see an example of this later in this chapter.

A *font* is a collection of glyphs. Fonts are usually only defined for some subset of the Unicode character set, usually corresponding to a single language. Aside from the glyph definitions, a font also includes information about how characters and glyphs match up. As you may remember from Chapter 2, *The Big Picture*, part of a `Graphics2D`'s state is its *current font*. This font is used to render text. You can set the current font by calling `setFont()`.

The 2D API gives your application access to all of the fonts installed on the underlying operating system. This is a big advantage over previous versions of the JDK, which only allowed access to a handful of fonts.

Font Metrics

Font metrics are a set of measurements that describe a font. Figure 6-2 shows several such measurements. The entire height of the font is the sum of the *leading*, *ascent*, and *descent* of the font. Ascent measures the height that character shapes rise above the baseline. Descent measures how far some shapes fall beneath the baseline (note the *y* in Figure 6-2). Leading is the extra space that is added between lines of text.* Ascent, descent, and leading are used for laying out multiple lines of text and do not actually impose any restrictions on a font's glyphs. For example, glyphs can extend higher than the ascent or lower than the descent. In general, however, a font's glyphs will stay within the confines of the ascent and descent.

---

* Leading gets its name from the days of metal typesetting, where a strip of lead was used to add space between lines of text.

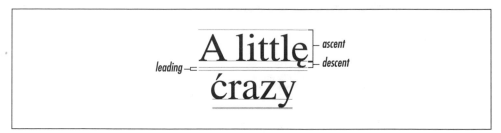

Figure 6-2. Some font metrics

Another important quantity is *advance*. The advance of a piece of text tells where on the baseline the next piece of text should be rendered. It is not the same as the bounding box width of the glyph shapes. For example, if you render the string "alf" followed by the string "redo," the "r" might be tucked under the top curve of the "f" to form the word "alfredo." In this case, the advance of the string "alf" would be a little less than the bounding box width of the glyphs.

Text Rendering Options

The 2D API offers a lot of flexibility in rendering text. Four basic techniques are available. The list below orders these techniques from least control to the greatest:

1. Use a Swing component like `JTextField`, `JTextArea`, or `JEditorPane`. These are all subclasses of `javax.swing.text.JTextComponent`. These components support editing, multiple fonts, and multiple styles, all without you having to lift a finger. For more information on Swing, see *Java Swing*, by Robert Eckstein, Marc Loy, and Dave Wood (O'Reilly).

2. Pass a character string to one of `Graphics2D`'s `drawString()` methods. The `Graphics2D` will use its current font to figure out which glyphs correspond to the characters in the string. Then it renders the shapes, just as it would render any other shapes. This allows you to take advantage of the elements of `Graphics2D`'s rendering pipeline, like transformations and compositing rules. This approach is covered in this chapter.

3. If you prefer to implement text editing yourself, use a `java.awt.font.TextLayout` object to take care of laying out your text. `TextLayout` includes nifty features like mixed styles, bidirectional text layout, carets, highlighting, and hit testing. Chapter 7 describes these features.

4. The lowest level of control is to manipulate glyphs yourself. In this technique, you use a font to determine the glyph shapes. Then you can do whatever you want with the shapes: fill them, transform them, stroke them, use them as clipping shapes, etc. Glyph-level manipulation is also discussed in Chapter 7.

Drawing Text

To render text, use one of Graphics2D's drawText() methods. There are four versions of this method. For now, let's look at the two simplest versions:

public abstract void drawString(String str, int x, int y)
public abstract void drawString(String s, float x, float y)

> This method draws the given string, using the current font, at the location specified by x and y. If the current font doesn't have glyphs for some of the characters in the string, the string may not be rendered properly.

The location specified by x and y is the location of the end of the string's *baseline*. The baseline is that line you had to write on in penmanship class in the first grade. A baseline is shown in Figure 6-3.

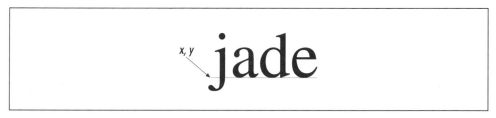

Figure 6-3. Baseline of a string

For languages that read from right to left, the point specified by x and y is still the left end of the baseline. Figure 6-4 shows some Arabic characters as rendered by drawString().

Figure 6-4. Baseline of a right-to-left string

Several different baselines may exist for a single glyph. The baseline shown in Figure 6-3 and Figure 6-4 is called the *Roman baseline*. The 2D API also includes the concepts of a *center baseline* and a *hanging baseline*. These are shown in Figure 6-5. The initial release of Java 2 (JDK 1.2) does not support the use of baselines other than the Roman baseline. There are methods that provide information about the other baselines, but they are not implemented in the initial release.

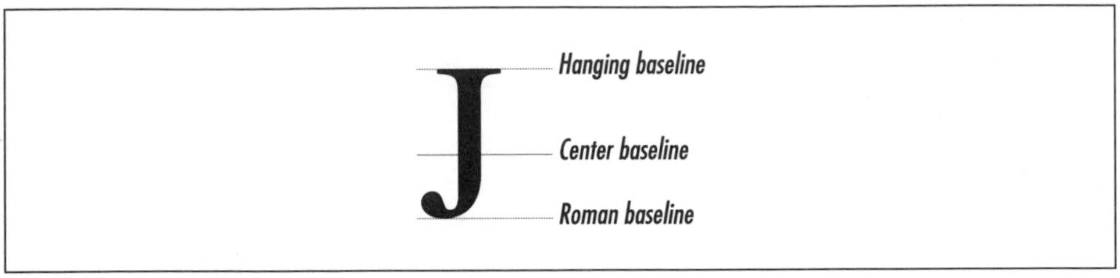

Figure 6-5. Three baseline types

The following example shows how to select a font and draw a simple string. Font selection is covered later in this chapter.

```java
import java.awt.*;
import java.awt.font.TextAttribute;
import java.text.*;

public class SimpleText {
  public static void main(String[] args) {
    Frame f = new ApplicationFrame("SimpleText v1.0") {
      public void paint(Graphics g) {
        Graphics2D g2 = (Graphics2D)g;

        g2.setRenderingHint(RenderingHints.KEY_ANTIALIASING,
            RenderingHints.VALUE_ANTIALIAS_ON);
        Font font = new Font("Serif", Font.PLAIN, 96);
        g2.setFont(font);

        g2.drawString("jade", 40, 120);
      }
    };
    f.setVisible(true);
  }
}
```

Close Enough?

The drawString(String s, float x, float y) method performs subtle approximations that you might not be expecting. To understand why, think about what this method has to do. It has to find the glyphs (shapes) that correspond to the characters in the given string. These glyphs come from Graphics2D's current font. Once these glyphs are obtained, they need to be filled, starting at the location given by x and y.

Here's where it gets tricky. Remember, from Chapter 2, *The Big Picture*, that something called a rasterizer converts shapes into alpha coverage values. The alpha values can then be used to color pixels on a drawing surface to fill the shape. To optimize the rendering of text, Java 2D's rasterizer caches rasterized glyphs. Instead of rasterizing every glyph every time it is drawn, the rendering engine uses its saved glyph rasterizations to speed things up.

The catch is that cached rasterizations are only valid for integer pixel positions. Consider a glyph for the character "R". If you rasterize this glyph when it is placed at 0, 0, the results are different than when the same glyph is rasterized at 0.5, 0 (assuming a User Space where one unit is the width of one pixel). To compensate for this, text is placed at integer pixel positions, even if you specify fractional pixel locations in `drawString()`. This process is called *grid fitting*—it ensures that the cached glyph rasterizations can be used to render text. Grid fitting is an approximation, a sacrifice of quality for speed.

The `KEY_FRACTIONALMETRICS` rendering hint (see Chapter 5, *Rendering*) modifies this behavior. When this hint is turned off, the advance of each glyph is rounded to an integer. The effect is that the entire string is adjusted to fit on the pixel grid. If the hint is on, the floating-point advances of the glyphs are used, so different parts of the string may fit to different parts of the pixel grid. If you animate a string through fractional pixel positions, this effect is readily apparent. With the fractional metric hint off, the entire string moves by pixel increments. With the hint on, different parts of the string move by pixel increments at different times, like an inchworm.

If you really want to position text with sub-pixel precision, don't rely on `drawString()`. Instead, use one of methods in Chapter 7 to obtain the string's `Shape`. Then render the `Shape` at whatever coordinates you want. This will, of course, be slower than `drawString()`. The `Shape` will be rasterized each time it is rendered, so you won't have the advantage of cached glyph rasterizations.

Stylin' with Styled Text

You can also render text using a `java.text.AttributedCharacterIterator`. `AttributedCharacterIterator` is an interface that lets you step through a string that has associated formatting information, like colors, text styles, or fonts.

Fortunately, you don't have to implement the `AttributedCharacterIterator` interface yourself. You can get an `AttributedCharacterIterator` from an instance of `java.text.AttributedString`.* Here's how it works:

1. Create an `AttributedString`. The simplest way to do this is using a plain old `String`:

   ```
   AttributedString as = new AttributedString("Future Love Paradise");
   ```

---

* `AttributedString` isn't really part of the 2D API. For more information on this class, see the JDK documentation.

What's an Iterator?

An *iterator* is something that you can use to step through another object's data. (The `java.util.Enumeration` interface is an iterator for a collection of objects.) A *character iterator* lets you walk through a string of characters. A `Graphics2D` can use a character iterator to step through a string of text, finding glyphs for each character and rendering the glyphs. Character iterators are represented by the `java.text.CharacterIterator` interface.

An *attributed character iterator* is simply an iterator for styled text. An attributed character iterator can be used to retrieve both character data and its attributes. The corresponding interface is `java.text.AttributedCharacter-Iterator`, which is an extension of `CharacterIterator`.

---

2. Add attributes to the `AttributedString`. The `java.awt.font.Text-Attribute` class contains a handy collection of attribute keys and values, shown in Table 6-1. You can add attributes to the whole string or just to a specific range of characters:

```
as.addAttribute(TextAttribute.FONT, serifFont);
as.addAttribute(TextAttribute.FONT, sansSerifFont, 2, 5);
```

3. Retrieve the iterator using `AttributedString`'s `getIterator()` method.

4. Pass the iterator to `drawString()`.

Table 6-1. Text Attribute Keys and Values

Key	Possible Values	Full Text Only?
BACKGROUND	a Paint	no
BIDI_EMBEDDING[a]	an Integer, either 1 to 15 or -15 to -1	no
CHAR_REPLACEMENT	a GraphicAttribute	no
FAMILY	a String containing a font family name	no
FONT	a Font	no
FOREGROUND	a Paint	no
INPUT_METHOD_HIGHLIGHT	an InputMethodHighlight[b]	no
JUSTIFICATION[c]	a Float from 0.0 to 1.0 JUSTIFICATION_FULL JUSTIFICATION_NONE	yes
POSTURE	a Float POSTURE_OBLIQUE POSTURE_REGULAR	no

Table 6-1. Text Attribute Keys and Values (continued)

Key	Possible Values	Full Text Only?
RUN_DIRECTION	a Boolean RUN_DIRECTION_LTR RUN_DIRECTION_RTL	yes
SIZE	a Float	no
STRIKETHROUGH	a Boolean STRIKETHROUGH_ON	no
SUPERSCRIPT	an Integer SUPERSCRIPT_SUB SUPERSCRIPT_SUPER	no
SWAP_COLORS	a Boolean SWAP_COLORS_ON	no
TRANSFORM[d]	a TransformAttribute	no
UNDERLINE	an Integer UNDERLINE_ON	no
WEIGHT	a Float WEIGHT_EXTRA_LIGHT WEIGHT_LIGHT WEIGHT_DEMILIGHT WEIGHT_REGULAR WEIGHT_SEMIBOLD WEIGHT_MEDIUM WEIGHT_DEMIBOLD WEIGHT_BOLD WEIGHT_HEAVY WEIGHT_EXTRABOLD WEIGHT_ULTRABOLD	no
WIDTH	a Float WIDTH_CONDENSED WIDTH_SEMI_CONDENSED WIDTH_REGULAR WIDTH_SEMI_EXTENDED WIDTH_EXTENDED	no

[a] Not implemented in the initial release of Java 2.
[b] This class is in the `java.awt.im` package, part of the Input Method Framework API. For more information, see the JDK documentation or *http://java.sun.com/products/jdk/1.2/docs/guide/intl/*.
[c] Not implemented in the initial release of Java 2.
[d] Not implemented in the initial release of Java 2.

The following `Graphics2D` methods support `AttributedCharacterIterators`:

public abstract void drawString(AttributedCharacterIterator iterator, int x, int y)

public abstract void drawString(AttributedCharacterIterator iterator, float x, float y)

These methods render the given iterator at the location given by x and y.

The following example shows how to associate different fonts and colors with different parts of an `AttributedString`:

```
import java.awt.*;
import java.awt.font.TextAttribute;
import java.text.*;

public class IteratorTest {
  public static void main(String[] args) {
    Frame f = new ApplicationFrame("IteratorTest v1.0") {
      public void paint(Graphics g) {
        Graphics2D g2 = (Graphics2D)g;

        String s = "a big surprise";
        Dimension d = getSize();

        g2.setRenderingHint(RenderingHints.KEY_ANTIALIASING,
            RenderingHints.VALUE_ANTIALIAS_ON);
        Font serifFont = new Font("Serif", Font.PLAIN, 48);
        Font sansSerifFont = new Font("Monospaced", Font.PLAIN, 48);

        AttributedString as = new AttributedString(s);
        as.addAttribute(TextAttribute.FONT, serifFont);
        as.addAttribute(TextAttribute.FONT, sansSerifFont, 2, 5);
        as.addAttribute(TextAttribute.FOREGROUND, Color.red, 2, 5);

        g2.drawString(as.getIterator(), 40, 80);
      }
    };
    f.setVisible(true);
  }
}
```

Figure 6-6 shows the results of this example.

Figure 6-6. Rendering styled text with a character iterator

Most of the attributes shown in Table 6-1 are self-explanatory. BACKGROUND and
FOREGROUND, for example, contain Paint objects for the background and foreground of the text. FONT, FAMILY, and SIZE refer to the font that will be used to
render text. And POSTURE, SUPERSCRIPT, WEIGHT, and WIDTH are used to determine the font's style. The STRIKETROUGH and UNDERLINE attributes determine
whether strikethrough lines and underlines will be drawn—there's an example
later in this chapter that demonstrates how these attributes are used.

Some of the attributes in the `TextAttributes` are more subtle. The `CHAR_REPLACEMENT` attribute is used to embed shapes and images in text. It is discussed in the next section. `SWAP_COLORS` is used to swap the foreground and background paints.

`JUSTIFICATION` is used to specify whether text should be fully *justified* or not. Full justification means that the text is stretched to fill a certain width. The stretching is accomplished by adding extra space between the glyphs of a string. The `TRANSFORM` attribute allows you to specify a transformation for some or all of the text. The `BIDI_EMBEDDING` attribute is used in bidirectional text and is outside the scope of this book. For more information on bidirectional text, see the Unicode Standard, available at *http://www.unicode.org/*. The `RUN_DIRECTION` attribute specifies whether the overall direction of a paragraph of text is right-to-left or left-to-right. `INPUT_METHOD_HIGHLIGHT` is a hook for the Input Method Framework— you should not apply this attribute yourself. For more information on the Input Method Framework, see *http://java.sun.com/products/jdk/1.2/docs/guide/intl/*.

Embedding Graphics in Text

Using an `AttributedString` for text rendering also gives you the opportunity to embed images and shapes in your text string. While this might seem obtuse (why not render the text, images, and shapes separately?), it is crucial for applications that render shapes and images embedded in bidirectional text. It's also handy in applications like web browsers that have graphic elements embedded in text. Using an `AttributedString`, you can substitute images and shapes for characters. In essence, the images and shapes behave like characters themselves, which can simplify your life—you can just let the 2D API worry about the formatting details.

To take advantage of this feature, use the `CHAR_REPLACEMENT` attribute defined in `TextAttributes` (see Table 6-1). You should apply this attribute to a single character of your `AttributedString`. The value of this attribute is any subclass of the `java.awt.font.GraphicAttribute` class. `GraphicAttribute` doesn't do anything by itself, but it does define constants that are used to indicate how a graphic attribute should be aligned with its accompanying text:

public static int TOP_ALIGNMENT
>   This constant aligns the graphic element with the top of the text. The top of the text is determined by subtracting the ascent from the baseline.

public static int BOTTOM_ALIGNMENT
>   This constant is used to align the graphic element with the bottom of the text, where the bottom is the baseline plus the descent.

public static int ROMAN_BASELINE
public static int CENTER_BASELINE
public static int HANGING_BASELINE

These constants are used to align the graphic element with the corresponding baseline.

GraphicAttribute is an abstract class, but it has two useful subclasses, ImageGraphicAttribute and ShapeGraphicAttribute. Their constructors are:

public ImageGraphicAttribute(Image image, int alignment)

This constructor creates an ImageGraphicAttribute from the supplied image. The alignment parameter should be one of the constants that are defined in the GraphicAttribute class. The top left corner of the image is placed at the text insertion point (subject to the alignment parameter). If you pass ROMAN_BASELINE, for example, the top left corner of the image will be placed on the text baseline. To adjust the position of the image, you can pass a different alignment or use the following constructor.

public ImageGraphicAttribute(Image image, int alignment, float originX, float originY)

This constructor is the same as above but accepts a pair of coordinate offsets, originX and originY. This coordinate pair determines what point of the image will be placed at the text insertion point. If you passed ROMAN_BASELINE for the alignment and 25, 25 for the origin coordinates, the image would be placed so that its 25, 25 point was at the text insertion point on the Roman baseline of the string. You can try this out to see what happens in the example below.

public ShapeGraphicAttribute(Shape shape, int alignment, boolean stroke)

This constructor creates a ShapeGraphicAttribute using the supplied shape. Again, the alignment parameter should be one of the alignment constants defined in the GraphicAttribute class. The stroke parameter determines whether the shape will be stroked or filled. It should be one of the constants defined in ShapeGraphicAttribute, either STROKE or FILL. If the shape is stroked, a default Stroke with a width of 1.0 will be used.

In the following example, two AttributedStrings are rendered with the CHAR_REPLACEMENT attribute. One displays an image; the other displays a stroked shape. This example makes use of ApplicationFrame, which you've seen before, in Chapter 1, *Introduction*. The image is loaded using a technique described in Chapter 9, *Images*.

```
import java.awt.*;
import java.awt.font.*;
import java.awt.geom.Ellipse2D;
import java.text.*;
```

```
public class InlineGraphics {
  public static void main(String[] args) {
    Frame f = new ApplicationFrame("InlineGraphics v1.0") {
      public void paint(Graphics g) {
        Graphics2D g2 = (Graphics2D)g;

        g2.setRenderingHint(RenderingHints.KEY_ANTIALIASING,
            RenderingHints.VALUE_ANTIALIAS_ON);
        Font serifFont = new Font("Serif", Font.PLAIN, 32);

        AttributedString as = new AttributedString("Star \ufffc pin");
        as.addAttribute(TextAttribute.FONT, serifFont);

        String filename = "roa2.jpg";
        Image image = new javax.swing.ImageIcon(filename).getImage();
        ImageGraphicAttribute imageAttribute = new ImageGraphicAttribute(
            image, GraphicAttribute.TOP_ALIGNMENT);
        as.addAttribute(TextAttribute.CHAR_REPLACEMENT,
            imageAttribute, 5, 6);
        g2.drawString(as.getIterator(), 20, 120);

        as = new AttributedString("Red \ufffc circle");
        as.addAttribute(TextAttribute.FONT, serifFont);

        Shape shape = new Ellipse2D.Float(0, -25, 25, 25);
        ShapeGraphicAttribute shapeAttribute = new ShapeGraphicAttribute(
            shape, GraphicAttribute.ROMAN_BASELINE,
            ShapeGraphicAttribute.STROKE);
        as.addAttribute(TextAttribute.CHAR_REPLACEMENT,
            shapeAttribute, 4, 5);
        as.addAttribute(TextAttribute.FOREGROUND, Color.red, 4, 5);
        g2.drawString(as.getIterator(), 20, 200);
      }
    };
    f.setVisible(true);
  }
}
```

A GraphicAttribute actually replaces a text character. This means that one character of text is not rendered as text; the graphic attribute is rendered instead. The Unicode Standard defines a special character for cases like this, called the *replacement character*, code FFFC. It's used in the example here as a placeholder for the image and the shape.

The results of this example are shown in Figure 6-7. The image uses TOP_ALIGNMENT, so its top edge is aligned with the ascent of the font. The shape, on the other hand, is aligned with the Roman baseline of the text. Because the shape is defined in negative y space, the bottom of the shape just grazes the Roman baseline. An ellipse defined as (0, 0, 25, 25) would actually sit below the Roman baseline.

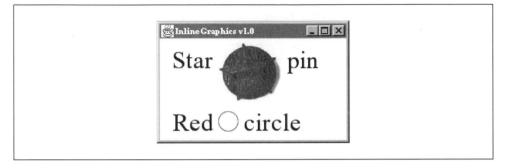

Figure 6-7. Images and shapes can act like characters

You can set the `Stroke` that is used for a `ShapeGraphicAttribute` by calling `setStroke()` before you render an attributed string. If you have multiple shapes that should be rendered with different `Strokes`, you will need to render them in separate attributed strings, setting the stroke before each one. You can, however, control the `Paint` on each `ShapeGraphicAttribute` individually, as shown in the previous example. Simply set the `FOREGROUND` attribute for the same character range as the shape graphic attribute to control what `Paint` is used.

Fun Stuff for Free!

Because text travels through the same rendering pipeline as shapes and images, you can do some neat stuff with text without breaking a sweat. (See Chapter 2 for an overview of the rendering pipeline.) Transforming text, for example, is just as easy as transforming shapes. As you saw in Chapter 2, drawing text is really a special case of drawing shapes: a font is used to determine the shapes, which are then filled. Any transformation that you set in a `Graphics2D` will be used when the text is rendered. In the following example, a rotational transformation is applied to the `Graphics2D` before text is drawn:

```
g2.transform(AffineTransform.getRotateInstance(Math.PI / 6));
g2.drawString("Rotated text", 150.0f, 50.0f);
```

Furthermore, the current paint of a `Graphics2D` is used to render text, so you already know how to fill text with a gradient or a pattern. The `Graphics2D`'s current transformation, compositing rule, clipping shape, and rendering hints are all applied to text rendering, as well. For more information on these parts of the rendering pipeline, see Chapter 5, *Rendering*.

Here's an example that shows how to transform text and make it partially transparent using a custom compositing rule. The output is shown in Figure 6-8.

Figure 6-8. Rendering text with rotation and transparency

```java
import java.awt.*;
import java.awt.geom.*;

public class TextRendering {
  public static void main(String[] args) {
    Frame frame = new ApplicationFrame("TextRendering v1.0") {
      public void paint(Graphics g) {
        Graphics2D g2 = (Graphics2D)g;
        g2.setRenderingHint(RenderingHints.KEY_ANTIALIASING,
            RenderingHints.VALUE_ANTIALIAS_ON);

        // Transform the origin to the bottom center of the window.
        Dimension d = getSize();
        AffineTransform ct = AffineTransform.getTranslateInstance(
            d.width / 2, d.height * 3 / 4);
        g2.transform(ct);

        // Get an appropriate font.
        String s = "jade";
        Font f = new Font("Serif", Font.PLAIN, 128);
        g2.setFont(f);

        int limit = 6;
        for (int i = 1; i <= limit; i++) {
          // Save the original transformation.
          AffineTransform oldTransform = g2.getTransform();
```

```
                float ratio = (float)i / (float)limit;
                g2.transform(AffineTransform.getRotateInstance(
                    Math.PI * (ratio - 1.0f)));
                float alpha = ((i == limit) ? 1.0f : ratio / 3);
                g2.setComposite(AlphaComposite.getInstance(
                    AlphaComposite.SRC_OVER, alpha));
                g2.drawString(s, 0, 0);

                // Restore the original transformation.
                g2.setTransform(oldTransform);
            }
          }
        };
        frame.setVisible(true);
    }
}
```

Here's another example that shows how a simple TexturePaint can make a word look snappy. Figure C-7 shows the results. (For more information on TexturePaint, refer back to Chapter 4, *Painting and Stroking*.) It would be even easier to use a GradientPaint when rendering text.

The example works by creating an image in the getTextureImage() method. A simple pattern of colored squares is drawn on this image. Then, in the paint() method, the image is used to build a TexturePaint. After passing the TexturePaint to Graphics2D's setPaint() method, a string is rendered with the familiar call to drawString().

```
import java.awt.*;
import java.awt.geom.Line2D;
import java.awt.image.BufferedImage;

public class TexturedText {
  public static void main(String[] args) {
    Frame f = new ApplicationFrame("TexturedText v1.0") {
      public void paint(Graphics g) {
        Graphics2D g2 = (Graphics2D)g;

        g2.setRenderingHint(RenderingHints.KEY_ANTIALIASING,
            RenderingHints.VALUE_ANTIALIAS_ON);
        Font font = new Font("Times New Roman", Font.PLAIN, 72);
        g2.setFont(font);

        String s = "Checkmate!";
        Dimension d = getSize();
        float x = 20, y = 100;

        BufferedImage bi = getTextureImage();
        Rectangle r = new Rectangle(0, 0, bi.getWidth(), bi.getHeight());
```

```
            TexturePaint tp = new TexturePaint(bi, r);
            g2.setPaint(tp);

            g2.drawString(s, x, y);
        }

        private BufferedImage getTextureImage() {
            // Create the test image.
            int size = 8;
            BufferedImage bi = new BufferedImage(size, size,
                BufferedImage.TYPE_INT_ARGB);
            Graphics2D g2 = bi.createGraphics();
            g2.setPaint(Color.red);
            g2.fillRect(0, 0, size / 2, size / 2);
            g2.setPaint(Color.yellow);
            g2.fillRect(size / 2, 0, size, size / 2);
            g2.setPaint(Color.green);
            g2.fillRect(0, size / 2, size / 2, size);
            g2.setPaint(Color.blue);
            g2.fillRect(size / 2, size / 2, size, size);
            return bi;
        }
    };
    f.setVisible(true);
  }
}
```

Bidirectional Text

Some languages, like Arabic and Hebrew, are read from right to left. It's a bit tricky to correctly render strings that have both left-to-right and right-to-left characters, but the 2D API handles all the details for you.[*] The following example shows how to display a string of English and Arabic characters. To run it, your system will need a font that can display both types of characters. The examples in this chapter use Lucida Sans, which is distributed as part of the Java 2 platform (more on this later).

```
    import java.awt.*;

public class BidirectionalText {
  public static void main(String[] args) {
    Frame f = new ApplicationFrame("BidirectionalText v1.0") {
      public void paint(Graphics g) {
        Graphics2D g2 = (Graphics2D)g;
        g2.setRenderingHint(RenderingHints.KEY_ANTIALIASING,
```

---

[*] For a clear explanation of bidirectional text rendering, see *International Text in JDK 1.2*, by Mark Davis, Doug Felt, and John Raley, at *http://www.ibm.com/java/education/international-text/*.

```
                RenderingHints.VALUE_ANTIALIAS_ON);

            Font font = new Font("Lucida Sans Regular", Font.PLAIN, 32);

            g2.setFont(font);
            g2.drawString("Please \u062e\u0644\u0639 slowly.", 40, 80);
          }
        };
      f.setVisible(true);
    }
  }
```

This program produces the window shown in Figure 6-9.

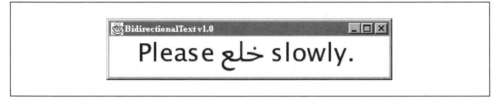

Figure 6-9. Bidirectional text

At first, you might be thinking that this is no big deal—all the rendering engine had to do was look up the glyphs for the characters in the string and render them. But it's more complicated than that. The Arabic characters are actually rendered so they read correctly from right to left. The order of the characters in the string is called the *logical order*. It's the order in which you want to read. As the example shows, it's distinct from the *visual order* of the glyphs. The rendering engine had to translate the logical order into a visual order according to glyph rules in its current font. The transformation is as follows, where italics represent the arabic characters:

- Logical order: Please *eat* slowly.

- Visual order: Please *tae* slowly.

The difference between the logical order and the visual order of a string is the fundamental concept of bidirectional text.

WARNING   The initial release of Java 2 (JDK 1.2) has a bug involving fonts, such that you cannot use certain fonts without calling the `getAll-Fonts()` method of `GraphicsEnvironment` first. Unfortunately, this method takes a long time to complete. This bug is fixed in JDK 1.2.1.

Same Character, Different Glyphs

As I mentioned before, there may be more than one glyph for a single character, depending on the character's context. The following example shows three Arabic characters separated by spaces, followed by the same three characters rendered as a single word. Once again, the 2D API takes care of the details to correctly render the text, as shown in Figure 6-10.

```java
import java.awt.*;
import java.awt.geom.Line2D;

public class MightyMorphingGlyphs {
  public static void main(String[] args) {
    Frame f = new ApplicationFrame("MightyMorphingGlyphs v1.0") {
      public void paint(Graphics g) {
        Graphics2D g2 = (Graphics2D)g;

        g2.setRenderingHint(RenderingHints.KEY_ANTIALIASING,
            RenderingHints.VALUE_ANTIALIAS_ON);
        Font font = new Font("Lucida Sans Regular", Font.PLAIN, 32);
        g2.setFont(font);

        g2.drawString("\u062e \u0644 \u0639", 40, 80);
        g2.drawString("\u062e\u0644\u0639", 40, 120);
      }
    };
    f.setVisible(true);
  }
}
```

Figure 6-10. Arabic characters use glyphs that depend on context

Fonts

Fonts, represented by instances of `java.awt.Font`, are a cornerstone of the 2D API's text rendering system. The `Font` class has existed since JDK 1.0, but it has evolved considerably since then. Fonts have three different names, like characters in a Dostoyevsky novel, and there are several paths you can follow to obtain a font.

Names

Fonts are identified by names. Fonts in the 2D API have three distinct names:

family name

> Several fonts may belong to the same family. For example, the bold and italic versions of a font have the same family name. You can find out a `Font`'s family using the `getFamily()` method.

face name or font name

> This name uniquely identifies a font. For example, "Garamond Italic" is a font face name for a font whose family is "Garamond." The face name is also called the *font name*. This name is returned from `Font`'s `getFontName()` method.

logical name

> Logical names were used before the 2D API to uniquely identify fonts. `Toolkit`'s `getFontList()` method returns a list of logical font names. Logical font names are mapped to an actual font on a particular machine. "Serif," for example, is a logical font name that corresponds to "Times New Roman" on my Windows NT machine. A font's logical name is retrieved using the `getName()` method. Don't get tripped up by the method names: `getFontName()` returns the font name, while `getName()` returns the logical name.

You can create a font from a name, a style, and a size:

public Font(String name, int style, int size)

> Use this constructor to create a `Font` for the given name, style, and size. The supplied name can be a face name or a logical name. Font styles are defined as constants in the `Font` class, either `PLAIN`, `ITALIC`, `BOLD`, or `ITALIC | BOLD`. The font size should be specified in typographic points, which are equal to 1/72 inch.* If the font you've requested is not available (or if you mistyped the font name), a default font will be returned.

Another approach is to ask for a font that matches some set of attributes, using `Font`'s static `getFont()` method:

public static Font getFont(Map attributes)

> This method returns a font that matches the attributes in the supplied `Map`. You should use the text attribute keys and values from the `java.awt.font. TextAttribute` class, which are shown in Table 6-1. (A `Map` is part of the Collections API; you can use a `Hashtable` if you wish.)

---

* True typographic points are .01383 inches, which is slightly less than 1/72 inch. The 2D API follows common usage in making points exactly 1/72 inch.

Finding Available Fonts

The following method in `java.awt.GraphicsEnvironment` returns all the fonts installed on your system. (I'll talk more about `GraphicsEnvironment` in Chapter 12, *Devices.*)

public abstract Font[] getAllFonts()

This method returns an array that contains every font installed in the `GraphicsEnvironment`. The Fonts returned by this method all have a size of 1. Unless you're planning to scale the fonts as they're rendered, these fonts will be very small. To obtain useful sizes, you can derive new fonts from these basic fonts, as you'll see later in this chapter. This method takes a while to complete, especially if you have a lot of fonts installed on your system. If you just want the names of the fonts, not Font objects, it's significantly faster to call `getAvailableFontFamilyNames()`, described below.

To call this method, you first need a `GraphicsEnvironment` instance that represents your system. You can get this instance by using the static `get-LocalGraphicsEnvironment()` method. The following example prints out the font name, family name, and logical name of every font installed on the local system:

```
import java.awt.*;

public class ShowFonts {
  public static void main(String[] args) {
    Font[] fonts;
    fonts = GraphicsEnvironment.getLocalGraphicsEnvironment().getAllFonts();
    for (int i = 0; i < fonts.length; i++) {
      System.out.print(fonts[i].getFontName() + " : ");
      System.out.print(fonts[i].getFamily() + " : ");
      System.out.print(fonts[i].getName());
      System.out.println();
    }
  }
}
```

The output includes names you'd expect to see, like "Times New Roman" and "Arial." It also includes the physical fonts, like "Lucida Bright Regular" and "Lucida Sans Typewriter Oblique." But there are some unfamiliar entries, like "monospaced" and "sansserif.italic." Where are these coming from? These are the logical font names, which are just aliases for other fonts on your system. Note that they will probably not be the same on different platforms. If you want to use a specific font, you should name it explicitly and recover gracefully if the system doesn't have that font.

The logical font names are mapped to real system fonts by the *font.properties* file. This file is found in the *jre/lib* subdirectory below the JDK installation directory. It lists all the logical font names and their equivalents on your particular platform. This mapping is platform-specific. On Windows, for example, the "sansserif" logical name is mapped to the "Arial" font. On other platforms, it will be mapped to whatever standard sans serif font is available.

`GraphicsEnvironment` also includes methods that return a list of the installed font family names:

public abstract String[] getAvailableFontFamilyNames()
public abstract String[] getAvailableFontFamilyNames(Locale l)

> These methods return an array of strings containing the family names of every available font. The family names can be localized using the second version of this method.

Physical Fonts

The Java 2 platform includes a dozen fonts, called *physical fonts.* These are tucked away in the *jre/lib/fonts* subdirectory; they are automatically available to your application, even though they are not installed into your underlying operating system. The face names are as follows:

- Lucida Sans Regular
- Lucida Sans Bold
- Lucida Sans Oblique
- Lucida Sans Bold Oblique
- Lucida Bright Regular
- Lucida Bright Bold
- Lucida Bright Italic
- Lucida Bright Bold Italic
- Lucida Sans Typewriter Regular
- Lucida Sans Typewriter Bold
- Lucida Sans Typewriter Oblique
- Lucida Sans Typewriter Bold Oblique

There are three groupings: Lucida Sans, Lucida Bright, and Lucida Sans Typewriter. What's interesting about these fonts is that you can depend on them being available in every Java 2 (JDK 1.2) environment.* For the first time, you can actually depend on the availability of a set of fonts across different system platforms.

---

* Actually, the full set of fonts will be distributed only with the JDK itself. The JRE will include only Lucida Sans Regular. You can distribute the other physical fonts with your application, if you wish.

The Lucida Sans fonts include Hebrew and Arabic characters, as you saw earlier in this chapter.

Using System Properties

Fonts may also be created from system properties. You can specify system properties on the command line when you run an application, like this:

```
java -Dshorts.font=Garamond-italic-64 Shorts
```

This sets a system property called "shorts.font" to the value "Garamond-italic-64." Inside the application, you can create a font from the property using the getFont() method:

public static Font getFont(String nm)
> This method creates a Font from the given property name. First, it finds the value of the system property whose name is nm. The property value should be in the form name–style–size, where name is a font face name or logical name; style is "plain," "italic," "bold," or "bolditalic;" and size is the desired font size. If the specified font cannot be found, a default font is returned.

public static Font getFont(String nm, Font font)
> This method is the same as above, but it returns the given font if the supplied system property is not defined.

A related method, decode(), knows how to parse a name–style–size string to create a font:

public static Font decode(String str)
> This method parses a string in the form name–style–size and returns a corresponding font.

Deriving Fonts

New fonts may be created by deriving them from existing fonts. This is useful when you already have a Font instance that is almost what you want:

public Font deriveFont(int style)
public Font deriveFont(float size)
public Font deriveFont(int style, float size)
> These methods return a derived Font with the given style, size, or both.

public Font deriveFont(AffineTransform trans)
public Font deriveFont(int style, AffineTransform trans)
> These methods return a derived Font whose glyphs have been transformed with the given AffineTransform. The second version also allows you to change the style of the font.

Hint, Hint

Fonts use a technique called *hinting* to ensure that they look good, no matter what font size you use. Font hinting is not the same as rendering hints, discussed back in Chapter 5.

You already know that a font is a collection of glyphs (shapes). The simplest way to get different sizes of a font would be to scale all the glyphs. But at very large or very small sizes, straight scaling doesn't always look good. Font designers, therefore, build hints into fonts that specify how the glyphs should be modified as they are scaled to large or small sizes.

This means that you may get different results from calling one of `Font`'s `deriveFont()` methods to scale a font than if you scaled the `Graphics2D` and rendered the text. The `deriveFont()` method takes account of the font hinting and will modify the glyphs accordingly. If you just scale the `Graphics2D`, instead, the glyphs for the font are simply transformed without regard for font hinting.

There's one last version of the `deriveFont()` method that can change almost anything about a font:

public Font deriveFont(Map attributes)

This method returns a derived font that matches the attributes in the supplied `Map`. Use the `FAMILY`, `POSTURE`, `SIZE`, and `WEIGHT` attribute keys and values given in Table 6-1. You can include other keys and values, but they will be ignored.

Here's an example that demonstrates how to derive fonts. Figure 6-11 shows the example in action.

```
import java.awt.*;
import java.awt.font.TextAttribute;
import java.awt.geom.AffineTransform;
import java.util.Hashtable;

public class FontDerivation {
  public static void main(String[] args) {
    Frame f = new ApplicationFrame("FontDerivation v1.0") {
      public void paint(Graphics g) {
        Graphics2D g2 = (Graphics2D)g;

        g2.setRenderingHint(RenderingHints.KEY_ANTIALIASING,
            RenderingHints.VALUE_ANTIALIAS_ON);

        // Create a 1-point font.
        Font font = new Font("Serif", Font.PLAIN, 1);
```

```
        float x = 20, y = 20;

        // Derive a 24-point font.
        Font font24 = font.deriveFont(24.0f);
        g2.setFont(font24);
        g2.drawString("font.deriveFont(24.0f)", x, y += 30);

        // Now make it italic.
        Font font24italic = font24.deriveFont(Font.ITALIC);
        g2.setFont(font24italic);
        g2.drawString("font24.deriveFont(Font.ITALIC)", x, y += 30);

        // Now make it slant backwards with a shearing transformation.
        AffineTransform at = new AffineTransform();
        at.shear(.2, 0);
        Font font24shear = font24.deriveFont(at);
        g2.setFont(font24shear);
        g2.drawString("font24.deriveFont(at)", x, y += 30);

        // Derive a bold font using an attribute Map.
        Hashtable attributes = new Hashtable();
        attributes.put(TextAttribute.WEIGHT, TextAttribute.WEIGHT_BOLD);
        Font font24bold = font24.deriveFont(attributes);
        g2.setFont(font24bold);
        g2.drawString("font24.deriveFont(attributes)", x, y += 30);
      }
    };
    f.setVisible(truc);
  }
}
```

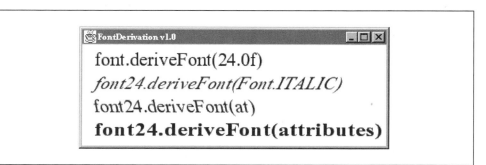

Figure 6-11. Deriving fonts

The example begins by obtaining a font from the logical name "Serif" with a point size of 1:

```
Font font = new Font("Serif", Font.PLAIN, 1);
```

Then a 24-point version of the font is derived:

```
Font font24 = font.deriveFont(24.0f);
```

An italic version of the 24-point font is then derived:

```
Font font24italic = font24.deriveFont(Font.ITALIC);
```

Then this example uses a transformation on the 24-point font to derive a backwards-leaning font:

```
AffineTransform at = new AffineTransform();
at.shear(.2, 0);
Font font24shear = font24.deriveFont(at);
```

Finally, a bold font is derived, using a hashtable of text attributes. (The hashtable contains only one item.)

```
Hashtable attributes = new Hashtable();
attributes.put(TextAttribute.WEIGHT, TextAttribute.WEIGHT_BOLD);
Font font24bold = font24.deriveFont(attributes);
```

NOTE   It's easy to confuse the deriveFont(int) and deriveFont(float) methods. If you just write deriveFont(24), the compiler interprets the 24 as an integer. This means that you'll be calling the version of deriveFont() that adjusts the style of the font. If you want to adjust the size of the font instead, then you need to explicitly call the floating-point version of the method by adding an "f" postfix to the number: deriveFont(24.0f). Alternately, you could just pass a float variable to the method.

Font Metrics

Before the 2D API, the java.awt.FontMetrics class provided font measurement information. In the old system, you would pass a Font to Toolkit's getFontMetrics() method. In the 2D API, FontMetrics still exists and is not deprecated; nevertheless, it has been replaced with the java.awt.font.LineMetrics class. Unless you have to work with old versions of the JDK, I suggest ignoring FontMetrics entirely.

In the new scheme, you can ask a Font for a LineMetrics object by calling one of its getLineMetrics() methods. Essentially, these methods accept a string and return a LineMetrics object that encapsulates the dimensions of the rendered string.

The FontRenderContext Class

Measuring text is a delicate operation. When the rendering engine (a Graphics2D) renders text, the results depend on the engine's rendering hints. In particular, the value of the KEY_ANTIALIASING hint and the KEY_FRACTIONAL-METRICS hints make subtle changes in the dimensions of rendered text. (For more information on rendering hints, see Chapter 5, *Rendering*.)

The bottom line is that you need to specify whether antialiasing and fractional metrics will be used when you ask for a LineMetrics object. This information is contained in a java.awt.font.FontRenderContext object. This class has one public constructor:

public FontRenderContext(AffineTransform tx, boolean isAntiAliased, boolean usesFractionalMetrics)

Use this constructor to create a FontRenderContext. The transformation that will be used to convert typographic points to device space is given by tx. The two boolean flags indicate whether the antialising and fractional metrics rendering hints will be used.

Usually, you won't need to create a FontRenderContext yourself. Graphics2D includes a handy method that produces a FontRenderContext:

public abstract FontRenderContext getFontRenderContext()

This method returns a FontRenderContext based on the current state of the Graphics2D. Make sure you call this method after you set rendering hints, as the current state of the Graphics2D's hints will affect the FontRenderContext that is returned by this method.

Getting Metrics from a Font

Once you have a FontRenderContext, getting font measurements is easy. The following methods in Font return the width and height of specific strings:

public Rectangle2D getStringBounds(String str, FontRenderContext frc)

This method returns the bounding rectangle of the given string, including leading and trailing whitespace. The returned rectangle should reflect the bounds of the given string if it is rendered at 0, 0.

public Rectangle2D getStringBounds(String str, int beginIndex, int limit, FontRenderContext frc)
public Rectangle2D getStringBounds(char[] chars, int beginIndex, int limit, FontRenderContext frc)
public Rectangle2D getStringBounds(CharacterIterator ci, int beginIndex, int limit, FontRenderContext frc)

These methods return the bounding box of the substring of limit characters, starting at beginIndex.

WARNING   In the initial release of Java 2 (JDK 1.2), the `getStringBounds()` methods do not work properly. In particular, leading and trailing white space is not included in the returned rectangle. Also, the bounds rectangle always has its origin at 0, 0. This bug is fixed in JDK 1.2.1.

The following example shows how to center text horizontally. The `paint-HorizontallyCenteredText()` method renders text using the given y coordinate as the baseline's vertical position. The text is centered on the given x coordinate.

```java
import java.awt.*;
import java.awt.font.*;
import java.awt.geom.*;

public class HorizontallyCenteredText {
  public static void main(String[] args) {
    Frame frame = new ApplicationFrame("HorizontallyCenteredText v1.0") {
      public void paint(Graphics g) {
        Graphics2D g2 = (Graphics2D)g;

        g2.setRenderingHint(RenderingHints.KEY_ANTIALIASING,
            RenderingHints.VALUE_ANTIALIAS_ON);

        g2.setFont(new Font("Serif", Font.PLAIN, 48));

        paintHorizontallyCenteredText(g2, "come", 100, 75);
        paintHorizontallyCenteredText(g2, "and", 100, 125);
        paintHorizontallyCenteredText(g2, "play", 100, 175);
      }

      protected void paintHorizontallyCenteredText(Graphics2D g2, String s,
          float centerX, float baselineY) {
        FontRenderContext frc = g2.getFontRenderContext();
        Rectangle2D bounds = g2.getFont().getStringBounds(s, frc);
        float width = (float)bounds.getWidth();
        g2.drawString(s, centerX - width / 2, baselineY);
      }
    };
    frame.setVisible(true);
  }
}
```

Figure 6-12 shows how `HorizontallyCenteredText` looks when it's running.

Figure 6-12. Horizontally centered text

The LineMetrics Class

For more detailed font measurements, the `getStringBounds()` methods don't get the job done. Fortunately, `Font` has another set of methods that return font metrics in the form of `java.awt.font.LineMetrics` objects. These methods are nearly identical to the `getStringBounds()` methods, but you get a `LineMetrics` object back instead of a `Rectangle2D`:

public LineMetrics getLineMetrics(String str, FontRenderContext frc)
public LineMetrics getLineMetrics(String str, int beginIndex, int limit,
    FontRenderContext frc)
public LineMetrics getLineMetrics(char[] chars, int beginIndex, int limit,
    FontRenderContext frc)
public LineMetrics getLineMetrics(CharacterIterator ci, int beginIndex, int limit,
    FontRenderContext frc)
> These methods return the metrics of the given string as rendered by this `Font`. As with the `getStringBounds()` methods, the `beginIndex` and `limit` parameters describe a subset of the given string, character array, or iterator.

What can you do with `LineMetrics`? Instances of this class contain information about the ascent, descent, and leading of a string, among other things:

public abstract float getAscent()
public abstract float getDescent()
public abstract float getLeading()
> These methods return the corresponding font metric for the string represented by this `LineMetrics` instance.

public abstract float getHeight()
> This method returns the total height, which is the sum of the ascent, descent, and leading.

The following example illustrates how these methods relate to rendered text. It draws a horizontal line representing the ascent, baseline, descent, and leading of a string.

```java
import java.awt.*;
import java.awt.font.FontRenderContext;
import java.awt.font.LineMetrics;
import java.awt.geom.Line2D;

public class LineMetricsIllustrated {
  public static void main(String[] args) {
    Frame frame = new ApplicationFrame("LineMetricsIllustrated v1.0") {
      public void paint(Graphics g) {
        Graphics2D g2 = (Graphics2D)g;

        g2.setRenderingHint(RenderingHints.KEY_ANTIALIASING,
            RenderingHints.VALUE_ANTIALIAS_ON);
        Font font = new Font("Serif", Font.PLAIN, 72);
        g2.setFont(font);

        String s = "Porphyry";
        float x = 50, y = 150;

        // Draw the baseline.
        FontRenderContext frc = g2.getFontRenderContext();
        float width = (float)font.getStringBounds(s, frc).getWidth();
        Line2D baseline = new Line2D.Float(x, y, x + width, y);
        g2.setPaint(Color.lightGray);
        g2.draw(baseline);

        // Draw the ascent.
        LineMetrics lm = font.getLineMetrics(s, frc);
        Line2D ascent = new Line2D.Float(x, y - lm.getAscent(),
            x + width, y - lm.getAscent());
        g2.draw(ascent);

        // Draw the descent.
        Line2D descent = new Line2D.Float(x, y + lm.getDescent(),
            x + width, y + lm.getDescent());
        g2.draw(descent);

        // Draw the leading.
        Line2D leading = new Line2D.Float(
            x, y + lm.getDescent() + lm.getLeading(),
            x + width, y + lm.getDescent() + lm.getLeading());
        g2.draw(leading);

        // Render the string.
        g2.setPaint(Color.black);
```

```
        g2.drawString(s, x, y);
      }
    };
    frame.setVisible(true);
  }
}
```

Figure 6-13. Ascent, baseline, descent, and leading in a rendered string

This small example produces the window shown in Figure 6-13. Note that font designers have quite a bit of flexibility in fitting the glyphs into the available space. In Figure 6-13, for example, the capital "P" only fills up some of the available space between the baseline and the ascent. This leaves some space for capital letters that have ornaments. Figure 6-14 shows the same example with a capital "H" with a circumflex.

Figure 6-14. A capital letter with an ornament takes up more of the font's ascent

Finally, LineMetrics can provide information about its baselines:

public abstract int getBaselineIndex()

This method returns the overall baseline of this LineMetrics as one of the constants in the Font class, either HANGING_BASELINE, CENTER_BASELINE, or ROMAN_BASELINE.

public abstract float[] getBaselineOffsets()

> Use this method to find the location of all three types of baselines for this
> `LineMetrics`. A three-element array of `float`s is returned by this method.
> Each value is an offset to a particular baseline. The array is indexed by the
> baseline type values defined in the `Font` class: `HANGING_BASELINE`, `CENTER_`
> `BASELINE`, or `ROMAN_BASELINE`. The offset for the `LineMetrics`'s overall
> baseline is always 0. This means that `getBaselinesOffsets()[get-`
> `BaselineIndex()]` will always be 0. The other baseline offsets are measured
> relative to the overall baseline for the `LineMetrics`.

In the initial release of Java 2, multiple baselines are not yet supported in `Font`
and `LineMetrics`. The `getBaselineOffsets()` method just returns an array of
three zeros.

Strikethrough and Underlining

An *underline* is a line that is drawn underneath text, not in the same location as the
baseline. A *strikethrough* line is a line that is drawn through text. As Table 6-1 shows,
underlining and strikethrough are included as attributes in the `TextAttribute`
class. This means that you can use an `AttributedCharacterIterator` to draw
these lines. The following example shows how to use these attributes. The results
are shown in Figure 6-15.

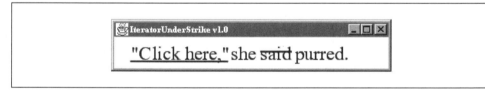

Figure 6-15. Underlining and strikethrough

```
import java.awt.*;
import java.awt.font.TextAttribute;
import java.text.*;

public class IteratorUnderStrike {
  public static void main(String[] args) {
    Frame f = new ApplicationFrame("IteratorUnderStrike v1.0") {
      public void paint(Graphics g) {
        Graphics2D g2 = (Graphics2D)g;

        String s = "\"Click here,\" she said purred.";

        g2.setRenderingHint(RenderingHints.KEY_ANTIALIASING,
            RenderingHints.VALUE_ANTIALIAS_ON);
        Font plainFont = new Font("Times New Roman", Font.PLAIN, 24);
```

```
            AttributedString as = new AttributedString(s);
            as.addAttribute(TextAttribute.FONT, plainFont);
            as.addAttribute(TextAttribute.UNDERLINE,
                TextAttribute.UNDERLINE_ON, 1, 11);
            as.addAttribute(TextAttribute.STRIKETHROUGH,
                TextAttribute.STRIKETHROUGH_ON, 18, 22);

            g2.drawString(as.getIterator(), 24, 70);
         }
      };
      f.setVisible(true);
   }
}
```

If your underlining and strikethough needs are more exotic, you can draw underlines and strikethrough lines yourself. The following methods in LineMetrics describe where underlines and strikethrough lines should be located. You can also find out how thick these lines should be:

public abstract float getUnderlineOffset()

This method returns a coordinate offset for the underline position. You can calculate the underline position by adding this offset to the baseline's y coordinate.

public abstract float getStrikethroughOffset()

This method returns an offset for the strikethrough position. Add this offset to the baseline's y coordinate to get the strikethrough line position. (Since strikethrough lines are above the baseline, the strikethrough offset is therefore negative.)

public abstract float getUnderlineThickness()
public abstract float getStrikethroughThickness()

These methods return the line thicknesses for underlines and strikethrough lines.

Keep in mind that it can be tricky to correctly draw underlines and strikethrough lines, especially in bidirectional text. If it's at all possible, rely on an AttributedCharacterIterator or a TextLayout (described in the next chapter) to draw the lines.

7

In this chapter:
- *Using the TextLayout Class*
- *Getting Close to the Metal*

Advanced Text Layout

Chapter 6, *Text*, described the basics of text rendering. This chapter dives deeper into the same subject. First, I'll talk about the `TextLayout` class, which provides support for rendering and editing text. The rest of the chapter is devoted to glyph-level manipulation with the `GlyphVector` and `GlyphMetrics` classes, which is useful if you want to implement custom text layout algorithms.

Using the TextLayout Class

The `drawString()` methods render simple pieces of text. If you're interested in support for a caret (cursor) and highlighting, you'll need to use the `java.awt.font.TextLayout` class. This class can be used as the basis for a sophisticated text editor. Most applications don't need the power of this customization and can simply use `JTextField`, `JTextArea`, or `JEditorPane`.

`TextLayout` offers the following features:

- text metrics
- hit testing
- caret support
- highlighting support
- paragraph layout on multiple lines (with the help of the `LineBreakMeasurer` class)

TextLayout Basics

Creating a `TextLayout` is pretty simple. You just need to supply the text itself, either as a string or a character iterator, and a `FontRenderContext` (which was described in Chapter 6):

public TextLayout(String string, Font font, FontRenderContext frc)
> Use this constructor to create a `TextLayout` using the supplied string and font.

public TextLayout(String string, Map attributes, FontRenderContext frc)
> This constructor creates a new `TextLayout` from the given string. The supplied `attributes` are applied to the entire string. (For a list of possible attributes, see Table 6-1.)

public TextLayout(AttributedCharacterIterator text, FontRenderContext frc)
> This constructor creates a `TextLayout` from the supplied iterator.

Once you've created a `TextLayout`, you can render it by calling its `draw()` method. This is a little different from the usual model. Usually you create something, like a shape or a string of text, and pass it to one of `Graphics2D`'s methods. In this case, you create a `TextLayout` and call its `draw()` method, passing in a `Graphics2D`:

public void draw(Graphics2D g2, float x, float y)
> This method renders the `TextLayout` at x, y. The point is used as the left end of the `TextLayout`'s baseline, just as for `drawString()` in the `Graphics2D` class.

The following example shows how to create a `TextLayout` and render it:

```
import java.awt.*;
import java.awt.font.*;

public class TextLayoutOne {
  public static void main(String[] args) {
    Frame f = new ApplicationFrame("TextLayoutOne v1.0") {
      public void paint(Graphics g) {
        Graphics2D g2 = (Graphics2D)g;

        g2.setRenderingHint(RenderingHints.KEY_ANTIALIASING,
            RenderingHints.VALUE_ANTIALIAS_ON);

        String s = "Always eat slowly.";
        Font font = new Font("Serif", Font.PLAIN, 32);

        TextLayout textLayout = new TextLayout(s, font,
            g2.getFontRenderContext());
        textLayout.draw(g2, 40, 80);
      }
    };
    f.setVisible(true);
  }
}
```

If you wish, you can obtain a Shape that corresponds to the contents of the TextLayout. The Shape can be filled, stroked, or manipulated just like any other Shape.

public Shape getOutline(AffineTransform tx)

> This method returns a Shape that represents the text contained by this TextLayout. The supplied transformation is applied to the shape before it is returned.

Metrics of a TextLayout

The TextLayout class includes methods that return the measurements of the entire layout:

public float getAscent()
public float getDescent()
public float getLeading()

> These methods return the ascent, descent, and leading of the entire TextLayout.

public byte getBaseline()

> This method returns the type of baseline used in this TextLayout. It should be one of the constants defined in Font, either ROMAN_BASELINE, HANGING_ BASELINE, or CENTER_BASELINE.

public float[] getBaselineOffsets()

> This method returns an array of baseline offsets. The array is indexed by the baseline type constants defined in the Font class. The offsets are relative to the baseline for this TextLayout.*

public float getAdvance()

> This method returns the advance of the TextLayout (which includes whitespace).

public float getVisibleAdvance()

> This method returns the visible advance of the TextLayout, which is the same as the advance minus trailing whitespace.

public Rectangle2D getBounds()

> This method returns the bounding rectangle of the TextLayout.

The TextLayout class supports bidirectional text. However, a piece of text with mixed right-to-left and left-to-right pieces still has an overall direction. For example, an English string that contains an Arabic word has an overall direction of

---

* Multiple baselines aren't implemented in the intial release of Java 2, so getBaselineOffsets() returns an array of three zeros.

left-to-right. You can find out the overall direction of a `TextLayout` with the following method:

public boolean isLeftToRight()

    This method returns `true` if the `TextLayout`'s overall text direction is left-to-right. Otherwise, `false` is returned for a right-to-left overall text direction.

Hit Testing

If you use the mouse to click on a rendered string, how do you find out which character is nearest to the mouse click? The answer is *hit testing*. It is fully supported by `TextLayout`. Given a set of coordinates, `TextLayout` returns a `java.awt.font.TextHitInfo` object. A `TextHitInfo` is basically a logical character index plus additional information about whether a hit is on the leading or trailing edge of the character.

public TextHitInfo hitTestChar(float x, float y)

    This method determines the character nearest the given coordinates.

public TextHitInfo hitTestChar(float x, float y, Rectangle2D bounds)

    This method is the same as the previous method, except that it uses the supplied rectangle as the bounds of the `TextLayout`. This is useful if you have several different `TextLayouts` on one line and you'd like them to use a common height.

The following example demonstrates how `TextLayout` can translate mouse coordinates into logical character indexes:

```
import java.awt.*;
import java.awt.event.*;
import java.awt.font.*;

public class HitMe
    extends ApplicationFrame {
  public static void main(String[] args) {
    Frame f = new HitMe();
    f.setTitle("HitMe v1.0");
    f.setVisible(true);
  }

  private TextLayout mTextLayout;
  private int mX = 40, mY = 80;

  public HitMe() {
    super("HitMe v1.0");
    addMouseListener(new MouseAdapter() {
      public void mouseClicked(MouseEvent me) {
        TextHitInfo hit = mTextLayout.hitTestChar(
```

```
                me.getX() - mX, me.getY() - mY);
            System.out.println(hit);
          }
        });
    }

    public void paint(Graphics g) {
      Graphics2D g2 = (Graphics2D)g;

      g2.setRenderingHint(RenderingHints.KEY_ANTIALIASING,
          RenderingHints.VALUE_ANTIALIAS_ON);

      String s = "Camelopardalis";
      Font font = new Font("Serif", Font.PLAIN, 32);

      if (mTextLayout == null) {
        FontRenderContext frc = g2.getFontRenderContext();
        mTextLayout = new TextLayout(s, font, frc);
      }

      mTextLayout.draw(g2, mX, mY);
    }
  }
```

This example converts mouse clicks into `TextHitInfo`s. To try it out, run the example and click on various points in the frame window. The results look something like this:

```
TextHitInfo[2L]
TextHitInfo[3L]
TextHitInfo[4L]
TextHitInfo[4T]
TextHitInfo[0L]
TextHitInfo[-1T]
TextHitInfo[14L]
TextHitInfo[13T]
TextHitInfo[14L]
TextHitInfo[6L]
TextHitInfo[7L]
```

The number in the brackets indicates the logical index. An "L" indicates the leading side, while a "T" indicates the trailing side. Notice that the output shows two special values. In left-to-right text, a -1 index indicates a hit off the left side of the string. Likewise, hits off the right side of the string are indicated by an index that is 1 more than the length of the string (14, in this case).

Of course, I don't recommend converting `TextHitInfo` to a string and examining the string. To find out the logical index of the hit, use the following method in `TextHitInfo`:

public int getInsertionIndex()

> This method returns a logical insertion index by considering the logical index of the hit and whether it is leading or trailing. For example, a hit on the leading edge of character 4 would produce an insertion index of 4. On the other hand, a hit on the trailing edge of character 4 would produce an insertion index of 5.

You can also examine the `TextHitInfo` with the following methods:

public int getCharIndex()

> This method returns the character index of the hit. This is not necessarily the same as the insertion index.

public boolean isLeadingEdge()

> This method returns `true` if the hit was on the leading edge of a character. It returns `false` if the hit was on the character's trailing edge.

A `TextHitInfo` is a useful thing. As you'll see in the coming sections, you can use `TextHitInfo`s to draw carets and highlight text.

Showing a Caret (or Two!)

A *caret*, also called a *cursor*, is that blinking vertical line in word processors that tells you where the next typed character will go. A more rigorous definition of a caret is that it is a visual representation of a logical position between two characters in a piece of text. If your application is going to support keyboard input, it should display a caret.

`TextLayout` won't draw a caret for you, but it will tell you how to draw one yourself. But there's a twist. How do you show a caret correctly in bidirectional text? Inside a left-to-right run of text, you can just put the caret between the glyphs. Likewise, you can place the caret between glyphs of right-to-left text. But what do you do at the boundaries? Take a look at Figure 7-1, which shows how the logical order of a character string is mapped to a visual order in rendered text. There are two problem spots, the directional transitions. At the end of the word "please," the caret appears to be in two places at once. It is simultaneously to the right of the "e" of "please" and to the right (visually) of first letter of the Arabic word.

How can the dual personality of a caret be resolved? It's simple—just draw two carets. Suppose the caret is placed after the end of "Please." A *primary caret* is shown in this location, and a *secondary caret* is shown at the beginning (the right side) of the Arabic word. Now, if the user types a character, what happens? English characters will be placed at the primary caret, while Arabic characters will be placed at the secondary caret. Regardless, the characters are inserted into the same logical position in the string. The dual carets are a visual representation of a single logical insertion point.

Figure 7-1. Caret schizophrenia

How does `TextLayout` determine which caret is primary and which is secondary? The default algorithm uses the line's dominant text direction to determine the primary caret. In Figure 7-1, for example, the primary line direction is left-to-right. The caret that corresponds to the English character insertion point will be the primary caret. The dominant line direction is determined using the bidirectional algorithm, which is part of the Unicode Standard (see *http://www.unicode.org/ unicode/publications.html* to order a copy).

`TextLayout` has several methods that return caret shapes, given a logical character offset:

public Shape[] getCaretShapes(int offset)
> This method returns a two-element array of caret shapes corresponding to the given character offset. The offset refers to logical order, not visual order. The first element of the array represents the primary caret and is never `null`. The second array element is the secondary caret; it may be `null` if there is no secondary caret defined at the given character offset. The shapes are defined in terms of the `TextLayout`'s bounding rectangle.

public Shape[] getCaretShapes(int offset, Rectangle2D bounds)
> This method is the same as the previous one, except the supplied bounding rectangle is used to bound the caret shapes. The height of the supplied rectangle is used to determine the height and shape of the returned caret shapes. You could use this method if you had several `TextLayouts` in a single line of text, and you wanted them all to have a common height.

public Shape[] getCaretShapes(int offset, Rectangle2D bounds,
TextLayout.CaretPolicy policy)
> This method is the same as the previous method except that it allows you to specify a *caret policy*. A caret policy determines which caret is the primary caret, if there are two. You can create your own caret policy by subclassing `TextLayout.CaretPolicy`. Or you can use one of the two previous methods, which use a default policy. The default policy uses the dominant line direction to determine the primary caret.*

---

* The `getNextLeftHit()` and `getNextRightHit()` methods have versions that accept a caret policy, as well. These methods are described in the next section.

You can also retrieve a caret corresponding to a `TextHitInfo`. These methods return only one caret, because a `TextHitInfo` is more specific than a logical character index:

public Shape getCaretShape(TextHitInfo hit)

    This method returns a shape representing a caret at the given hit point.

public Shape getCaretShape(TextHitInfo hit, Rectangle2D bounds)

    This method is the same as the previous method, but it uses the supplied rectangle as the bounds of the `TextLayout`.

These methods are demonstrated in the next section.

Moving the Caret

How should a caret move through bidirectional text? Usually, the caret moves right and left as the user presses the corresponding arrow keys on the keyboard. But in bidirectional text, you have to remember the difference between logical and visual order. When the user moves the caret with the arrow keys, you want to move the caret in a visually sensible way. In bidirectional text, this means that the logical insertion index may jump around as the caret moves. Fortunately, the `TextLayout` and `TextHitInfo` classes take care of the details. `TextLayout` includes the following handy methods for navigating visually through a string of rendered text:

public TextHitInfo getNextRightHit(TextHitInfo hit)
public TextHitInfo getNextRightHit(int offset)

    Given a `TextHitInfo` or a logical index, these methods find the next visual hit to the right.

public TextHitInfo getNextLeftHit(TextHitInfo hit)
public TextHitInfo getNextLeftHit(int offset)

    These methods find the next visual hit to the left, starting at the specified hit or logical index.

The following example responds to the arrow keys to move a caret through a string of bidirectional text. The primary cursor is shown as a solid line, the secondary is dashed. As you can see when you run the example, the secondary cursor only shows up at the boundaries between left-to-right and right-to-left text. Figure 7-2 shows a snapshot of this example.

```
import java.awt.*;
import java.awt.event.*;
import java.awt.font.*;
import java.awt.geom.AffineTransform;
import java.text.*;
```

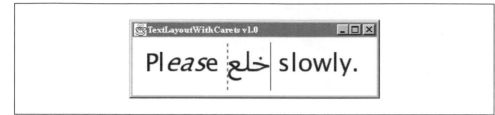

Figure 7-2. Dual carets

```
public class TextLayoutWithCarets
    extends ApplicationFrame {
  public static void main(String[] args) {
    TextLayoutWithCarets f = new TextLayoutWithCarets();
    f.setVisible(true);
  }

  private TextHitInfo mHit;
  private TextLayout mLayout;
  private boolean mInitialized = false;

  public TextLayoutWithCarets() {
    super("TextLayoutWithCarets v1.0");
  }

  private void initialize(Graphics2D g2) {
    String s = "Please \u062e\u0644\u0639 slowly.";
    // Create a plain and italic font.
    int fontSize = 32;
    Font font = new Font("Lucida Sans Regular", Font.PLAIN, fontSize);
    Font italicFont = new Font("Lucida Sans Oblique", Font.ITALIC, fontSize);
    // Create an Attributed String
    AttributedString as = new AttributedString(s);
    as.addAttribute(TextAttribute.FONT, font);
    as.addAttribute(TextAttribute.FONT, italicFont, 2, 5);
    // Get the iterator.
    AttributedCharacterIterator iterator = as.getIterator();
    // Create a TextLayout.
    FontRenderContext frc = g2.getFontRenderContext();
    mLayout = new TextLayout(iterator, frc);

    mHit = mLayout.getNextLeftHit(1);

    // Respond to left and right arrow keys.
    addKeyListener(new KeyAdapter() {
      public void keyPressed(KeyEvent ke) {
        if (ke.getKeyCode() == KeyEvent.VK_RIGHT) {
          mHit = mLayout.getNextRightHit(mHit.getInsertionIndex());
          if (mHit == null) mHit = mLayout.getNextLeftHit(1);
```

```
          repaint();
        }
        else if (ke.getKeyCode() == KeyEvent.VK_LEFT) {
          mHit = mLayout.getNextLeftHit(mHit.getInsertionIndex());
          if (mHit == null)
            mHit = mLayout.getNextRightHit(mLayout.getCharacterCount() - 1);
          repaint();
        }
      }
    });

    mInitialized = true;
  }

  public void paint(Graphics g) {
    Graphics2D g2 = (Graphics2D)g;
    g2.setRenderingHint(RenderingHints.KEY_ANTIALIASING,
        RenderingHints.VALUE_ANTIALIAS_ON);
    g2.setRenderingHint(RenderingHints.KEY_FRACTIONALMETRICS,
        RenderingHints.VALUE_FRACTIONALMETRICS_ON);

    if (mInitialized == false) initialize(g2);

    float x = 20, y = 80;
    mLayout.draw(g2, x, y);

    // Create a plain stroke and a dashed stroke.
    Stroke[] caretStrokes = new Stroke[2];
    caretStrokes[0] = new BasicStroke();
    caretStrokes[1] = new BasicStroke(1,
        BasicStroke.CAP_BUTT, BasicStroke.JOIN_ROUND, 0,
        new float[] { 4, 4 }, 0);

    // Now draw the carets
    Shape[] carets = mLayout.getCaretShapes(mHit.getInsertionIndex());
    for (int i = 0; i < carets.length; i++) {
      if (carets[i] != null)  {
        AffineTransform at = AffineTransform.getTranslateInstance(x, y);
        Shape shape = at.createTransformedShape(carets[i]);
        g2.setStroke(caretStrokes[i]);
        g2.draw(shape);
      }
    }
  }
}
```

This example shows how to render carets on a TextLayout. The paint() method has the following five steps in it.

1. The rendering hints are set.

2. The first time `paint()` is called, the `initialize()` method is called to create the `TextLayout` and the `TextHitInfo` that represent the current logical position in the text.

3. The text itself is drawn.

4. A two-element array of `Strokes` is created, for drawing the carets. The first `Stroke` is a solid line. The second is dashed.

5. Finally, the carets are drawn. The shapes returned from `getCaretShapes()` have to be translated to the same location as the text. After setting the stroke, the translated caret is drawn.

The `TextLayoutWithCarets` application demonstrates another nice feature of `TextLayout`'s carets: they conform to the posture of the text. In italic text, for example, the caret is slanted on the same angle as the italics, as shown in Figure 7-3.

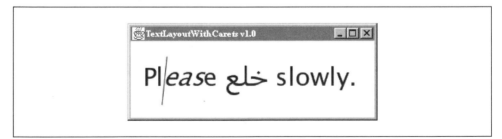

Figure 7-3. A slanted caret in italic text

Between italic and regular text, the caret picks a happy medium between vertical and slanted, as shown in Figure 7-4.

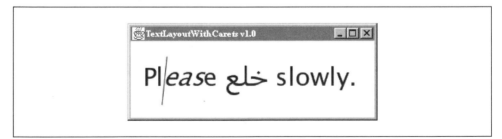

Figure 7-4. A partially slanted caret at the boundary between plain and italic text

Highlighting Text

A *highlight* is a shape drawn behind a certain portion of text. In a word processor, you can highlight text by clicking and dragging the mouse. TextLayout includes several handy methods that calculate highlight shapes for you:

public Shape getVisualHighlightShape(TextHitInfo firstEndpoint,
> *TextHitInfo secondEndpoint)*

> This method returns the highlight shape for the visual selection between the supplied endpoints. Because the highlight shape is based on a visual range, the corresponding logical selection may be discontinuous in bidirectional strings.

public Shape getVisualHighlightShape(TextHitInfo firstEndpoint,
> *TextHitInfo secondEndpoint, Rectangle2D bounds)*

> This method calculates a highlight shape using the supplied rectangle as the bounds of the TextLayout.

public Shape getLogicalHighlightShape(int firstEndpoint, int secondEndpoint)

> Use this method to obtain a highlight shape corresponding to the logical selection described by firstEndpoint and secondEndpoint. If you are highlighting a bidirectional string, the shape may be visually discontinuous.

public Shape getLogicalHighlightShape(int firstEndpoint, int secondEndpoint,
> *Rectangle2D bounds)*

> This method calculates a highlight shape for the given logical endpoints. The supplied rectangle is used as the bounds of the TextLayout.

The following example shows how to interactively draw a highlight shape. It uses both hit testing and highlighting. You can click and drag a highlighted selection as you would in a word processor. Figure 7-5 shows how this example looks when it's running.

Figure 7-5. Highlighted text

```
import java.awt.*;
import java.awt.event.*;
import java.awt.font.*;
```

```java
import java.awt.geom.AffineTransform;

public class Highlights
    extends ApplicationFrame {
  public static void main(String[] args) {
    Frame f = new Highlights();
    f.setVisible(true);
  }

  private TextLayout mTextLayout;
  private TextHitInfo mFirstHit, mSecondHit;
  private int mX = 40, mY = 80;

  public Highlights() {
    super("Highlights v1.0");
    addMouseListener(new MouseAdapter() {
      public void mousePressed(MouseEvent me) {
        mFirstHit = mTextLayout.hitTestChar(
            me.getX() - mX, me.getY() - mY);
        mSecondHit = null;
      }
      public void mouseReleased(MouseEvent me) {
        mSecondHit = mTextLayout.hitTestChar(
            me.getX() - mX, me.getY() - mY);
        repaint();
      }
    });
    addMouseMotionListener(new MouseMotionAdapter() {
      public void mouseDragged(MouseEvent me) {
        mSecondHit = mTextLayout.hitTestChar(
            me.getX() - mX, me.getY() - mY);
        repaint();
      }
    });
  }

  public void paint(Graphics g) {
    Graphics2D g2 = (Graphics2D)g;

    g2.setRenderingHint(RenderingHints.KEY_ANTIALIASING,
        RenderingHints.VALUE_ANTIALIAS_ON);
    g2.setRenderingHint(RenderingHints.KEY_FRACTIONALMETRICS,
        RenderingHints.VALUE_FRACTIONALMETRICS_ON);

    String s = "Camelopardalis";
    Font font = new Font("Serif", Font.PLAIN, 32);
```

```
    if (mTextLayout == null) {
      FontRenderContext frc = g2.getFontRenderContext();
      mTextLayout = new TextLayout(s, font, frc);
    }

    // Draw the highlight.
    if (mFirstHit != null && mSecondHit != null) {
      Shape base = mTextLayout.getLogicalHighlightShape(
          mFirstHit.getInsertionIndex(), mSecondHit.getInsertionIndex());
      AffineTransform at = AffineTransform.getTranslateInstance(mX, mY);
      Shape highlight = at.createTransformedShape(base);
      g2.setPaint(Color.green);
      g2.fill(highlight);
    }

    g2.setPaint(Color.black);
    mTextLayout.draw(g2, mX, mY);
  }
}
```

As with caret shapes, a highlight shape needs to be translated to the same location as the rendered text. In this example, the highlight shape is obtained from the TextLayout in the paint() method as follows:

```
Shape base = mTextLayout.getLogicalHighlightShape(
    mFirstHit.getInsertionIndex(), mSecondHit.getInsertionIndex());
```

This highlight shape is translated so it is at the same location as the text string itself:

```
AffineTransform at = AffineTransform.getTranslateInstance(mX, mY);
 Shape highlight = at.createTransformedShape(base);
```

The translated highlight shape is filled with green:

```
g2.setPaint(Color.green);
g2.fill(highlight);
```

And finally, the text itself is drawn in black on top of the highlight:

```
g2.setPaint(Color.black);
mTextLayout.draw(g2, mX, mY);
```

Rendering Multiline Text

TextLayout has some impressive capabilities, but it only represents a single line of text. If your text won't fit on one line, you need some way to break the text into multiple TextLayout objects. Fortunately, the 2D API provides a class that does this work for you, java.awt.font.LineBreakMeasurer.

You can create a `LineBreakMeasurer` from an entire paragraph of text:

public LineBreakMeasurer(AttributedCharacterIterator text, FontRenderContext frc)
Use this constructor to create a `LineBreakMeasurer` from the paragraph represented by `text`. The `FontRenderContext` is used to ensure that characters are measured properly.

public LineBreakMeasurer(AttributedCharacterIterator text, BreakIterator breakIter,
FontRenderContext frc)
This constructor is the same as the previous one, but it also accepts a `java.text.BreakIterator` that will be used to determine where line breaks are permitted. Use this constructor if you need to define a line breaking policy that is different from the default. `BreakIterator` is part of the internationalization classes in the `java.text` package. For more information, see *http://java.sun.com/products/jdk/1.2/docs/guide/internat/*.

Once you have a `LineBreakMeasurer`, you can retrieve each line of text as a `TextLayout`:

public TextLayout nextLayout(float maxAdvance)
This method returns the next line of text. The `maxAdvance` parameter should contain the maximum allowed advance for the returned `TextLayout`. It is the width into which you are trying to fit the text. This width is also called the *wrapping width.*

public TextLayout nextLayout(float wrappingWidth, int offsetLimit,
boolean requireNextWord)
This method is the same as the last method, but it adds more constraints on the line breaking algorithm.* The returned line can contain only characters up to the supplied `offsetLimit`, which is a logical character offset. Furthermore, if `requireNextWord` is `true`, the entire next word of the `LineBreakMeasurer` must be returned in the `TextLayout`. If the next word is too large to fit in the given wrapping width, `null` will be returned.

The following example shows how to create a `LineBreakMeasurer` and render the `TextLayouts` that it generates:

```
import java.awt.*;
import java.awt.font.*;
import java.text.*;

public class ParagraphLayout {
  public static void main(String[] args) {
    Frame f = new ApplicationFrame("ParagraphLayout v1.0") {
```

---

* Although the `maxAdvance` parameter is called `wrappingWidth` in the second method, it is exactly the same thing.

```
         public void paint(Graphics g) {
           Graphics2D g2 = (Graphics2D)g;

           g2.setRenderingHint(RenderingHints.KEY_ANTIALIASING,
               RenderingHints.VALUE_ANTIALIAS_ON);

           // From _One Hundred Years of Solitude_ by Gabriel Garcia Marquez.
           String s = "Jos\u00e9 Arcadio Buend\u00eda spent the long months " +
               "of the rainy season shut up in a small room that he " +
               "had built in the rear of the house so that no one " +
               "would disturb his experiments. Having completely abandoned " +
               "his domestic obligations, he spent entire nights in the " +
               "courtyard watching the course of the stars and he almost " +
               "contracted sunstroke from trying to establish an exact method " +
               "to ascertain noon. When he became an expert in the use and " +
               "manipulation of his instruments, he conceived a notion of " +
               "space that allowed him to navigate across unknown seas, " +
               "to visit uninhabited territories, and to establish " +
               "relations with splendid beings without having to leave " +
               "his study. That was the period in which he acquired the habit " +
               "of talking to himself, of walking through the house without " +
               "paying attention to anyone...";
           Font font = new Font("Serif", Font.PLAIN, 24);
           AttributedString as = new AttributedString(s);
           as.addAttribute(TextAttribute.FONT, font);
           AttributedCharacterIterator aci = as.getIterator();

           FontRenderContext frc = g2.getFontRenderContext();
           LineBreakMeasurer lbm = new LineBreakMeasurer(aci, frc);
           Insets insets = getInsets();
           float wrappingWidth = getSize().width - insets.left - insets.right;
           float x = insets.left;
           float y = insets.top;

           while (lbm.getPosition() < aci.getEndIndex()) {
             TextLayout textLayout = lbm.nextLayout(wrappingWidth);
             y += textLayout.getAscent();
             textLayout.draw(g2, x, y);
             y += textLayout.getDescent() + textLayout.getLeading();
             x = insets.left;
           }
         }
       };
     f.setVisible(true);
   }
 }
```

Figure 7-6 shows this example in action. If you resize the frame window, the text will automatically adjust to the width of the window.

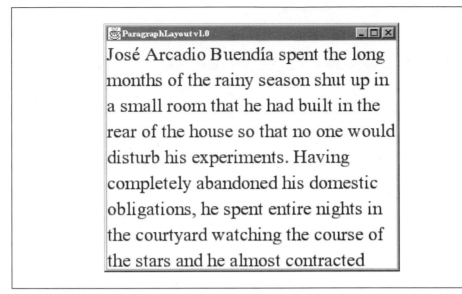

Figure 7-6. Multiline text

You can find out information about the next line of text using the following methods:

public int nextOffset(float maxAdvance)
>   This method returns the logical character offset of the next line. However, this method does not update the current offset.

public int nextOffset(float wrappingWidth, int offsetLimit, boolean requireNextWord)
>   This method corresponds to the `nextLayout()` method with the same parameters. It figures out the logical offset of the beginning of the next line after a call to `nextLayout(wrappingWidth, offsetLimit, requireNextWord)`. Like the previous method, this method does not update the current offset.

You can find out a `LineBreakMeasurer`'s current logical offset or set it using the following methods:

public int getPosition()
>   This method returns the current logical offset.

public void setPosition(int newPosition)
>   This method sets the current logical offset of this `LineBreakMeasurer`. Usually you won't ever need to call this method, as `nextLayout()` updates the current position each time it is called.

Finally, `LineBreakMeasurer` includes methods for adding and removing single characters. Although you could create an entirely new `LineBreakMeasurer` each time the source text changed, these methods should be faster:

public void insertChar(AttributedCharacterIterator newParagraph, int insertPos)

> Use this method to insert a single character. The `newParagraph` parameter should contain the entire paragraph, including the new character. The location of the new character is given by `insertPos`.

public void deleteChar(AttributedCharacterIterator newParagraph, int deletePos)

> Use this method to remove a single character. The `newParagraph` parameter should contain the entire paragraph without the removed character. The location of the removal is given by `deletePos`.

Getting Close to the Metal

The 2D API gives you absolute control over glyphs and their layout, if you want it. The text rendering methods I've described so far all take advantage of automatic layout mechanisms. You pass a string to `drawString()` or to a `TextLayout` and the 2D API worries about the details of laying out the glyphs. For total control, you can manipulate the shapes yourself.

Why would you want to do this? It's possible you won't be satisfied with the way `TextLayout` or `drawString()` is formatting your text and you'd rather use your own layout algorithm. Another possibility is that you may want to achieve funky text effects, like text with a curved baseline. You need glyph-level control for that kind of effect.

There are two classes that relate directly to glyphs. The `java.awt.font.GlyphVector` class represents a set of glyphs, each with its own position. The `java.awt.font.GlyphMetrics` class encapsulates measurements for a single glyph.

To actually render glyphs individually, you can retrieve them from a `GlyphVector` as a `Shape` and pass them to `Graphics2D`'s `fill()` or `draw()` methods, as for any other shape. `Graphics2D` also has a method for drawing an entire `GlyphVector`:

public abstract void drawGlyphVector(GlyphVector g, float x, float y)

> This method renders the glyphs contained in the supplied `GlyphVector`, using x and y as the baseline location.

Creating GlyphVectors

A `GlyphVector` holds only glyphs from a single font. If you are trying to render styled text using `GlyphVectors`, you'll have to break the text up into pieces that use a single font and font style before creating `GlyphVectors`. These pieces are sometimes called *style runs*.

GlyphVector is an abstract class, so you can't instantiate a GlyphVector yourself. The Font class, however, has methods that instantiate GlyphVector subclasses. GlyphVectors are created using the following methods in Font:

public GlyphVector createGlyphVector(FontRenderContext frc, String str)
public GlyphVector createGlyphVector(FontRenderContext frc, char[] chars)
public GlyphVector createGlyphVector(FontRenderContext frc, CharacterIterator ci)

> Use these methods to create a GlyphVector that represents the given characters. The characters may be contained in a String or a character array, or represented by a CharacterIterator. In general, the GlyphVectors returned by these methods are not adequate for bidirectional text and may not include other advanced features. For more sophisticated text formatting, use a TextLayout.

Note that GlyphVectors can only be created from regular character iterators, not from AttributedCharacterIterators. GlyphVectors can only represent text in a single font, with a single text style. TextLayout, by contrast, can represent a line of text with any number of different styles, fonts, and colors.

A GlyphVector contains an array of *glyph codes* that represent specific glyph shapes in a font. If you happen to have an array of glyph codes, you can use a Font to create a GlyphVector as follows:

public GlyphVector createGlyphVector(FontRenderContext frc, int[] glyphCodes)

> This method creates a GlyphVector that contains the glyphs represented by the supplied array of glyph codes. Glyph codes are specific to fonts and don't correspond to Unicode character codes.

The following example shows how to create and render a GlyphVector:

```
import java.awt.*;
import java.awt.font.*;

public class VictorVector {
  public static void main(String[] args) {
    Frame f = new ApplicationFrame("VictorVector v1.0") {
      public void paint(Graphics g) {
        Graphics2D g2 = (Graphics2D)g;

        g2.setRenderingHint(RenderingHints.KEY_ANTIALIASING,
          RenderingHints.VALUE_ANTIALIAS_ON);

        String s = "What's our vector, Victor?";
        Font font = new Font("Serif", Font.PLAIN, 24);
        FontRenderContext frc = g2.getFontRenderContext();

        GlyphVector gv = font.createGlyphVector(frc, s);
        g2.drawGlyphVector(gv, 40, 60);
```

```
      }
    };
    f.setVisible(true);
  }
}
```

When run, this example looks just like the results of a call to `drawString()`, as shown in Figure 7-7.

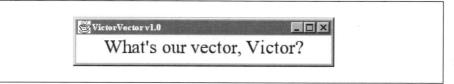

Figure 7-7. Using a GlyphVector to render a string

Retrieving Glyph Shapes

A glyph is just a shape that represents one or more characters. `GlyphVector` includes methods that return the shapes of individual glyphs or of all the glyphs together:

public abstract Shape getOutline()
> Use this method to obtain a `Shape` representing all of the glyphs in this `GlyphVector`. This is useful if you want to use a string for a clipping path or as an outline.

public abstract Shape getOutline(float x, float y)
> This method returns a shape representing all of this `GlyphVector`'s glyphs, translated to the point specified by x and y. The translation just applies to the location of the start of the baseline. Each glyph shape is positioned relative to this location.

public abstract Shape getGlyphOutline(int glyphIndex)
> This method returns a `Shape` that represents a single glyph.

Each of the glyphs in a `GlyphVector` has an associated position:

public abstract Point2D getGlyphPosition(int glyphIndex)
> Use this method to find the baseline location of a single glyph.

To find out how many glyphs are in a `GlyphVector`, use the `getNumGlyphs()` method. Remember, the number of glyphs is not always the same as the number of characters you are rendering. Some pairs of characters can be represented by a single glyph (a ligature), while other characters may be represented by multiple glyphs (composing glyphs).

public abstract int getNumGlyphs()

> This method returns the number of glyphs in this `GlyphVector`. This is one more than the greatest glyph index value that can be passed to `getGlyphOutline()` and `getGlyphPosition()`.

You can also find out the bounding rectangle of the `GlyphVector`:

public abstract Rectangle2D getVisualBounds()

> This method returns a rectangle that exactly encloses the glyphs in this `GlyphVector`.

public abstract Rectangle2D getLogicalBounds()

> This method returns a rectangle that can be used for positioning this `GlyphVector` visually with adjacent `GlyphVectors`. It takes leading and trailing whitespace into account.*

The following example retrieves, transforms, and renders each glyph shape in a `GlyphVector`. Each glyph is rotated through an angle between 0 and $\pi/4$. The angle is determined by the glyph's index, such that the first glyph isn't rotated at all, and the last glyph is rotated by $\pi/4$.

```java
import java.awt.*;
import java.awt.font.*;
import java.awt.geom.*;

public class RollingText {
  public static void main(String[] args) {
    Frame f = new ApplicationFrame("RollingText v1.0") {
      public void paint(Graphics g) {
        Graphics2D g2 = (Graphics2D)g;

        g2.setRenderingHint(RenderingHints.KEY_ANTIALIASING,
            RenderingHints.VALUE_ANTIALIAS_ON);

        String s = "What's our vector, Victor?";
        Font font = new Font("Serif", Font.PLAIN, 24);
        FontRenderContext frc = g2.getFontRenderContext();
        g2.translate(40, 80);

        GlyphVector gv = font.createGlyphVector(frc, s);
        int length = gv.getNumGlyphs();
        for (int i = 0; i < length; i++) {
          Point2D p = gv.getGlyphPosition(i);
          double theta = (double)i / (double)(length - 1) * Math.PI / 4;
          AffineTransform at = AffineTransform.getTranslateInstance(
```

---

* It's supposed to, anyhow. In the initial release of Java 2, I still get the same rectangle from `getVisualBounds()` and `getLogicalBounds()`.

```
                    p.getX(), p.getY());
            at.rotate(theta);
            Shape glyph = gv.getGlyphOutline(i);
            Shape transformedGlyph = at.createTransformedShape(glyph);
            g2.fill(transformedGlyph);
        }
    }
};
f.setVisible(true);
}
}
```

This example is shown in Figure 7-8.

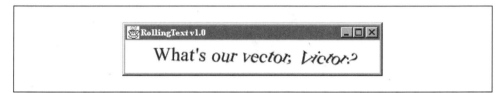

Figure 7-8. Transforming individual glyphs

Modifying a GlyphVector

There are two methods that modify the location and transformation associated with a single glyph in a GlyphVector. As of JDK 1.2.1, however, the method to modify a glyph's transformation is not implemented. If you want to transform individual glyphs, retrieve the glyph shapes and perform the modifications yourself, as demonstrated in the RollingText example.

public abstract void setGlyphPosition(int glyphIndex, Point2D newPos)
   This method changes the location of the glyph at the given index to the specified point.

public abstract void setGlyphTransform(int glyphIndex, AffineTransform newTX)
   This method sets the transform associated with the given glyph index to the supplied transformation.

Glyph Metrics

You can find out measurement information about individual glyphs using the GlyphMetrics class. To obtain metrics for a glyph, call GlyphVector's getGlyphMetrics() method:

public abstract GlyphMetrics getGlyphMetrics(int glyphIndex)
   This method returns glyph metrics for the glyph at the given index in this GlyphVector.

What can you do with a `GlyphMetrics` object? This class serves two purposes. First, it describes the exact relationship between a glyph's width and its advance. The other thing `GlyphMetrics` can do is describe a type of glyph.

The width of a glyph is simply the width of the glyph's shape. The advance of a glyph, on the other hand, describes where the next glyph should be rendered. Some glyphs are designed to overlap, which means that the width of the glyph may be greater than the advance. Glyphs that need to be separate should have advances that are greater than their widths.

The width and advance of a glyph are related by two quantities, the *left side bearing* (LSB) and the *right side bearing* (RSB). Figure 7-9 shows these quantities for an uppercase "A".

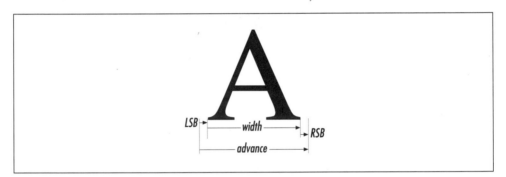

Figure 7-9. Advance, width, and side bearings of a glyph

The following equation describes the relationship between a glyph's advance, width, and side bearings:

$$advance \ = \ width + LSB + RSB$$

Interestingly, the side bearings may be negative quantities. Figure 7-10 shows the advance, width, and side bearings for a lower-case "f". Because the advance for this glyph is less than its width, the top of the "f" will actually hang over into the space of the next rendered glyph. This is done for aesthetic reasons.

It's easy to extract these measurements from a `GlyphMetrics` object:

public Rectangle2D getBounds2D()
> This method returns the bounds of the glyph's shape. The width of this rectangle is the actual width of the glyph.

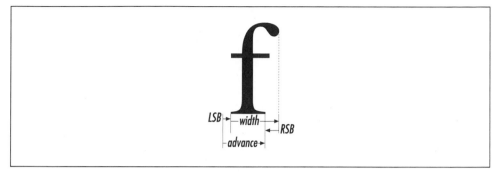

Figure 7-10. A glyph with a negative right side bearing

public float getAdvance()
public float getLSB()
public float get RSB()

These methods return the advance, left side bearing, and right side bearing of the glyph represented by this GlyphMetrics.

The rest of GlyphMetrics's methods are devoted to describing the type of a glyph. GlyphMetrics includes five constants representing different glyph types:

public static final byte STANDARD

Standard glyphs have this type.

public static final byte LIGATURE

Ligature glyphs have this type. A ligature is a glyph that represents more than one character, like "fi".

public static final byte COMBINING

This type represents a glyph that can be combined with other standard glyphs to represent a character. An accented character, for example, is created from a combining glyph that might be put together with an "a" or an "e".

public static final byte COMPONENT

This type of glyph is used to make visual modifications to existing glyphs, which is necessary in cases like Arabic text justification.

public static final byte WHITESPACE

This type of glyph has no visual representation.

You can find out the type of a glyph using the following method in Glyph-Metrics:

public int getType()

This method returns the glyph type, which is one or more of the type constants described above.

`GlyphMetrics` also includes the following methods for testing the glyph type:

public boolean isStandard()
public boolean isLigature()
public boolean isCombining()
public boolean isComponent()
public boolean isWhitespace()

There's another class related to glyph metrics, called `java.awt.font.`
`GlyphJustificationInfo`. It's used for advanced features like text justification,
but it's not implemented in the initial release of Java 2. See the JDK documentation for details on this class.

8

Color

In this chapter, I'll cover the following topics:

- the `java.awt.Color` class

- how humans perceive light and color

- color spaces and absolute color spaces

- device profiles

Color is a tricky thing. If you don't believe me, try this exercise. Take a piece of construction paper in your favorite color—let's say green. Scan the paper into a computer and look at the image on the screen. It's a different green. Try looking at it on another monitor. Now print the image on a color printer. Try another color printer. Take a photograph of the paper and get the print developed. Now try it with slide film. At this point, you have six images of the original paper, probably none with the same color.

The architects of the Java 2D API realized how hard it is to deal with color, and they went to a lot of trouble to craft a correct solution. Java 2D was designed with two seemingly incompatible goals in mind:

1. Support high-end, correct color management through the use of standard color spaces and color profiles.

2. Make it easy to use colors without worrying about color spaces and device dependencies.

If You're Not Too Picky...

Many applications don't need high quality color reproduction. Standard user interface components like buttons and scrolling lists don't demand accurate color reproduction—it doesn't matter if buttons are a slightly different color on different machines. Likewise, for charts and figures, it may not matter if the colors vary from machine to machine. But if you're writing desktop publishing software, or image manipulation software, you will need to be more careful. I'll talk about 2D's support for correct color handling later in this chapter.

If your application doesn't demand that colors look exactly the same everywhere, you don't have to read most of this chapter. It's easy to work with color without worrying about color spaces or profiles.

Creating Colors

The `java.awt.Color` class represents a color in a default RGB color space. To create a `Color`, just specify its red, green, and blue components:

public Color(int r, int g, int b)
> This constructor creates a new `Color` using the specified values for red, green and blue. The values should range from 0 to 255, inclusive.

public Color(float r, float g, float b)
> This constructor creates a new `Color` using the specified values for red, green and blue. The values should range from 0.0 to 1.0, inclusive.

public Color(int rgb)
> This constructor accepts the red, green, and blue values in a *packed* integer. This means that the red, green, and blue values, which are 8 bits each, are stored inside a Java integer, which is 32 bits wide. Figure 8-1 shows where all the bits should be.

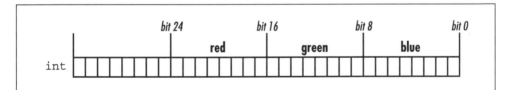

Figure 8-1. Red, green, and blue values in a packed integer

Colors are opaque by default. To create a partially transparent color, specify an alpha value when the color is created:

public Color(int r, int g, int b, int a)
> This constructor creates a new `Color` using the specified values for red, green, blue, and alpha. For the alpha value, 0 is totally transparent, while 255 is opaque.

public Color(float r, float g, float b, float a)

> This constructor creates a new `Color` using the specified values for red, green, blue, and alpha. The values should range from 0.0 to 1.0, inclusive.

public Color(int rgba, boolean hasalpha)

> This constructor accepts red, green, blue, and alpha values in a packed integer. Figure 8-2 shows where the different values live in the packed integer. If the `hasalpha` parameter is `false`, the alpha value is ignored, and the color will be created opaque.

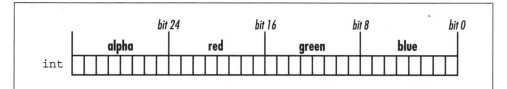

Figure 8-2. Red, green, blue, and alpha values in a packed integer

Retrieving Color Values

You can retrieve a color's components with the following methods:

public int getRed()
public int getGreen()
public int getBlue()
public int getAlpha()

> These methods return the components of this `Color`.

public int getRGB()

> This method returns a packed integer with the alpha, red, green, and blue color components of this `Color`. The returned integer is formatted as shown in Figure 8-2.

Canned Colors

The `Color` class comes with predefined colors in the form of static member variables. I talked about these in Chapter 4, *Painting and Stroking*. Table 8-1 lists these colors again and shows their exact red, green, and blue values.

Table 8-1. Color Constants

Name	Equivalent
`Color.white`	`new Color(255, 255, 255)`
`Color.lightGray`	`new Color(192, 192, 192)`
`Color.gray`	`new Color(128, 128, 128)`

Table 8-1. Color Constants (continued)

Name	Equivalent
Color.darkGray	new Color(64, 64, 64)
Color.black	new Color(0, 0, 0)
Color.red	new Color(255, 0, 0)
Color.pink	new Color(255, 175, 175)
Color.orange	new Color(255, 200, 0)
Color.yellow	new Color(255, 255, 0)
Color.green	new Color(0, 255, 0)
Color.magenta	new Color(255, 0, 255)
Color.cyan	new Color(0, 255, 255)
Color.blue	new Color(0, 0, 255)

If you'd like to give your users the chance to pick colors, Swing includes a very nice color chooser dialog. It's very easy to use—refer back to Chapter 4 for details and an example.

An Example

I'll conclude this section with an example that demonstrates the use of the java.awt.Color class. Remember (from Chapter 4) that the Color class implements the java.awt.Paint interface. This means that you can pass a Color to Graphics2D's setPaint() method. The color will be used to fill shapes, including shape outlines and text.

This example draws three rows of colored blocks. The first row shows all the predefined colors described in Table 8-1. The second row shows a linear gradient between two colors. The third row shows a single color with different levels of alpha:

```
import java.awt.*;
import java.awt.geom.Rectangle2D;

public class ColorBlocks {
  public static void main(String[] args) {
    ApplicationFrame f = new ApplicationFrame("ColorBlocks v1.0") {
      public void paint(Graphics g) {
        Graphics2D g2 = (Graphics2D)g;
        // Center User Space.
        Dimension d = getSize();
        g2.translate(d.width / 2, d.height / 2);

        Color[] colors = {
            Color.white, Color.lightGray, Color.gray, Color.darkGray,
```

```
      Color.black, Color.red, Color.pink, Color.orange,
      Color.yellow, Color.green, Color.magenta, Color.cyan, Color.blue
};

int limit = colors.length;
float s = 20;
float x = -s * limit / 2;
float y = -s * 3 / 2;

// Show all the predefined colors.
for (int i = 0; i < limit; i++) {
  Rectangle2D r = new Rectangle2D.Float(
      x + s * (float)i, y, s, s);
  g2.setPaint(colors[i]);
  g2.fill(r);
}

// Show a linear gradient.
y += s;
Color c1 = Color.yellow;
Color c2 = Color.blue;
for (int i = 0; i < limit; i++) {
  float ratio = (float)i / (float)limit;
  int red = (int)(c2.getRed() * ratio + c1.getRed() * (1 - ratio));
  int green = (int)(c2.getGreen() * ratio +
                    c1.getGreen() * (1 - ratio));
  int blue = (int)(c2.getBlue() * ratio +
                   c1.getBluc() * (1 - ratio));
  Color c = new Color(red, green, blue);
  Rectangle2D r = new Rectangle2D.Float(
      x + s * (float)i, y, s, s);
  g2.setPaint(c);
  g2.fill(r);
}

// Show an alpha gradient.
y += s;
c1 = Color.red;
for (int i = 0; i < limit; i++) {
  int alpha = (int)(255 * (float)i / (float)limit);
  Color c = new Color(c1.getRed(), c1.getGreen(),
                      c1.getBlue(), alpha);
  Rectangle2D r = new Rectangle2D.Float(
      x + s * (float)i, y, s, s);
  g2.setPaint(c);
  g2.fill(r);
}
```

```
            // Draw a frame around the whole thing.
            y -= s * 2;
            Rectangle2D frame = new Rectangle2D.Float(x, y, s * limit, s * 3);
            g2.setPaint(Color.black);
            g2.draw(frame);
        }
    };
    f.setSize(300, 200);
    f.center();
    f.setVisible(true);
    }
}
```

Figure C-8 shows the results of this example.

By now, you know how to create and use colors. If you're still not satisfied, read on. In the remainder of this chapter, I'll talk about color in detail.

Physics and Physiology

Color is a property of light, which is electromagnetic radiation. Light has a magnitude, which corresponds to the sensation of brightness. The color of the light is determined by the light's wavelength. Typically, light has some distribution of wavelengths, with a dominant wavelength that determines the perceived color.

In the human eye, the retina contains cells that respond to light. There are two main types of cells: rods and cones. The rods only respond to the intensity of light, more or less without regard to its wavelength. It's the cones that interest us here, because they respond to different colors of light.

According to the *tristimulus theory*, there are three varieties of cones. Each type of cone has a characteristic response to light of different wavelengths. On a graph, each cone type's response is a curve over the range of visible wavelengths. We'll call these the response functions. Each curve peaks at a different wavelength. The three peak wavelengths correspond roughly to red, green, and blue. (They are not exactly red, green, and blue, and this will cause us trouble later.) Thus, any wavelength (color) of light can be expressed in terms of the responses of the three types of cones.

This is probably starting to sound familiar. A computer monitor produces colors by mixing different amounts of red, green, and blue light (RGB). In a more tidy universe, this would be the end of the story. Using red, green, and blue lights, a monitor should be able to produce any color that the human eye can see. Unfortunately, it doesn't work this way.

To figure out why, let's consider a hypothetical monitor. Instead of mixing red, green, and blue, it mixes the colors corresponding to the peak wavelengths of the three cone response functions. If we want to match a color at a particular wave-length, we just need to find the values of the three response functions at that wavelength. Then we can mix proportional amounts of our lights to produce the desired color.

Real monitors, however, mix red, green, and blue, not the cone response peak colors. In an RGB monitor, the situation is a little more complicated. There is a set of equations, called color matching functions, that tell how much red, green, and blue should be mixed to produce a color at a given wavelength. Unfortunately, one of these functions is negative over part of the range of visible wavelengths. Since a monitor can only produce colors by adding primary colors together, it cannot subtract one of the primary colors as implied by the negative range of the matching function. An RGB monitor, therefore, has a range of colors that it cannot reproduce.

Color Spaces

A *color space* is a collection of all colors that can be shown by a particular device. An RGB monitor, for example, has a certain range of colors that it can display, based on its red, green, and blue lights and the ranges of intensity for each. A different RGB monitor will have a different color space, because of variations in the colors of the red, green, and blue lights and other variations in electronics and manufacture. Both monitors use the same *color space type*, RGB, but each has a device-dependent color space. Similarly, some printers use combinations of cyan, magenta, yellow, and black ink to create colors. These types of printers have a CMYK color space type, but each printer defines its own CMYK color space.

If you specify an RGB color, then, you can easily display it on any device with an RGB color space, but it may look different on each device. To show a color on two different devices and have it look the same, you need some way to specify the color in absolute terms. Then it can be translated into the specific color spaces of each device.

CIEXYZ

The *Commission Internationale de l'Eclairage* (CIE) designed an absolute color space in 1931. They defined three primary colors, called X, Y, and Z, instead of red, green, and blue. Any visible color can be reproduced using only positive amounts of X, Y, and Z. The name of this color space is CIEXYZ.

It's usually not convenient for devices to deal with CIEXYZ. A monitor creates colors by mixing red, green, and blue light, so an RGB system is very natural. In the same way, many printers work by mixing colored inks—they "think" in CMYK. Nevertheless, CIEXYZ is a useful system for two reasons:

• CIEXYZ is absolute. It does not depend on a particular device.

• Every visible color can be represented using CIEXYZ.

What if you have an RGB color that you want to show on two different monitors? Because of differences in design and manufacture, the two monitors define different RGB spaces, so the color looks different. A device-independent color space, CIEXYZ, can be used to map from one monitor's RGB space to the other monitor's RGB space. This is accomplished through the use of color profiles, which I'll discuss later in this chapter.

sRGB

A more recent absolute color space is sRGB (standard RGB). It uses the familiar red, green, and blue primaries but defines them absolutely. Like CIEXYZ, it's a standard, device-independent color space. It's easier to use than CIEXYZ, since it uses the familiar RGB color space type, but it's also less capable than CIEXYZ—sRGB cannot represent all visible colors. You can read more about sRGB at *http://www.w3.org/pub/WWW/Graphics/Color/sRGB.html.*

sRGB is the default color space in Java 2D. Whenever you create a `Color` without specifying a color space, the color is created in sRGB.

java.awt.color.ColorSpace

The `java.awt.color.ColorSpace` class encapsulates a specific color space. An instance of this class may represent a device-dependent color space, like the RGB color space of a particular monitor. An instance of this class may also represent one of the absolute color spaces, like CIEXYZ and sRGB. `ColorSpace` includes constants that represent common color space types. Below are a few of the more famous types.

Color space types

public static final int TYPE_XYZ

This constant represents a color space with X, Y, and Z components, like CIEXYZ.

public static final int TYPE_RGB

This is the familiar color space of monitors that create colors by mixing red, green, and blue light.

public static final int TYPE_GRAY

This constant represents a grayscale color space type. This color space type defines colors that are evenly spaced between black and white. Colors in a grayscale color space have a single component.

public static final int TYPE_HSV

This constant represents a color space type that is defined by hue, saturation, and value components. These color spaces are useful because HSV is an intuitive way to specify colors. While RGB evolved from the way monitors and televisions work, HSV was designed around how people think about color.

public static final int TYPE_CMY

This constant represents a color space where cyan, magenta, and yellow inks are combined to create different colors. Black is created by mixing the maximum amount of all three components.

public static final int TYPE_CMYK

CMYK devices mix color in the same way as CMY devices, except there is an additional black ink (K) that can be used. CMYK printers are useful for printing things like magazines, where color images are intermingled with black text.

Predefined color spaces

`ColorSpace` itself is an abstract class. However, you can use the `get-Instance()` method to retrieve a `ColorSpace` representing one of the absolute color spaces:

public static ColorSpace getInstance(int colorspace)

This method returns a `ColorSpace` that represents an absolute color space of the supplied type. The type should be one of the following five constants.

public static final int CS_sRGB

This constant represents the sRGB color space.

public static final int CS_CIEXYZ

This constant represents the CIEXYZ color space.

public static final int CS_GRAY

This constant represents an ideal grayscale color space.

public static final int CS_PYCC

This constant represents a color space used on Kodak Photo CDs.

public static final int CS_LINEAR_RGB

This constant represents a specialized RGB color space.

Color components

Different color space types use different numbers of color *components* to define a color. An RGB color, for example, has three different components, one each for red, green, and blue. A grayscale color has only one component—it describes the brightness of the color on a scale from black to white. The `ColorSpace` class includes a method that tells how many color components are used:

public int getNumComponents()
> This method returns the number of color components used by this `ColorSpace`.

You can retrieve the components of a particular color using one of the following methods in the `Color` class:

public float[] getColorComponents(float[] compArray)
> This method returns the components of this `Color` as an array of `float`s. The components returned are valid for the `ColorSpace` of this `Color`. If the supplied array is not `null`, it is filled with the color components and returned. If the array parameter is `null`, a new array will be created and filled with the color components. No alpha component is returned by this method.

public float[] getColorComponents(ColorSpace cspace, float[] compArray)
> This method returns the components of this `Color` in the supplied `ColorSpace` as an array of `float`s. Calling this method is equivalent to getting the color components using the previous method and converting them to the supplied `ColorSpace` (see the next section). If the supplied array is not `null`, it is filled with the color components and returned. No alpha component is returned by this method.

public float[] getRGBColorComponents(float[] compArray)
> This method returns the components of this `Color` in the sRGB color space. It is almost the same as calling `getColorComponents(ColorSpace.get-Instance(ColorSpace.CS_sRGB), compArray)`.*

Conversion methods

The most important methods in `ColorSpace` are the methods that convert to and from standard color spaces. In particular, `ColorSpace` can convert a color to and from CIEXYZ:

public abstract float[] toCIEXYZ(float[] colorvalue)
> This method converts a color in this `ColorSpace` to CIEXYZ. The supplied array should contain as many components as are used in this color space. The

---

* Due to rounding errors in floating point arithmetic, the resulting color component arrays are slightly different.

returned array will always have three elements, corresponding to the X, Y, and Z in CIEXYZ.

public abstract float[] fromCIEXYZ(float[] colorvalue)

This method converts a color in CIEXYZ to this `ColorSpace`. The supplied array should contain three elements, corresponding to X, Y, and Z. The returned array will have as many components as are in this `ColorSpace`.

`ColorSpace` has a similar pair of functions that deal with the sRGB color space:

public abstract float[] toRGB(float colorvalue[])
public abstract float[] fromRGB(float rgbvalue[])

Remember, sRGB is not capable of representing all visible colors. Therefore, it is possible to lose color information if you use sRGB as a conversion color space. If you need to be sure you won't lose any information, use CIEXYZ instead.

And back to color, finally

By default, `Colors` are created in the sRGB color space. But the `Color` class provides one last constructor that allows you to use other color spaces:

public Color(ColorSpace cspace, float[] components, float alpha)

This constructor creates a new `Color` in the given color space, using the supplied components and alpha value. The component array should have `cspace.getNumComponents()` elements, and the `alpha` parameter should be between 0.0 and 1.0, inclusive.

Every color lives in a particular color space. It's easy to retrieve a `Color`'s `ColorSpace`:

public ColorSpace getColorSpace()

This method returns the `ColorSpace` in which this `Color` is defined.

If you want to convert colors from one color space to another, you won't usually have to convert in and out of CIEXYZ or sRGB yourself. Instead, you can use the `getColorComponents()` method in the `Color` class. The following method converts any color, in any color space, into grayscale:

```
public static Color convertToGrayscale(Color color) {
  ColorSpace graySpace = ColorSpace.getInstance(ColorSpace.CS_GRAY);
  float[] gray = color.getColorComponents(graySpace, null);
  return new Color(graySpace, gray, 1.0f);
}
```

Profiles

One way to compensate for device dependencies is by using a *profile*. A profile is a set of information that describes how to map from a standard color space (like

CIEXYZ or sRGB) to the color space of a particular device. A color specified in CIEXYZ could be mapped, through the use of profiles, to the RGB spaces of each monitor. Assuming the profiles were correct, the color would appear the same on both monitors. The International Color Consortium (ICC) has a standard format for profiles (see *http://www.color.org/*). Figure 8-3 shows how a CIEXYZ color can be shown on two different output devices. The first profile is used to translate from a CIEXYZ color to an RGB color that the monitor can display. The second profile translates from CIEXYZ to the printer's CMYK color space.

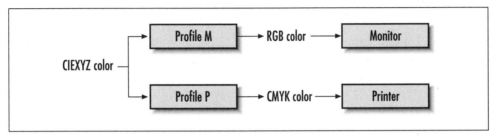

Figure 8-3. Using profiles with output devices

Color profiles are also useful for input devices. Figure 8-4 shows how a color can be accurately scanned and reproduced using color profiles. Initially, the color is defined in the scanner's color space. Profile S is used to convert this color to CIEXYZ. From there, it can be displayed on any output device, using an appropriate profile.

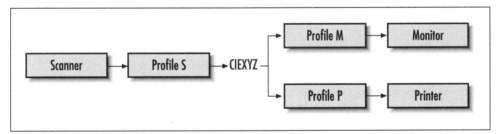

Figure 8-4. Profiles are useful with input devices, too

So where do profiles come from? The manufacturer of an input or an output device may offer profiles for their products. However, this profile will not be entirely accurate, as it doesn't take into account the variations of each device. Typically you'll have to go through some sort of calibration procedure to generate a more accurate profile for a specific device. This can be time-consuming, but if you're serious about color handling, it's essential.

java.awt.color.ICC_Profile

In Java 2D, profiles are represented by instances of `java.awt.color.ICC_Profile`. You can instantiate this class from an array of bytes or an input stream, using one of the `getInstance()` methods:

public static ICC_Profile getInstance(byte[] data)
> This method constructs a profile from the supplied array of data. The data should be in the format described by the ICC, at *http://www.color.org/*.

public static ICC_Profile getInstance(InputStream s) throws IOException
> This method constructs a profile by reading the profile data from the supplied input stream.

public static ICC_Profile getInstance(String fileName) throws IOException
> This method constructs a profile by reading the profile data from the given file. If `fileName` is a relative path, `getInstance()` looks in three places for the file: the directory specified by the `java.iccprofile.path` system property, any directory in the `java.class.path` system property, and in the *jre/lib/cmm* directory underneath the JDK installation directory. (Profiles for the absolute color spaces, like sRGB and CIEXYZ, live in this directory.)

In the following example, a profile is constructed from a file:

```
FileInputStream in = new FileInputStream("Dp17txc1.icm");
ICC_Profile profile = ICC_Profile.getInstance(in);
in.close();
```

You can also construct a profile that corresponds to one of the absolute color spaces:

public static ICC_Profile getInstance(int cspace)
> This method constructs a profile for the given absolute color space. The `cspace` parameter should be one of `ColorSpace`'s constants, either `CS_sRGB`, `CS_CIEXYZ`, `CS_YCC`, or `CS_GRAY`. You probably won't need this method—if you want an instance of one of the absolute color spaces, use `ColorSpace`'s `getInstance()` method instead.

java.awt.color.ICC_ColorSpace

`java.awt.color.ICC_ColorSpace` is a concrete subclass of `ColorSpace`. If you happen to have ICC profiles for your input and output devices, you can construct appropriate `ColorSpaces` for them using this class. An `ICC_ColorSpace` profile is constructed as follows:

public ICC_ColorSpace(ICC_Profile profile)
> This constructor creates a new color space from the given profile.

Putting It All Together

Most of 2D's color handling is behind-the-scenes work. You'll hardly ever need to deal with CIEXYZ or sRGB conversions yourself. You can control 2D's color handling with a rendering hint (see Chapter 5, *Rendering*). The name of the hint key is KEY_COLOR_RENDERING. It has three possible values:

VALUE_COLOR_RENDER_QUALITY
> With this hint setting, the 2D API will do its very best to represent colors correctly. The API accomplishes this by attempting to find a color profile for your screen. Every color that is shown will be converted to a color space constructed from this profile. The way that profiles are located depends on the underlying operating system.

VALUE_COLOR_RENDER_SPEED
> This hint value specifies that 2D should render things speedily, not worrying about a screen profile. This means that sRGB colors will be transferred directly to an RGB screen, even though this is not quite a correct match.

VALUE_COLOR_RENDER_DEFAULT
> This hint value tells 2D to do whatever it usually does for color rendering.

Remember, rendering hints are only suggestions. Even if you tell 2D to use the VALUE_COLOR_RENDER_QUALITY hint, you still might not get colors that have been corrected for a particular screen, for either of these reasons:

- If the 2D implementation doesn't support the color rendering hint, no color correction will be done.

- If 2D can't find a color profile for your screen, it can't do color correction.

The initial release of Java 2 does not do any special processing if the VALUE_ COLOR_RENDER_QUALITY hint has been set. However, it should be implemented in the future, so if correct color handling is important to your application, use this hint.

If your application has access to a screen color profile, you could always perform the color conversions yourself. For example, if your application wants to show a color-corrected image, you could convert the image to a color space based on the screen profile. Then you could render the image with the VALUE_COLOR_RENDER_ SPEED hint, to make sure that no additional conversion is performed.

9

Images

This is the first of three chapters about images in the 2D API. In this chapter, you'll learn the basics of loading and displaying images. Chapter 10, *Image Processing*, shows how you can modify the appearance of images using the 2D API's image processing classes. Finally, Chapter 11, *Image Guts*, peels the skin off images to show you how everything works inside.

If you're already familiar with image handling in JDK 1.1 and earlier, some of this chapter is review. But some of it isn't, so pay attention.

Overview

An *image* is a two-dimensional array of colors. Each element in the array is called a *pixel*. Although this sounds like a description of a drawing surface, the two concepts are distinct. The pixels of the image do not necessarily correspond directly to the pixels of a drawing surface. The image has a width and height, measured in pixels, and a coordinate system that is independent of any drawing surface.

java.awt.Image

The `java.awt.Image` class is the center of Java's image universe. It represents a rectangle of colored pixels. The image data is not directly accessible. In essence, then, an `Image` is just a box for image data. You can retrieve the width and height of the image, if they are available:

public abstract int getWidth(ImageObserver observer)
> This method returns the width of the `Image`, measured in pixels. If the width is not available (because the image data has not yet been loaded), -1 is returned. The supplied `ImageObserver` will be notified as image data

becomes available. You can pass null for the ImageObserver parameter if you wish. (I'll talk more about ImageObservers soon.)

public abstract int getHeight(ImageObserver observer)

> This method returns the height of the Image, measured in pixels. It behaves just like getWidth().

The Graphics2D class knows how to render an Image to a drawing surface, using one of its many drawImage() methods. As an image makes its way through the rendering pipeline, it is transformed, clipped, and composited, just like shapes and text.

java.awt.image.BufferedImage

Prior to Java 2, the only way to manipulate image data was through the use of a sometimes awkward image producer and consumer model. The 2D API, introduced in the Java 2 platform, includes an extension of Image, java.awt.image. BufferedImage, which allows direct access to the image's data.

One of the really nice things about BufferedImage is that its image data is always immediately accessible. This means that you never have to mess around with ImageObservers when you're using BufferedImages. Like Image, Buffered-Image has methods that return the width and height of the image. But they always return valid values; there's no ImageObserver messing things up:

public int getWidth()
public int getHeight()

> These methods return the width and height of this BufferedImage.

As I mentioned, the image data is directly accessible. In Chapter 11, I'll explain the getRGB() and setRGB() methods, which allow you to retrieve pixel colors or set them.

If you want to create a new image from some subset of a current BufferedImage, it's only a method call away:

public BufferedImage getSubimage(int x, int y, int w, int h)

> This method returns an image representing the data in the rectangle defined by x, y, w, and h.

Just remember that whatever you can do with an Image, you can do with a BufferedImage. I'll describe the BufferedImage class in detail in Chapter 11.

Where Do Images Come From?

You can either load an image from an input stream or create a fresh image.

Loading Images

The JDK knows how to create images from GIF and JPEG data. There are four methods that load these types of images from URLs or files. Note that these methods do, in fact, return `Image`s and not `BufferedImage`s. If you want to create writable versions of these `Image`s, you'll have to convert the `Image` to a `BufferedImage` first. I'll describe how to do that later in this chapter.

In applets

Applets can load images from URLs using two methods in the `java.applet.Applet` class.

public Image getImage(URL url)
> This method returns an `Image` that represents image data located at the supplied URL. This method returns immediately. The image data is not loaded until you try to display the image. Interestingly, this method does not throw any exceptions, because the data loading is not performed when the `Image` is created.

public Image getImage(URL url, String name)
> This is the same as the method above, except that the image data is located at the file name, relative to the given URL.

Let's say you have an image called *oreilly.gif*, located in the same place as the HTML page that contains your applet. You might, therefore, obtain an `Image` like this:

```
Image tarsier = getImage(getDocumentBase(), "oreilly.gif");
```

The following complete applet loads the image and displays it:

```
import java.applet.*;
import java.awt.*;

public class ShowImage
    extends Applet {
  private Image mImage;

  public void init() {
    mImage = getImage(getDocumentBase(), "oreilly.gif");
  }

  public void paint(Graphics g) {
    g.drawImage(mImage, 0, 0, this);
  }
}
```

Although we create the `Image` object in the `init()` method, the image data does not begin loading until we try to display the image in `paint()`. The details of loading and displaying are a bit peculiar; we'll get to them soon.

In applications

Applications can obtain images in much the same way, using a pair of methods in `java.awt.Toolkit`:

public abstract Image getImage(URL url)
> This method returns an `Image` that represents image data located at the supplied URL. As with `Applet`'s `getImage()`, this method returns immediately and the image data is not loaded until you try to display the image.

public abstract Image getImage(String filename)
> This method returns an `Image` that represents image data in the given file.

Although these methods are `abstract`, you can obtain a `Toolkit` subclass appropriate for your runtime platform by calling `Toolkit.getDefaultToolkit()`. To create an `Image` from a file called *oreilly.gif*, for example, you would do something like this:

```
Image tarsier = Toolkit.getDefaultToolkit().getImage("oreilly.gif");
```

Interestingly, the `getImage()` methods described above place loaded images into a cache. If you ask for the same image again, the image is returned to you from the cache, rather than being reloaded. If you don't need the cache feature, use the corresponding `createImage()` methods instead:

public abstract Image createImage(URL url)
public abstract Image createImage(String filename)
> These methods return an `Image` representing the data at the given URL or file name. The returned image is a new object and is not cached.

If you already have the image data in a byte array, `Toolkit` has two other methods that can be used to create an `Image` from the image data:

public Image createImage(byte[] imagedata)
> This method creates a new `Image` object from the supplied image data. The data should be in GIF or JPEG format.

public abstract Image createImage(byte[] imagedata, int imageoffset, int imagelength)
> This method uses `imagelength` bytes of the given byte array, starting at `imageoffset`, to create a new `Image` object. Again, the data should be in GIF or JPEG format.

Using the JPEG codecs

The Java 2 platform includes support for loading and saving JPEG images with classes tucked away in the com.sun.image.codec.jpeg package. *Codec* is a word somebody made up that stands for "encoder/decoder." The basic idea is that you can create a file from an input stream of JPEG data (decoding) or write an image's data out to a JPEG file (encoding).

NOTE   The JPEG classes are not part of the core JDK. This means that you can't depend on these classes to be available in JDK implementations from vendors other than Sun. Originally Sun included the JPEG classes in the core API, but this ignited a firestorm of controversy, including allegations that Sun violated the "open process" of API development. Most of this noise came from employees of Activated Intelligence, a company that sells Java image codec software. Regardless, Sun backed off and moved the classes out of the core into the com.sun.image.codec package. Sun is in the process of crafting a longer-term solution for image codecs. In the meantime, the JPEG codecs are a stopgap measure to allow for loading and saving images.

To load an image, you need a decoder. To save an image, you need an encoder. The JPEGCodec class has factory methods that return these objects:

public static JPEGImageDecoder createJPEGDecoder(InputStream src)
    This method returns an object that can read JPEG image data from the given stream.

public static JPEGImageEncoder createJPEGEncoder(OutputStream dest)
    This method returns an object that can write JPEG image data to the supplied stream.

Once you have a JPEGImageDecoder, you can read an image with the following method:

public BufferedImage decodeAsBufferedImage() throws IOException, ImageFormatException
    Use this method to read a JPEG image from this JPEGImageDecoder. If the file does not have the correct format, an ImageFormatException is thrown. If any other problem occurs, an IOException is thrown.

The following code, for example, reads an image from the file *Venus of Urbino.jpg*:

```
String filename = "Venus of Urbino.jpg";
FileInputStream in = new FileInputStream(filename);
JPEGImageDecoder decoder = JPEGCodec.createJPEGDecoder(in);
BufferedImage image = decoder.decodeAsBufferedImage();
in.close();
```

It's that simple. Saving an image is straightforward, too. Once you've gotten a `JPEGImageEncoder`, use its `encode()` method:

public void encode(BufferedImage bi) throws IOException, ImageFormatException
> This method writes the data for the given `BufferedImage`. If something goes wrong, an exception will be thrown.

There's quite a bit of complexity that's hidden behind the JPEG classes. JPEG is a lossy compression algorithm, which means that it tries to save only the parts of the image that are important in an attempt to keep file sizes to a minimum. There are a lot of knobs and dials that you can fiddle with to affect how the JPEG algorithm works. If you just use the methods I've described, you are using all the default settings for these parameters. If you need more control, I suggest you check out the documentation for the `JPEGEncodeParam` and `JPEGDecodeParam` interfaces.

NOTE   The initial release of Java 2 (JDK 1.2) didn't include the JPEG codec documentation. If you want to read more about the JPEG codec package, the documentation is available from the 2D web page at *http://java.sun.com/products/java-media/2D/.*

Creating Images

There are several ways to create a brand-new image. The easiest way is to call `Component`'s `createImage()` method:

public Image createImage(int width, int height)
> This method creates a new `Image` with the given width and height. In the 2D API, the returned object can be safely cast to a `BufferedImage`.

You can create a `BufferedImage` using one of its constructors, but you'll have to know some more details about images first. I'll explain the `BufferedImage` class in Chapter 11. For now, I'll whet your appetite with the following code, which creates an empty `BufferedImage` that is 100 pixels wide and 200 pixels high:

```
BufferedImage bi = new BufferedImage(100, 200, BufferedImage.TYPE_INT_RGB);
```

The `java.awt.GraphicsConfiguration` class offers a different way to create new `BufferedImages`. `GraphicsConfiguration` represents a collection of settings for one of your output devices. For example, a `GraphicsConfiguration` could represent the configuration of a particular window on a monitor.

public abstract BufferedImage createCompatibleImage(int width, int height)
> This method creates an image that is *compatible* with this `Graphics-Configuration` and has the supplied width and height. A compatible image has a data structure and color model that is the same (or almost the same) as

the underlying device, which allows the image to be rendered efficiently. (We'll talk more about image data and color models in Chapter 11.)

public abstract BufferedImage createCompatibleImage(int width, int height, int transparency)
This method is the same as the previous method, except it accepts one of the constants from the `java.awt.Transparency` interface, described in Chapter 4, *Painting and Stroking*.

To create a compatible image for your monitor, you could do something like this:

```
GraphicsEnvironment local = GraphicsEnvironment.
getLocalGraphicsEnvironment();
GraphicsDevice screen = local.getDefaultScreenDevice();
GraphicsConfiguration configuration = screen.getDefaultConfiguration();
BufferedImage image = configuration.createCompatibleImage(200, 200);
```

For more information on 2D's device classes, see Chapter 12, *Devices*.

Displaying Images

`Images` are rendered on a drawing surface using `drawImage()` in the `Graphics` and `Graphics2D` classes. This method comes in many flavors, as you'll see. To understand how `drawImage()` works, you first need to understand the concept of an *image observer*. This concept has been in the AWT since Java 1.0, so I'll just review it briefly.*

ImageObserver

The Java platform was designed to be savvy about networks. For images, this boils down to the premise that it could take a significant amount of time to load an image over the network. The `drawImage()` methods in `Graphics` and `Graphics2D`, therefore, support the concept of an *image observer*, an object which monitors the progress of loading image data. When you call `drawImage()` to place an image on a component, it draws as much of the image as is available and returns. If none of the image data is available, the method returns immediately. In a separate thread, however, the image data is loading. The `drawImage()` method accepts an image observer parameter. As image data is loaded, the image observer is notified. Typically the image observer will `repaint()` the component, which calls `drawImage()` again. Since the image data is loaded, the image will be painted immediately.

In the `ShowImage` applet, earlier in this chapter, `this` is passed to `drawImage()` as the `ImageObserver`. How can this work? It turns out that `Component` (`Applet's`

---

* For more information, see John Zukowski's *Java AWT Reference* (O'Reilly) or *Exploring Java*, by Pat Niemeyer and Josh Peck (O'Reilly).

ancestor) itself is an image observer. Its default behavior is to `repaint()` itself whenever it's notified that image data has been received. Here's how it happens in the applet:

1. The applet is initialized, which sets up an `Image` object. No image data is loaded yet.

2. The applet's `paint()` method is called when the applet is first displayed. In this method, we call `drawImage()`. The method returns immediately without drawing anything, but the image data begins loading.

3. As the image data loads, the applet (acting as an image observer) repaints itself. The image appears on the screen, piece by piece, until it is fully loaded.

The `java.awt.image.ImageObserver` interface encapsulates the behavior of an image observer. It defines a single method, `imageUpdate()`, that is called as the image data is loaded.

public boolean imageUpdate(Image img, int infoflags, int x, int y, int width, int height)

This callback method is invoked as data for an image is loaded. The image in question is passed as a parameter. The `infoflags` parameters will contain some combination of the `ImageObserver` constants `WIDTH`, `HEIGHT`, `PROPERTIES`, `SOMEBITS`, `FRAMEBITS`, `ALLBITS`, `ERROR`, and `ABORT`. The `x`, `y`, `width`, and `height` parameters will be filled in as appropriate; if they are not available yet, their values are -1. Return `false` from this method if the image has finished loading or if there was an error. Otherwise, return `true` to receive further `imageUpdate()` calls.

The `Component` class implements the `ImageObserver` interface. Basically, it repaints itself when `imageUpdate()` is called. Thus, it's common to see `this` passed as the `ImageObserver` parameter to `drawImage()`.

The following example demonstrates the use of `ImageObserver` in a small application. It's a subclass of `Frame`, called `RightSizer`, that displays a single image. When the image's dimensions are known, the `RightSizer` is resized to fit the image exactly.*

```
import java.awt.*;
import java.awt.event.*;
import java.awt.image.*;
import java.net.URL;

public class RightSizer
    extends ApplicationFrame {
```

---

* By default, this application loads an image from O'Reilly's web site, so it won't work right unless you're hooked up to the Internet.

```java
  private Image mImage;

  public static void main(String[] args) throws Exception {
    String url = "http://java.oreilly.com/" +
        "news/knudsen/graphics/bite-size_banner.gif";
    if (args.length > 0) url = args[0];
    new RightSizer(new URL(url));
  }

  public RightSizer(URL url) {
    super("RightSizer v1.0");
    mImage = Toolkit.getDefaultToolkit().getImage(url);
    rightSize();
  }

  private void rightSize() {
    int width = mImage.getWidth(this);
    int height = mImage.getHeight(this);
    if (width == -1 || height == -1) return;
    addNotify();
    Insets insets = getInsets();
    setSize(width + insets.left + insets.right,
        height + insets.top + insets.bottom);
    center();
    setVisible(true);
  }

  public boolean imageUpdate(Image img, int infoflags,
      int x, int y, int width, int height) {
    if ((infoflags & ImageObserver.ERROR) != 0) {
      System.out.println("Error loading image!");
      System.exit(-1);
    }
    if ((infoflags & ImageObserver.WIDTH) != 0 &&
        (infoflags & ImageObserver.HEIGHT) != 0)
      rightSize();
    if ((infoflags & ImageObserver.SOMEBITS) != 0)
      repaint();
    if ((infoflags & ImageObserver.ALLBITS) != 0) {
      rightSize();
      repaint();
      return false;
    }
    return true;
  }

  public void update(Graphics g) {
    paint(g);
  }
```

```
    public void paint(Graphics g) {
      Insets insets = getInsets();
      g.drawImage(mImage, insets.left, insets.top, this);
    }
  }
```

There are several aspects of this application that are not obvious. First, the sequence of operations is a bit unusual:

1. The main() method creates a new instance of RightSizer, a Frame subclass.

2. In RightSizer's constructor, a new Image is created using Toolkit's getImage() method. Note that this does not begin loading the image data.

3. RightSizer's constructor calls the rightSize() method. This method calls the image's getWidth() and getHeight() methods. These calls tell the image to begin loading its data. When these methods are first called, however, they return -1 because the width and height of the image are not known. rightSize(), recognizing that the image is not loaded, returns immediately.

4. As the image data is loaded, imageUpdate() is called. When the width and height of the image are known, rightSize() is called again. This time, it sizes the frame to fit the image size, centers that frame, and makes it visible.

Why does rightSize() call addNotify()? The addNotify() method creates the frame's peer, its actual resource in whatever native window toolkit you're working on. Calling this method ensures that the frame's insets will be reported correctly, which is critical to making the frame the correct size.

Why is the update() method redefined in RightSizer? Normally, the update() method of a component clears its drawing area and calls paint(). In this case, clearing the background before painting the image causes the image to flicker as it is loaded. RightSizer's implementation of update() calls paint() directly, without clearing the background first.

Waiting for Images with a MediaTracker

java.awt.MediaTracker is a handy utility class that does some of the dirty work of an ImageObserver. It can monitor the progress of any number of images. You can wait for all the images to load, or just specific images, and you can check for errors. Here's the constructor:

public MediaTracker(Component comp)

Use this constructor to create a new MediaTracker for images that will be displayed on comp. It's actually not too important which Component gets passed to the constructor. If you look at the source code for ImageIcon in Swing, for example, you'll see the following:

```
protected final static Component component = new Component() {};
protected final static MediaTracker tracker = new MediaTracker(component);
```

To modify which images the `MediaTracker` is interested in, use the following methods:

public void addImage(Image image, int id)

This method adds the supplied `Image` to this `MediaTracker`'s pile of images. The given identification number should be used with subsequent method calls concerning this `Image`. Note that you may assign the same identification number to more than one image.

public void removeImage(Image image)

This method removes all instances of the given image from this `MediaTracker`.

To wait for images to load, use the following method:

public void waitForID(int id) throws InterruptedException

This method waits for the image or images associated with the given identification number to finish loading. If this thread is interrupted while waiting, an `InterruptedException` is thrown.

If something goes wrong while image data is loading, you don't find out about it unless you ask:

public boolean isErrorID(int id)

If any of the images associated with the given identification number encountered errors while loading, this method returns `true`.

Suppose you were willing to wait for an `Image` to load completely. The following method does just this:

```
private static final Component sComponent = new Component() {};
private static final MediaTracker sTracker = new MediaTracker(sComponent);
private static int sID = 0;

public static boolean waitForImage(Image image) {
    int id;
    synchronized(sComponent) { id = sID++; }
    sTracker.addImage(image, id);
    try { sTracker.waitForID(id); }
    catch (InterruptedException ie) { return false; }
    if (sTracker.isErrorID(id)) return false;
    return true;
}
```

Basically, the image gets added to the `MediaTracker`. Then `waitForID()` is called to wait for image loading to finish. If everything goes well, this method returns `true`. If the `MediaTracker` is interrupted or there's an error loading the image, this method returns `false`. This method is actually part of a class called `Utilities`, which is presented at the end of this chapter.

Waiting for Images the Easy Way

Java's new Swing toolkit has a class that creates an image and waits for it to load. Instead of reinventing the wheel with a `MediaTracker`, try this approach instead. The `javax.swing.ImageIcon` class represents an image in a Swing user interface component. Three of its constructors are useful for loading images:

public ImageIcon(String filename)
public ImageIcon(URL location)
public ImageIcon(byte[] imageData)
> These constructors create a new `ImageIcon` by loading the image represented by the supplied filename, URL, or byte array. The image will be fully loaded before the constructor returns.

After you create an `ImageIcon`, you can retrieve the `Image` it represents using the following method:

public Image getImage()
> This method returns the `Image` represented by this `ImageIcon`.

Fully loading an image from a file is a one-line process:

```
Image image = new javax.swing.ImageIcon("tarsier.gif").getImage();
```

Displaying Images with Graphics

The old `Graphics` class offers six overloaded versions of `drawImage()`. These can be categorized as three pairs. The first pair renders the image at a given location at its original size. The second pair scales the image to fit in a rectangle. The third set renders a portion of the image, scaling it to fit in a supplied rectangle. These methods are:

public boolean drawImage(Image img, int x, int y, ImageObserver observer)
> This method renders the supplied image at the given location. The `ImageObserver` will be notified as the image data is loaded. If any areas of the image are transparent, the background color of the drawing surface will show through.

public boolean drawImage(Image img, int x, int y, Color bgcolor, ImageObserver observer)
> This method is the same as above, but the supplied color is used for the transparent areas of the image. In effect, this method fills the image rectangle with the given color and draws the image on top.

public boolean drawImage(Image img, int x, int y, int width, int height,
    ImageObserver observer)
public boolean drawImage(Image img, int x, int y, int width, int height, Color bgcolor,
    ImageObserver observer)

Use these methods to render the given image, scaling it to fit in the rectangle described by `x`, `y`, `width`, and `height`. As before, the version with a `Color` parameter uses the supplied color for the transparent areas of the image. The scaling algorithm is either nearest neighbor or bilinear interpolation, both of which are described in Chapter 10. The `KEY_INTERPOLATION` rendering hint controls which algorithm will be used. For more information on rendering hints, see Chapter 5.

public boolean drawImage(Image img, int dx1, int dy1, int dx2, int dy2, int sx1, int sy1,
    int sx2, int sy2, ImageObserver observer)
public boolean drawImage(Image img, int dx1, int dy1, int dx2, int dy2, int sx1, int sy1,
    int sx2, int sy2, Color bgcolor, ImageObserver observer)

These methods render a portion of the supplied image into a rectangle on the drawing surface, scaling if necessary. `sx1`, `sy1`, `sx2`, and `sy2` describe the top left and bottom right corners of the portion of the image that you want to use. They should be specified in the coordinate system of the image. `dx1`, `dy1`, `dx2`, and `dy2` represent the corners of the rectangle, in User Space, where the image portion will be rendered.

These methods have two confusing features. First, the rectangles are specified in different coordinate spaces. The source rectangle lives in the image's coordinate space, while the destination rectangle lives in User Space. Second, the rectangles themselves are described by their corners. In the other `drawImage()` methods, rectangles are always described by a corner point, a width, and a height.

Displaying Images with Graphics2D

Java 2D's `Graphics2D` offers two other options for rendering images:

public void drawImage(Image img, AffineTransform xform, ImageObserver obs)

This method renders an image after transforming it. The supplied transformation is applied to the image before it enters the pipeline. Therefore, the supplied transformation supplements whatever transformation is installed in the `Graphics2D`.

public void drawImage(BufferedImage img, BufferedImageOp op, int x, int y)

Use this method to render a processed version of a `BufferedImage`. The original image is not changed. I'll talk about image processing in detail in Chapter 10.

The Graphics2D class also includes the drawRenderableImage() and drawRenderedImage() methods, but these are related to the Java Advanced Imaging API (JAI). For more information, see *http://java.sun.com/products/java-media/jai/*.

Cashing In with Graphics2D

Remember all that cool stuff a Graphics2D can do, like transformations, clipping, and alpha compositing? It all works with images, too. To illustrate, here's an example that uses a text string as a clipping path and draws an image. The whole thing is rotated, too. Figure C-9 shows how the example looks.

Here's the code that rotates User Space. The rotation is performed around the center of the window:

```
Dimension d = getSize();
g2.rotate(-Math.PI / 12, d.width / 2, d.height / 2);
```

Getting the text clipping string is a little more involved. This code is in the getClippingShape() method. A Font is used to create a GlyphVector for the clipping shape string. Then the shape is retrieved by calling GlyphVector's getOutline() method:

```
String s = "bella";
Font font = new Font("Serif", Font.PLAIN, 192);
FontRenderContext frc = g2.getFontRenderContext();
GlyphVector gv = font.createGlyphVector(frc, s);
mClippingShape = gv.getOutline(10, 200);
```

Setting the clipping shape and rendering the image is easy:

```
g2.clip(getClippingShape(g2));
g2.drawImage(image, 0, 0, null);
```

Here's the entire example. It uses the JPEG classes (discussed earlier in this chapter) to load the image.

```
import java.awt.*;
import java.awt.font.*;
import java.awt.image.BufferedImage;
import java.io.*;

import com.sun.image.codec.jpeg.*;

public class ClipImage {
    public static void main(String[] args) throws IOException {
        String filename = "Venus of Urbino.jpg";
        InputStream in = ClipImage.class.getResourceAsStream(filename);
        JPEGImageDecoder decoder = JPEGCodec.createJPEGDecoder(in);
        final BufferedImage image = decoder.decodeAsBufferedImage();
        in.close();
```

```
      ApplicationFrame f = new ApplicationFrame("ClipImage v1.0") {
        private Shape mClippingShape;

        public void paint(Graphics g) {
          Graphics2D g2 = (Graphics2D)g;
          Dimension d = getSize();
          g2.rotate(-Math.PI / 12, d.width / 2, d.height / 2);
          g2.clip(getClippingShape(g2));
          g2.drawImage(image, 0, 0, null);
        }

        private Shape getClippingShape(Graphics2D g2) {
          if (mClippingShape != null) return mClippingShape;
          String s = "bella";
          Font font = new Font("Serif", Font.PLAIN, 192);
          FontRenderContext frc = g2.getFontRenderContext();
          GlyphVector gv = font.createGlyphVector(frc, s);
          mClippingShape = gv.getOutline(10, 200);
          return mClippingShape;
        }
      };
      f.setSize(400, 250);
      f.center();
      f.setVisible(true);
  }
}
```

Drawing on Images

Up until now, I've treated an image as something that gets rendered on a drawing surface. But the image itself can be a drawing surface. The Image class provides the following method for this purpose:

public abstract Graphics getGraphics()
> This method returns a Graphics instance that renders to this Image. This method is supported only for application-created offscreen images. In particular, images that represent external image data, like those returned from the getImage() methods in Applet and Toolkit, will throw an Illegal-AccessError from this method.

BufferedImage, as a subclass of Image, also has a getGraphics() method. However, it is deprecated. You should use the createGraphics() method instead, as it explicitly returns a Graphics2D instead of a Graphics:

public Graphics2D createGraphics()
> Use this method to obtain a Graphics2D that represents this BufferedImage as a drawing surface.

The following example shows the two-faced nature of Images. It creates an image, draws on it, and then renders the modified image to the screen. It demonstrates that an image can be rendered on a drawing surface as well as being a drawing surface itself.

```java
import java.awt.*;
import java.awt.event.*;
import java.awt.image.*;
import java.io.*;

import com.sun.image.codec.jpeg.*;

public class ImageDuplicity
    extends Component {
  public static void main(String[] args) {
    ApplicationFrame f = new ApplicationFrame("ImageDuplicity v1.0");
    f.setLayout(new BorderLayout());
    Component c = new ImageDuplicity();
    f.add(c, BorderLayout.CENTER);
    f.setSize(200, 250);
    f.center();
    f.setVisible(true);
  }

  private BufferedImage mImage;

  public void paint(Graphics g) {
    Graphics2D g2 = (Graphics2D)g;
    // If the offscreen image is not defined, create it.
    if (mImage == null) createOffscreenImage();
    // Render the offscreen image.
    g2.drawImage(mImage, 0, 0, this);
  }

  private void createOffscreenImage() {
    // Create a BufferedImage the same size as this component.
    Dimension d = getSize();
    int w = d.width, h = d.height;
    mImage = new BufferedImage(w, h, BufferedImage.TYPE_INT_RGB);
    // Obtain the Graphics2D for the offscreen image.
    Graphics2D g2 = mImage.createGraphics();
    g2.setRenderingHint(RenderingHints.KEY_ANTIALIASING,
        RenderingHints.VALUE_ANTIALIAS_ON);
    // Load an image from a file.
    try {
      String filename = "Raphael.jpg";
      InputStream in = getClass().getResourceAsStream(filename);
      JPEGImageDecoder decoder = JPEGCodec.createJPEGDecoder(in);
      BufferedImage image = decoder.decodeAsBufferedImage();
```

```
            in.close();
            // Draw the loaded image on the offscreen image.
            g2.drawImage(image, 0, 0, w, h, null);
        }
        catch (Exception e) { System.out.print(e); }
        // Draw some concentric ellipses.
        g2.setStroke(new BasicStroke(2));
        Color[] colors = { Color.red, Color.blue, Color.green };
        for (int i = -32; i < 40; i += 8) {
            g2.setPaint(colors[Math.abs(i) % 3]);
            g2.drawOval(i, i, w - i * 2, h - i * 2);
        }
    }
}
```

The main() method sets up a frame window to contain the example. All of the
action is in the paint() and createOffscreenImage() methods. All paint()
has to do is create the offscreen image, if necessary, and render it to the screen.
The createOffscreenImage() method first creates a new offscreen image that
will fit inside the ImageDuplicity component. Then it loads another image from
a file and renders the loaded image on the offscreen image, scaling it to fit.
Finally, createOffscreenImage() draws some colored concentric ellipses on the
offscreen image. Figure C-10 shows what this looks like.

Double Buffering

One important application of offscreen images is *double buffering*. This is a technique that eliminates flicker in animated graphics. Double buffering gets its name
from the fact that there are two graphics areas (buffers) involved—the onscreen
buffer and the offscreen image. Animation is just the process of showing one
frame after another. Without double buffering, you simply clear the drawing area
and draw the new frame. Repeated clearing and redrawing produces flicker, as
shown in the next example, Annoyance. This class simply renders a filled rectangle at the coordinates of the last mouse motion event. When you move the
mouse around in the window, you'll notice the flicker.

```
import java.awt.*;
import java.awt.event.*;

public class Annoyance
    extends ApplicationFrame
    implements MouseMotionListener {
  public static void main(String[] args) {
    new Annoyance();
  }

    private int mX, mY;
```

```
      public Annoyance() {
        super("Annoyance v1.0");
        addMouseMotionListener(this);
        setVisible(true);
      }

      public void mouseMoved(MouseEvent me) {
        mX = (int)me.getPoint().getX();
        mY = (int)me.getPoint().getY();
        repaint();
      }

      public void mouseDragged(MouseEvent me) { mouseMoved(me); }

    public void paint(Graphics g) {
      int s = 100;
      g.setColor(Color.blue);
      g.fillRect(mX - s / 2, mY - s / 2, s, s);
    }
  }
```

Double buffering eliminates the flicker from this example. Basically, I'll render the rectangle into an offscreen image and then transfer the image to the screen. This erases the old picture and draws the new one in one step. The new paint() method looks like this:

```
    public void paint(Graphics g) {
      // Clear the offscreen image.
      Dimension d = getSize();
      checkOffscreenImage();
      Graphics offG = mImage.getGraphics();
      offG.setColor(getBackground());
      offG.fillRect(0, 0, d.width, d.height);
      // Draw into the offscreen image.
      paintOffscreen(mImage.getGraphics());
      // Put the offscreen image on the screen.
      g.drawImage(mImage, 0, 0, null);
    }
```

Note that we have to clear the offscreen image first. Normally, a drawing surface is cleared in Component's update() method. However, since our real drawing happens offscreen, we have to manually clear the offscreen image.

But update() is still clearing the onscreen drawing surface. Since our offscreen image will completely replace the onscreen drawing surface, we don't want update() to clear the onscreen drawing surface every time the image is rendered. Our new class, therefore, overrides update() so that all it does is call paint().

```
    import java.awt.*;
    import java.awt.event.*;
```

```java
public class SmoothMove
    extends ApplicationFrame
    implements MouseMotionListener {
  public static void main(String[] args) {
    new SmoothMove();
  }

  private int mX, mY;
  private Image mImage;

  public SmoothMove() {
    super("SmoothMove v1.0");
    addMouseMotionListener(this);
    setVisible(true);
  }

  public void mouseMoved(MouseEvent me) {
    mX = (int)me.getPoint().getX();
    mY = (int)me.getPoint().getY();
    repaint();
  }

  public void mouseDragged(MouseEvent me) { mouseMoved(me); }

  public void update(Graphics g) { paint(g); }

  public void paint(Graphics g) {
    // Clear the offscreen image.
    Dimension d = getSize();
    checkOffscreenImage();
    Graphics offG = mImage.getGraphics();
    offG.setColor(getBackground());
    offG.fillRect(0, 0, d.width, d.height);
    // Draw into the offscreen image.
    paintOffscreen(mImage.getGraphics());
    // Put the offscreen image on the screen.
    g.drawImage(mImage, 0, 0, null);
  }

  private void checkOffscreenImage() {
    Dimension d = getSize();
    if (mImage == null ||
        mImage.getWidth(null) != d.width ||
        mImage.getHeight(null) != d.height) {
      mImage = createImage(d.width, d.height);
    }
  }
```

```
   public void paintOffscreen(Graphics g) {
     int s = 100;
     g.setColor(Color.blue);
     g.fillRect(mX - s / 2, mY - s / 2, s, s);
   }
 }
```

Swing components, by default, perform double-buffered drawing. If you want to use double buffering, the easiest way to do it is to use a Swing component.

A Useful Class

As promised earlier, this section contains a class that's full of handy static methods. The class is called `Utilities` and contains the following methods:

public static boolean waitForImage(Image image)
> This method waits for the given image to load fully. If everything goes well, it returns `true`. If there is an error loading the image, it returns `false`.

public static Image blockingLoad(String path)
public static Image blockingLoad(URL url)
> These methods load an image from the given file path or URL. These methods will not return until the image data is fully loaded. If there is an error while loading, `null` is returned.

public static BufferedImage makeBufferedImage(Image image)
> This method creates a `BufferedImage` from the supplied `Image`.

public static Frame getNonClearingFrame(String name, Component c)
> This method returns a `Frame` subclass whose `update()` method does not clear the `Frame`'s drawing surface. The `name` parameter becomes the `Frame`'s title, and the `Frame` is sized to fit the preferred size of the given component. Then the component is added to the `Frame`'s contents. The `Frame` is disposed if the user tries to close it.

public static void sizeContainerToComponent(Container container, Component component)
> This method resizes the given container so that it just encloses the preferred size of the given component.

public static void centerFrame(Frame f)
> Use this method to place the given `Frame` in the center of the screen.

Here is the `Utilities` class itself. Its methods will be useful in the next chapter.

```
import java.awt.*;
import java.awt.event.*;
import java.awt.image.BufferedImage;
import java.net.URL;
```

```
public class Utilities {
  private static final Component sComponent = new Component() {};
  private static final MediaTracker sTracker = new MediaTracker(sComponent);
  private static int sID = 0;

  public static boolean waitForImage(Image image) {
    int id;
    synchronized(sComponent) { id = sID++; }
    sTracker.addImage(image, id);
    try { sTracker.waitForID(id); }
    catch (InterruptedException ie) { return false; }
    if (sTracker.isErrorID(id)) return false;
    return true;
  }

  public static Image blockingLoad(String path) {
    Image image = Toolkit.getDefaultToolkit().getImage(path);
    if (waitForImage(image) == false) return null;
    return image;
  }

  public static Image blockingLoad(URL url) {
    Image image = Toolkit.getDefaultToolkit().getImage(url);
    if (waitForImage(image) == false) return null;
    return image;
  }

  public static BufferedImage makeBufferedImage(Image image) {
    return makeBufferedImage(image, BufferedImage.TYPE_INT_RGB);
  }

  public static BufferedImage makeBufferedImage(Image image, int imageType) {
    if (waitForImage(image) == false) return null;

    BufferedImage bufferedImage = new BufferedImage(
        image.getWidth(null), image.getHeight(null),
        imageType);
    Graphics2D g2 = bufferedImage.createGraphics();
    g2.drawImage(image, null, null);
    return bufferedImage;
  }

  public static Frame getNonClearingFrame(String name, Component c) {
    final Frame f = new Frame(name) {
      public void update(Graphics g) { paint(g); }
    };
    sizeContainerToComponent(f, c);
    centerFrame(f);
    f.setLayout(new BorderLayout());
```

```
    f.add(c, BorderLayout.CENTER);
    f.addWindowListener(new WindowAdapter() {
      public void windowClosing(WindowEvent e) { f.dispose(); }
    });
    return f;
  }

  public static void sizeContainerToComponent(Container container,
      Component component) {
    if (container.isDisplayable() == false) container.addNotify();
    Insets insets = container.getInsets();
    Dimension size = component.getPreferredSize();
    int width = insets.left + insets.right + size.width;
    int height = insets.top + insets.bottom + size.height;
    container.setSize(width, height);
  }

  public static void centerFrame(Frame f) {
    Dimension screen = Toolkit.getDefaultToolkit().getScreenSize();
    Dimension d = f.getSize();
    int x = (screen.width - d.width) / 2;
    int y = (screen.height - d.height) / 2;
    f.setLocation(x, y);
  }
}
```

Figure C-1: *Showing off with the 2D API*

Figure C-2: *A new kind of gradient*

Figure C-3: *Partially transparent text*

Figure C-4: *Using SrcOut with an onscreen drawing surface*

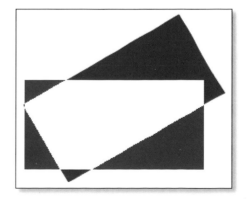

Figure C-5: *Using SrcOut with an offscreen drawing surface*

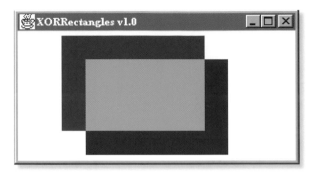

Figure C-6:   *XOR mode in action*

Figure C-7:   *Using a texture to render text*

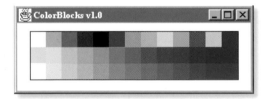

Figure C-8:   *ColorBlocks output*

Figure C-9:   *Venus peeks out from a text clipping shape*

Figure C-10:   *An image can be a drawing surface*

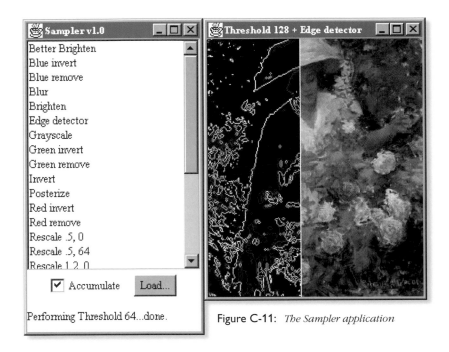

Figure C-11: *The Sampler application*

Figure C-12: *Ethol with Roses, by Edmund Greacen*

Figure C-13: *Blurry Ethol*

Figure C-14: *Edge detection*

Figure C-15: *Sharpening*

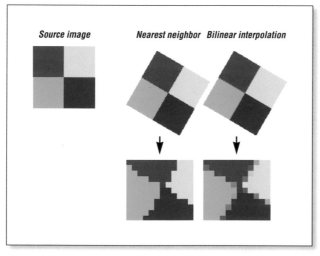

Figure C-16: *AffineTransformOp algorithms compared*

Figure C-17: *Ethol, rotated using bilinear interpolation*

Figure C-18: *Where did the corner go?*

Figure C-19: *Inverted Ethol*

Figure C-20: *Inverting the red component*

Figure C-21: *Ethol without her green color component*

Figure C-22: *Increasing brightness by 50%*

Figure C-23: *Reducing brightness by 50% and adding an offset*

Figure C-24: *Brightening with a linear function*

Figure C-25: *Brightening using a square root function*

Figure C-26: *Converting to a grayscale color space*

Figure C-27: *Thresholding*

Figure C-28:
PNGDecoder in action

Figure C-29: *The FilePrinter application*

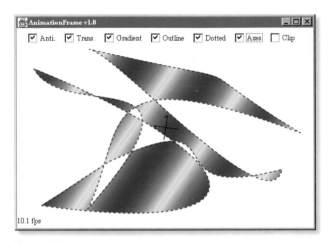

Figure C-30: *Animating a complex shape*

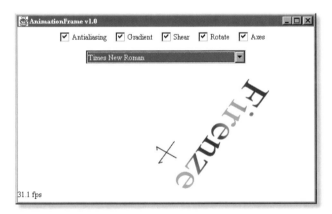

Figure C-31: *Animated text*

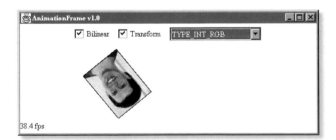

Figure C-32: *Animating an image*

10

Image Processing

Image processing is a field distinct from the rest of computer graphics. It describes how digital images can be manipulated mathematically. Image processing is also called *image filtering*, a term that originated with the use of filters in photography. Digital filters tend to be more capable and precise than their physical counterparts. The terminology persists, however; when we look at the `BufferedImageOp` interface, you'll see that its central method is named `filter()`.

This chapter describes image processing in the 2D API. First, I'll talk about the new image processing model in the 2D API. After that, there's a long example that demonstrates 2D's image processing capabilities. The remainder of the chapter is a sort of cookbook that describes the types of image operations that are included in the `java.awt.image` package. I'll explain each operation briefly in mathematical terms and try to show its effect on different images.

The New Model

The 2D API has a simple image processing model based on the `BufferedImage` class. Image processing operations are represented by the `java.awt.image.BufferedImageOp` interface. Classes that implement this interface know how to process an existing `BufferedImage`, called the *source image*, to produce a new image, the *destination image*. It's very easy. Figure 10-1 shows a schematic representation of this model.

Once you have a `BufferedImage` to use as the source, processing the image is simple. You just instantiate your favorite `BufferedImageOp` implementation and call its `filter()` method with the source image. This method returns the destination image to you as another `BufferedImage`:

public BufferedImage filter(BufferedImage src, BufferedImage dst)

> This method processes the source image, src, using some image operation. If dst is not null, it will contain the processed image when this method returns. If dst is null, a new BufferedImage will be created containing the processed image. In either case, the processed image is returned.

Figure 10-1. Image processing the 2D way

In some cases, the source and destination image can be the same. This means that the operator processes a source image, placing the results back into the same image. At the end of the operation, the source image has become the destination image. This is called *in place* processing. Not all image operators can do it.

Here's a simple example that converts an image to grayscale. I'll talk about ColorConvertOp and the other predefined image processing operations later in this chapter.

```
public static BufferedImage convertToGrayscale(BufferedImage source) {
  BufferedImageOp op = new ColorConvertOp(
      ColorSpace.getInstance(ColorSpace.CS_GRAY), null);
  return op.filter(source, null);
}
```

Combining the Old and New Methods

Before Java 2, image processing involved image producers, consumers, and the java.awt.image.ImageFilter class. If you have an application that uses this model extensively, you might be interested in combining the old paradigm of image processing with the new BufferedImageOp paradigm. Luckily, the 2D API provides a class for this purpose, java.awt.image.BufferedImageFilter. This class extends ImageFilter but wraps a BufferedImageOp. This process allows you to embed the functionality of a BufferedImageOp in a ImageFilter.

An Appetizer

This section contains an example application, Sampler, that demonstrates all of the image operators that are discussed in the remainder of the chapter. Sampler provides a palette of image operators and performs them on an image loaded from a file. You can specify this file on the command line. If you don't specify the file, a default will be loaded. The application displays two windows, as shown in Figure C-11. As you select image operations from the list, they are performed on the image in the window on the right. Don't be surprised if some of the operations take a few seconds to complete. To see the effects of the operation, click and drag the mouse in the image window. This adjusts a white line that divides the processed image from the original.

If you want to perform operations cumulatively, check off the **Accumulate** checkbox. In Figure C-11, for example, the original image has been processed by a thresholding operation followed by an edge detection operation. I'll talk about these operations, and others, in the coming sections.

This example consists of two classes: `Sampler` and `SplitImageComponent`. It also uses the methods from `Utilities`, presented at the end of Chapter 9, *Images*.

`SplitImageComponent` displays the original image and the processed image, separated by a white vertical line. It responds to mouse events by adjusting the location of the split between the two images. The window on the right side of Figure C-11 contains a `SplitImageComponent`.

`SplitImageComponent` subclasses `JPanel` to take advantage of Swing's automatic double buffering. This means that the motion is smooth when you use the mouse to drag the split bar around.

The class itself is pretty straightforward. You can set and retrieve the two images that `SplitImageComponent` displays, using `setImage()`, `setSecondImage()`, `getImage()`, and `getSecondImage()`. Most of the exciting stuff is in the `paint()` method, which uses a clipping rectangle to draw portions of the two images. It also draws the white line representing the split between the two images. Finally, `getPreferredSize()` returns the largest image size.

```
import java.awt.*;
import java.awt.event.*;
import java.awt.image.BufferedImage;
import java.awt.geom.Line2D;

import javax.swing.*;

public class SplitImageComponent
    extends JPanel {
  private BufferedImage mImage;
  private BufferedImage mSecondImage;
  private int mSplitX;

  public SplitImageComponent(String path) {
```

```
    setImage(path);
    init();
  }

  public SplitImageComponent(BufferedImage image) {
    setImage(image);
    init();
  }

  public void setImage(String path) {
    Image image = Utilities.blockingLoad(path);
    mImage = Utilities.makeBufferedImage(image);
  }

  public void setImage(BufferedImage image) { mImage = image; }

  public void setSecondImage(BufferedImage image) {
    mSecondImage = image;
    repaint();
  }

  public BufferedImage getImage() { return mImage; }
  public BufferedImage getSecondImage() { return mSecondImage; }

  private void init() {
    setBackground(Color.white);
    addMouseListener(new MouseAdapter() {
      public void mousePressed(MouseEvent me) {
        mSplitX = me.getX();
        repaint();
      }
    });
    addMouseMotionListener(new MouseMotionAdapter() {
      public void mouseDragged(MouseEvent me) {
        mSplitX = me.getX();
        repaint();
      }
    });
  }

  public void paint(Graphics g) {
    Graphics2D g2 = (Graphics2D)g;
    int width = getSize().width;
    int height = getSize().height;

    // Explicitly clear the window.
    Rectangle clear = new Rectangle(0, 0, width, height);
    g2.setPaint(getBackground());
    g2.fill(clear);
```

```
      // Clip the first image, if appropriate,
      //   to be on the right side of the split.
      if (mSplitX != 0 && mSecondImage != null) {
        Rectangle firstClip = new Rectangle(mSplitX, 0,
            width - mSplitX, height);
        g2.setClip(firstClip);
      }
      g2.drawImage(getImage(), 0, 0, null);

      if (mSplitX == 0 || mSecondImage == null) return;

      Rectangle secondClip = new Rectangle(0, 0, mSplitX, height);
      g2.setClip(secondClip);
      g2.drawImage(mSecondImage, 0, 0, null);

      Line2D splitLine = new Line2D.Float(mSplitX, 0, mSplitX, height);
      g2.setClip(null);
      g2.setColor(Color.white);
      g2.draw(splitLine);
    }

    public Dimension getPreferredSize() {
      int width = getImage().getWidth();
      int height = getImage().getHeight();
      if (mSecondImage != null) {
        width = Math.max(width, mSecondImage.getWidth());
        height = Math.max(height, mSecondImage.getHeight());
      }
      return new Dimension(width, height);
    }
  }
```

The Sampler class itself displays a list of image processing operations. It's the window on the left side of Figure 10-2. Most of the Sampler class is concerned with mundane details, like setting up the two frame windows and the user controls. The part that does the image processing is very small. Look in the createUI() method—the event handler for the List contains all the magic. Basically, we use the name from the List as the key to an internal Hashtable of image operations.

```
String key = list.getSelectedItem();
BufferedImageOp op = (BufferedImageOp)mOps.get(key);
```

The source image is either the original image or the last processed image, depending on the state of the **Accumulate** checkbox:

```
BufferedImage source = mSplitImageComponent.getSecondImage();
boolean accumulate = accumulateCheckbox.getState();
if (source == null || accumulate == false)
  source = mSplitImageComponent.getImage();
```

Once we've determined the source image and the operation, it's a snap to process
the image:

```
BufferedImage destination = op.filter(source, null);
mSplitImageComponent.setSecondImage(destination);
```

The `Sampler` class has the following major pieces:

- The `main()` method creates a new `Sampler` that processes the image file
  named on the command line. If no file is specified, the default *Ethol with Roses.
  small.jpg* is used.

- `Sampler`'s constructor performs three important initializations. First, it calls
  `createOps()` to create a table of image processing operators. Second, it calls
  `createImageFrame()` to create a separate frame window to hold the image.
  Finally, the constructor calls `createUI()` to create the user interface for the
  main `Sampler` window.

- The `createOps()` method calls helper methods—`createConvolutions()`,
  `createTransformations()`, `createLookups()`, `createRescales()`, and
  `createColorOps()`—to create a cornucopia of image operators. The contents of these methods will be explained in the rest of this chapter.

- The `createUI()` method creates the user interface for the `Sampler` window
  and adds event handlers to the controls.

Here is the entire class:

```
import java.awt.*;
import java.awt.color.*;
import java.awt.event.*;
import java.awt.geom.AffineTransform;
import java.awt.image.*;
import java.util.*;

public class Sampler
    extends Frame {
  private Frame mImageFrame;
  private SplitImageComponent mSplitImageComponent;
  private Hashtable mOps;

  public static void main(String[] args) {
    String imageFile = "Ethol with Roses.small.jpg";
    if (args.length > 0) imageFile = args[0];
    new Sampler(imageFile);
  }

  public Sampler(String imageFile) {
    super("Sampler v1.0");
    createOps();
```

```
      createImageFrame(imageFile);
      createUI();
      setVisible(true);
  }

  private void createOps() {
    mOps = new Hashtable();
    createConvolutions();
    createTransformations();
    createLookups();
    createRescales();
    createColorOps();
  }

  private void createConvolutions() {
    float ninth = 1.0f / 9.0f;
    float[] blurKernel = {
        ninth, ninth, ninth,
        ninth, ninth, ninth,
        ninth, ninth, ninth
    };
    mOps.put("Blur", new ConvolveOp(
        new Kernel(3, 3, blurKernel),
        ConvolveOp.EDGE_NO_OP, null));

    float[] edge = {
        0f, -1f, 0f,
        -1f, 4f, -1f,
        0f, -1f, 0f
    };
    mOps.put("Edge detector", new ConvolveOp(
        new Kernel(3, 3, edge),
        ConvolveOp.EDGE_NO_OP, null));

    float[] sharp = {
        0f, -1f, 0f,
        -1f, 5f, -1f,
        0f, -1f, 0f
    };
    mOps.put("Sharpen", new ConvolveOp(
        new Kernel(3, 3, sharp)));
  }

  private void createTransformations() {
    AffineTransform at;
    at = AffineTransform.getRotateInstance(Math.PI / 6, 0, 285);
    mOps.put("Rotate nearest neighbor", new AffineTransformOp(at, null));

    RenderingHints rh = new RenderingHints(
```

```
            RenderingHints.KEY_INTERPOLATION,
            RenderingHints.VALUE_INTERPOLATION_BILINEAR);
      mOps.put("Rotate bilinear", new AffineTransformOp(at, rh));

      at = AffineTransform.getScaleInstance(.5, .5);
      mOps.put("Scale .5, .5", new AffineTransformOp(at, null));

      at = AffineTransform.getRotateInstance(Math.PI / 6);
      mOps.put("Rotate bilinear (origin)", new AffineTransformOp(at, rh));
  }

  private void createLookups() {
      short[] brighten = new short[256];
      short[] betterBrighten = new short[256];
      short[] posterize = new short[256];
      short[] invert = new short[256];
      short[] straight = new short[256];
      short[] zero = new short[256];
      for (int i = 0; i < 256; i++) {
        brighten[i] = (short)(128 + i / 2);
        betterBrighten[i] = (short)(Math.sqrt((double)i / 255.0) * 255.0);
        posterize[i] = (short)(i - (i % 32));
        invert[i] = (short)(255 - i);
        straight[i] = (short)i;
        zero[i] = (short)0;
      }
      mOps.put("Brighten", new LookupOp(new ShortLookupTable(0, brighten),
                null));
      mOps.put("Better Brighten", new LookupOp(
          new ShortLookupTable(0, betterBrighten), null));
      mOps.put("Posterize", new LookupOp(
          new ShortLookupTable(0, posterize), null));
      mOps.put("Invert", new LookupOp(new ShortLookupTable(0, invert), null));

      short[][] redOnly = { invert, straight, straight };
      short[][] greenOnly = { straight, invert, straight };
      short[][] blueOnly = { straight, straight, invert };
      mOps.put("Red invert", new LookupOp(new ShortLookupTable(0, redOnly),
                null));
      mOps.put("Green invert", new LookupOp(
          new ShortLookupTable(0, greenOnly), null));
      mOps.put("Blue invert", new LookupOp(
          new ShortLookupTable(0, blueOnly), null));

      short[][] redRemove = { zero, straight, straight };
      short[][] greenRemove = { straight, zero, straight };
      short[][] blueRemove = { straight, straight, zero };
      mOps.put("Red remove", new LookupOp(
          new ShortLookupTable(0, redRemove), null));
```

```
      mOps.put("Green remove", new LookupOp(
          new ShortLookupTable(0, greenRemove), null));
      mOps.put("Blue remove", new LookupOp(
          new ShortLookupTable(0, blueRemove), null));
    }

    private void createRescales() {
      mOps.put("Rescale .5, 0", new RescaleOp(.5f, 0, null));
      mOps.put("Rescale .5, 64", new RescaleOp(.5f, 64, null));
      mOps.put("Rescale 1.2, 0", new RescaleOp(1.2f, 0, null));
      mOps.put("Rescale 1.5, 0", new RescaleOp(1.5f, 0, null));
    }

    private void createColorOps() {
      mOps.put("Grayscale", new ColorConvertOp(
          ColorSpace.getInstance(ColorSpace.CS_GRAY), null));
    }

    private void createImageFrame(String imageFile) {
      // Create the image frame.
      mSplitImageComponent = new SplitImageComponent(imageFile);
      mImageFrame = new Frame(imageFile);
      mImageFrame.setLayout(new BorderLayout());
      mImageFrame.add(mSplitImageComponent, BorderLayout.CENTER);
      Utilities.sizeContainerToComponent(mImageFrame, mSplitImageComponent);
      Utilities.centerFrame(mImageFrame);
      mImageFrame.setVisible(true);
    }

    private void createUI() {
      setFont(new Font("Serif", Font.PLAIN, 12));
      setLayout(new BorderLayout());
      // Set our location to the left of the image frame.
      setSize(200, 350);
      Point pt = mImageFrame.getLocation();
      setLocation(pt.x - getSize().width, pt.y);

      final Checkbox accumulateCheckbox = new Checkbox("Accumulate", false);
      final Label statusLabel = new Label("");

      // Make a sorted list of the operators.
      Enumeration e = mOps.keys();
      Vector names = new Vector();
      while (e.hasMoreElements())
        names.addElement(e.nextElement());
      Collections.sort(names);
      final java.awt.List list = new java.awt.List();
      for (int i = 0; i < names.size(); i++)
        list.add((String)names.elementAt(i));
```

```
    add(list, BorderLayout.CENTER);

    // When an item is selected, do the corresponding transformation.
    list.addItemListener(new ItemListener() {
      public void itemStateChanged(ItemEvent ie) {
        if (ie.getStateChange() != ItemEvent.SELECTED) return;
        String key = list.getSelectedItem();
        BufferedImageOp op = (BufferedImageOp)mOps.get(key);
        BufferedImage source = mSplitImageComponent.getSecondImage();
        boolean accumulate = accumulateCheckbox.getState();
        if (source == null || accumulate == false)
          source = mSplitImageComponent.getImage();
        String previous = mImageFrame.getTitle() + " + ";
        if (accumulate == false)
          previous = "";
        mImageFrame.setTitle(previous + key);
        statusLabel.setText("Performing " + key + "...");
        list.setEnabled(false);
        accumulateCheckbox.setEnabled(false);
        BufferedImage destination = op.filter(source, null);
        mSplitImageComponent.setSecondImage(destination);
        mSplitImageComponent.setSize(
            mSplitImageComponent.getPreferredSize());
        mImageFrame.setSize(mImageFrame.getPreferredSize());
        list.setEnabled(true);
        accumulateCheckbox.setEnabled(true);
        statusLabel.setText("Performing " + key + "...done.");
      }
    });

    Button loadButton = new Button("Load...");
    loadButton.addActionListener(new ActionListener() {
      public void actionPerformed(ActionEvent ae) {
        FileDialog fd = new FileDialog(Sampler.this);
        fd.show();
        if (fd.getFile() == null) return;
        String path = fd.getDirectory() + fd.getFile();
        mSplitImageComponent.setImage(path);
        mSplitImageComponent.setSecondImage(null);
        Utilities.sizeContainerToComponent(
            mImageFrame, mSplitImageComponent);
        mImageFrame.validate();
        mImageFrame.repaint();
      }
    });

    Panel bottom = new Panel(new GridLayout(2, 1));
    Panel topBottom = new Panel();
    topBottom.add(accumulateCheckbox);
    topBottom.add(loadButton);
```

```
        bottom.add(topBottom);
        bottom.add(statusLabel);
        add(bottom, BorderLayout.SOUTH);

        addWindowListener(new WindowAdapter() {
          public void windowClosing(WindowEvent e) {
            mImageFrame.dispose();
            dispose();
            System.exit(0);
          }
        });
    }
}
```

Have fun with this application. When you want to know more about the image processing operations that it demonstrates, read on.

Predefined Operations

The 2D API comes complete with a handful of useful image operators. These are implementations of the `BufferedImageOp` interface. Table 10-1 summarizes the image operator classes that are defined in `java.awt.image`. I'll talk about each type of operator in the coming sections. The "In Place?" column indicates whether the operator is capable of in-place processing, where the source and destination image are the same.

Table 10-1. Image Processing Classes

Class Name	Supporting Classes	Effect	In Place?
ConvolveOp	Kernel	blurring, sharpening, edge detection	no
AffineTransformOp	java.awt.geom. AffineTransform	geometric transformation	no
LookupOp	LookupTable, ByteLookupTable, ShortLookupTable	posterizing, inversion	yes
RescaleOp		brightening, darkening	yes
ColorConvertOp	java.awt.color. ColorSpace	color space conversion	yes

Blurring and Sharpening

`ConvolveOp` is one of the most versatile image operators in the 2D API. It represents a *spatial convolution*, which is a fancy mathematical term that means that the color of each destination pixel is determined by combining the colors of the corresponding source pixel and its neighbors. A convolution operator can be used to blur or sharpen an image, among other things.

Kernels

The convolution operator uses a *kernel* to specify how a source pixel and its neighbors are combined. A kernel is simply a matrix, where the center of the matrix represents the source pixel and the other elements correspond to the neighboring source pixels. The destination color is calculated by multiplying each pixel color by its corresponding kernel coefficient and adding the results together.* The following kernel transfers the color of each source pixel directly to the corresponding destination pixel. It has no effect on an image because it does not use any of the neighboring source pixels (their coefficients are all zero). I call this kernel an *identity kernel*:

$$\begin{bmatrix} 0.0 & 0.0 & 0.0 \\ 0.0 & 1.0 & 0.0 \\ 0.0 & 0.0 & 0.0 \end{bmatrix}$$

The identity kernel doesn't do anything to an image, so it's really only useful as an illustration. Figure 10-2 shows how this kernel is superimposed on a source image to produce a destination pixel color. This process is repeated for every destination pixel.

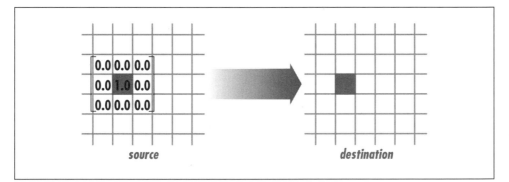

Figure 10-2. Convolution on a single source pixel

Kernels are represented by instances of `java.awt.image.Kernel`, which can be constructed from a one dimensional array as follows:

public Kernel(int width, int height, float[] data)
> This constructor creates a new `Kernel` from the supplied data. The data should be arranged in rows, where the first `width` elements of the array are the first row of the kernel.

---

* The results of this calculation are bounded. Any calculated color components that are less than 0 are set to 0, while color component values greater than their maximum values are set to the maximum.

For example, the following code creates a 3 x 3 identity kernel:

```
float[] identity = {
    0.0f, 0.0f, 0.0f,
    0.0f, 1.0f, 0.0f,
    0.0f, 0.0f, 0.0f
};
Kernel identityKernel = new Kernel(3, 3, identity);
```

Creating the convolution operator

Once you have a kernel, it's easy to create a convolution operator that uses the kernel. There's one additional question that must be addressed first, though. How does the convolution operator behave at the edges of an image? When the kernel is positioned over pixels at the edge of the image, some elements of the kernel are hanging off the image. ConvolveOp provides two constants that represent possible edge behaviors:

public static final int EDGE_ZERO_FILL
> This constant specifies that destination pixels at the image's edges are filled with 0, or black.

public static final int EDGE_NO_OP
> This constant states that edge pixels are unchanged from the source image to the destination image.

You can construct a ConvolveOp using just a Kernel, or you can specify an edge behavior too:

public ConvolveOp(Kernel kernel)
> This constructor creates a ConvolveOp using the given kernel. The edge behavior defaults to EDGE_ZERO_FILL.

public ConvolveOp(Kernel kernel, int edgeHint)
> This constructor creates a ConvolveOp using the given kernel. edgeHint determines the behavior of the ConvolveOp at the edges of the image. It should be EDGE_ZERO_FILL or EDGE_NO_OP.

Some nifty kernels

Now you know how to create a Kernel and a ConvolveOp. That's fine, but the only kernel I've showed you so far (the identity kernel) doesn't do anything! What fun is that?

Let's see what happens when we fill a kernel with a single value. To preserve the brightness of the image, make sure that all the elements of the kernel add up to 1. If they add up to more than 1, the processed image will be brighter than the original. If the sum of the kernel coefficients is less than one, the processed image will be darker. This is because the colors of all the pixels used by the kernel are combined to form a single destination pixel color. The following kernel's coefficients are all the same and add up to 1:

$$\begin{bmatrix} \frac{1}{9} & \frac{1}{9} & \frac{1}{9} \\[4pt] \frac{1}{9} & \frac{1}{9} & \frac{1}{9} \\[4pt] \frac{1}{9} & \frac{1}{9} & \frac{1}{9} \end{bmatrix}$$

The following code shows how to create a `ConvolveOp` around this kernel:

```
float ninth = 1.0f / 9.0f;
float[] blurKernel = {
    ninth, ninth, ninth,
    ninth, ninth, ninth,
    ninth, ninth, ninth
};
ConvolveOp blurOp = new ConvolveOp(
    new Kernel(3, 3, blurKernel),
    ConvolveOp.EDGE_NO_OP, null);
```

As you may have guessed, this `ConvolveOp` blurs the source image. Figure C-12 shows an image of a painting, *Ethol with Roses*, painted by Edmund Greacen in 1907.* The next figure, Figure C-13, shows how this image is affected by the blurring kernel.

Why would you do this to an image? Blurring is useful for images that are *noisy*, meaning the source of the image data was not very reliable. Suppose, for example, that a weather satellite takes a digital photograph and transmits it back to earth. Errors in the radio communications link between the satellite and earth can introduce noise into the image data. A blurring filter can reduce the visibility of these errors.

Edge detection, another common convolution operation, is used to highlight abrupt color changes in images. The following kernel can be used for this purpose:

$$\begin{bmatrix} 0.0 & -1.0 & 0.0 \\ -1.0 & 4.0 & -1.0 \\ 0.0 & -1.0 & 0.0 \end{bmatrix}$$

This kernel's coefficients add up to less than 1, so the processed image is much darker than the original. Figure C-14 shows our original image after an edge

---

* I got this image from Carol Gerten's Fine Art web site at *http://sunsite.unc.edu/cjackson/*.

Space and Time

Mathematically speaking, an image is a function. For any x and y coordinates, the function tells you the color of the image:

color = imageFunction(x, y)

This function lives in the *spatial domain*, because x and y are variables that indicate position in a plane. The result of the function, the color, is said to be a signal that depends on x and y.

Another way to look at an image is in the *frequency domain*. This means that you look at how rapidly the colors change as you vary one of the spatial variables. There's a nifty method that translates spatial functions into frequency domain functions, called the *Fourier Transform*.

What does this have to do with anything? A convolution is actually easier to understand in the frequency domain. It acts as a frequency filter. The blurring convolution, for example, filters out high frequencies in an image. This makes sense, intuitively. High frequencies in an image correspond to rapid spatial changes in color (sharp edges). When you apply the blurring filter, the sharp edges are obliterated, and you're left with just blurry, low frequency color changes. Likewise, a sharpening convolution simply emphasizes the high frequencies in an image.

Signal processing is the official name for the study of Fourier Transforms and related mathematics. Interestingly, signal processing techniques apply equally well to images and sound signals. Sound is a function that lives in the time domain. But you can apply the same Fourier Transform to examine sound in the frequency domain. The same filter that blurs images also removes the high frequencies from sounds, reducing their "shimmer." The math is the same; it's just applied differently.

---

detection convolution has been applied. The original painting was Impressionistic, so there aren't many edges to be highlighted. But you can pick out the edge of Ethol's hat and her right shoulder, as well as some smaller details.

A simple variation on the edge detection kernel is a *sharpening* kernel. This kernel is formed by adding an edge detection kernel and the identity kernel:

$$\begin{bmatrix} 0.0 & -1.0 & 0.0 \\ -1.0 & 4.0 & -1.0 \\ 0.0 & -1.0 & 0.0 \end{bmatrix} + \begin{bmatrix} 0.0 & 0.0 & 0.0 \\ 0.0 & 1.0 & 0.0 \\ 0.0 & 0.0 & 0.0 \end{bmatrix} = \begin{bmatrix} 0.0 & -1.0 & 0.0 \\ -1.0 & 5.0 & -1.0 \\ 0.0 & -1.0 & 0.0 \end{bmatrix}$$

The sharpening kernel emphasizes the image's sharp color changes while retaining much of its original data. Figure C-15 shows the effect of this sharpening kernel on our test image.

Geometric Transformations

Images can be geometrically transformed using the `AffineTransformOp` class. This class uses an `AffineTransform` to create a destination image that is a geometrically transformed version of the source image. This is different from setting a transformation in a `Graphics2D` and then rendering an image. The `AffineTransformOp` actually creates a new image that represents a transformed version of the source image.

How is the image transformed, exactly? Remember that an image is a rectangle of colored pixels. Think of it as a bunch of little colored squares, where each square is a pixel. To calculate a new image, `AffineTransformOp` transforms each of the pixels and calculates a new image. Figure 10-3 shows an example in which a source image is rotated. The transformed pixel grid of the source image is overlaid on the pixel grid of the destination.

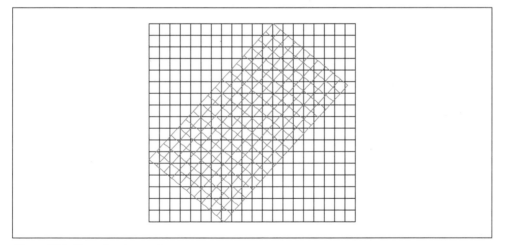

Figure 10-3. Transforming an image

The job of `AffineTransformOp` is to figure out a color for each of the destination image pixels. Unless the destination pixels line up with the transformed source pixels (for instance, if you scaled the image to make it exactly twice as wide), the destination image is an approximation of the source image. The `AffineTransformOp` class supports two algorithms for calculating destination pixel colors:

Nearest neighbor

> Using this algorithm, the color of each destination pixel is determined by finding the transformed source pixel that is nearest to the destination pixel. The color of the nearest transformed source pixel is transferred directly into the destination pixel.

Bilinear interpolation

> In this algorithm, the colors of transformed source pixels that overlap the destination pixel are combined to form the destination pixel color.

The nearest neighbor algorithm is faster than bilinear interpolation. But bilinear interpolation produces higher quality images. Figure C-16 shows a simple image that has been rotated using both algorithms. The pixels in the center of the image have been enlarged to show the difference between the two algorithms.

These algorithms apply to any transformation, not just to rotations. Whether it's scaling or shearing a source image, `AffineTransformOp` still has the same job: to figure out the destination pixel colors based on the source pixel colors.

`AffineTransformOps` are constructed with an `AffineTransform` and a set of rendering hints:

public AffineTransformOp(AffineTransform xform, RenderingHints hints)

> This constructor creates an `AffineTransformOp` that will process images using the given transformation. By default, the nearest neighbor algorithm is used. If hints is not `null` and contains an entry for `RenderingHints.KEY_INTERPOLATION`, then the value of that hint will determine the transformation algorithm.[*]

For example, the following code creates an `AffineTransformOp` that represents a rotation using bilinear interpolation. Notice how the transformation itself is specified using a plain old `AffineTransform`, which is then used to create an image operator:

```
AffineTransform at = AffineTransform.getRotateInstance(Math.PI / 6, 0, 80);
RenderingHints rh = new RenderingHints(
    RenderingHints.KEY_INTERPOLATION,
    RenderingHints.VALUE_INTERPOLATION_BILINEAR);
AffineTransformOp bilinearRotateOp = new AffineTransformOp(at, rh);
```

There are two things that may be surprising when you work with `Affine-TransformOps`. First, as shown in Figure C-17, you may get some unexpected black regions. Where are these coming from?

---

[*] For more information on rendering hints, refer back to Chapter 5.

The regions in the destination image that are not defined in the source image are filled with zeros. In this case, we're rotating an RGB image, so filling with zeros means filling with black. Since an RGB image has no alpha channel, it is treated as entirely opaque. If you rotated an ARGB* image instead, filling with zeros would make the black areas transparent (because pixels there would have alpha values of 0). When you rendered the processed image, these areas would be completely transparent, which is a more intuitive result.

The second unexpected effect of an `AffineTransformOp` is that portions of the source image may "disappear" in the destination image. Figure C-18 shows the result of rotating an image about its origin. The bottom left corner has been rotated clear out of the destination image. The reason this happens is that the image is being transformed in Image Space. The origin of the destination image must be the same as the origin of the source image. The rotation about the origin is actually transforming parts of the image into negative Image Space, which can't be shown in the destination image. To work around this issue, make sure that the transformation you want to use doesn't put any part of the source image in negative coordinate space. For positive rotations up to 90°, rotation around the bottom left corner is safe. For negative rotations up to -90°, rotation around the top right corner is safe.

Lookup Tables

Convolution is an interesting and useful operation, but it is sometimes hard to look at a kernel and figure out what's going to happen to the source image. Another operation, the *lookup table*, provides more direct control over pixel color transformations. The table is an array that contains destination pixel color values. Source pixel color values serve as indices to this table. The lookup is performed for each of the red, green, and blue color components. You can provide one table for each component, or use a single table for all three. The table itself is represented by an instance of the `LookupTable` class, which is really nothing more than a thin wrapper for arrays of data. `LookupTable` has subclasses representing `short` and `byte` arrays, called `ShortLookupTable` and `ByteLookupTable`. The two constructors for `ShortLookupTable` are shown below; the constructors for `ByteLookupTable` are identical except that they use `bytes` instead of `shorts`:

public ShortLookupTable(int offset, short[] data)

> Use this constructor to create a `ShortLookupTable` based on the given array. Each source pixel color component is used as an index into the given array. The corresponding destination pixel color component is the value at the given index. All color components use the given array. The supplied offset

---

* An ARGB image is an RGB image with an additional byte per pixel specifying transparency or alpha.

value is subtracted from the input before indexing the array. If you expect your input data to be in the range from 50 to 150, for example, you might create a ShortLookupTable using a 100 element array with an offset of 50. Note that if any input value is less than the offset, an exception will be thrown. Normally, color components range from 0 to 255, so the array should contain 256 elements for an input offset of 0.

public ShortLookupTable(int offset, short[][] data)

This constructor works like the last one, but it uses a separate array (from the supplied two-dimensional array) for each color component. The offset works the same way, too. Note that the same offset is used for all of the arrays. Make sure you supply an array for each color component. If you're processing RGB images, for example, you should pass three arrays. ARGB images require four arrays.

The LookupOp class represents an image operation based on a lookup table:

public LookupOp(LookupTable lookup, RenderingHints hints)

This constructor creates a lookup table operator using the given table.

The lookup table is a very versatile operator. I'll start with a simple table that inverts its values. Here's the code that creates the data array, the LookupTable, and the lookup operator:

```
short[] invert = new short[256];
for (int i = 0; i < 256; i++)
  invert[i] = (short)(255 - i);
LookupTable table = new ShortLookupTable(0, invert);
LookupOp invertOp = new LookupOp(table, null);
```

Figure C-19 shows the effect of this operator, which is much like a photographic negative.

Now suppose we only want to affect one color component. The following code shows how to create an operator that inverts just the red component in an RGB image:

```
short[] invert = new short[256];
short[] straight = new short[256];
for (int i = 0; i < 256; i++) {
  invert[i] = (short)(255 - i);
  straight[i] = (short)i;
}
short[][] redInvert = { invert, straight, straight };
LookupTable table = new ShortLookupTable(0, redInvert);
LookupOp redInvertOp = new LookupOp(table, null);
```

Figure C-20 shows the effect of this operator. A very simple modification of this can be used to remove an entire color component from an image. The next example shows how to create an operator that removes the green component from an RGB image.

```
short[] zero = new short[256];
short[] straight = new short[256];
for (int i = 0; i < 256; i++) {
  zero[i] = (short)0;
  straight[i] = (short)i;
}
short[][] greenRemove = { straight, zero, straight };
LookupTable table = new ShortLookupTable(0, greenRemove);
LookupOp greenRemoveOp = new LookupOp(table, null);
```

An RGB image without its green component has only blue and red components, which makes it predominantly magenta. Figure C-21 shows the effect of removing the green color component from our test image.

Adjusting Brightness

Using a rescaling operator

The simplest way to adjust the brightness of an image is to use a *rescaling* operator. Rescaling is a fancy name for multiplying every color component of every pixel by a scale factor. A scale factor of 1.0 leaves the image unchanged.

Rescaling is encapsulated in the `java.awt.image.RescaleOp` class. This class supports an *offset* in addition to the scale factor. The offset is added to the color component values after they have been scaled. The formula is shown here, where c is the new value of the color component and c_o is the original value:

$$c = scaleFactor \cdot c_o + offset$$

The results of this calculation are bounded. If the new color component exceeds the maximum value, the maximum is used instead. If you repeatedly process an image with a `RescaleOp` using a scale factor greater than 1.0, eventually you'll end up with a completely white image.[*]

Here are the constructors for `RescaleOp`:

public RescaleOp(float scaleFactor, float offset, RenderingHints hints)
> Use this constructor to create a `RescaleOp` using the given scale factor and offset. The rendering hints may be used when images are filtered using this operator.

---

[*] Well, that's almost true. If any of the color components of the original image's pixels are zero, they will not be affected by the rescaling operation.

public RescaleOp(float[] scaleFactors, float[] offsets, RenderingHints hints)

This constructor accepts a separate scale factor and offset for each color component. The array parameters should have at least as many elements as the number of color components in the image that you intend to process. If you want to process an RGB image, for example, you should supply three scale factors and three offsets.

To increase the brightness of an image by 50%, create a `RescaleOp` as follows:

```
RescaleOp brighterOp = new RescaleOp(1.5f, 0, null);
```

Figure C-22 shows the effect of this brightness operator. Similarly, the following code reduces the brightness of the image by 50% and adds an offset:

```
RescaleOp dimOffsetOp = new RescaleOp(.5f, 64f, null);
```

Figure C-23 shows the result of applying this reduction operator to *Ethol with Roses*.

Using a lookup table

Lookup tables can also be used to adjust the brightness of an image. There are a few different ways to do this. One way is to map the full range of input values, 0 to 255, to a smaller range, say 128 to 255. Figure 10-4 shows this relationship.

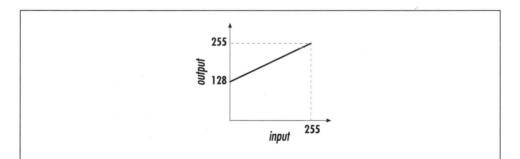

Figure 10-4. Brightening an image with a linear mapping

It's simple to implement this scheme with a lookup table:

```
short[] brighten = new short[256];
for (int i = 0; i < 256; i++)
  brighten[i] = (short)(128 + i / 2);
LookupTable table = new ShortLookupTable(0, brighten);
LookupOp brightenOp = new LookupOp(table, null);
```

Although this technique does brighten images, the brightened images may appear washed out, as shown in Figure C-24. And in fact, you could achieve exactly the same effect using a `RescaleOp`.

Let's try a different approach to brightening. Instead of a linear change, we'll use a square root function, as shown in Figure 10-5. This has the effect of boosting the middle range of input values more than the top or bottom. Another few lines of code is all it takes to implement this brightening scheme:

```
short[] rootBrighten = new short[256];
for (int i = 0; i < 256; i++)
  rootBrighten[i] = (short)(Math.sqrt((double)i / 255.0) * 255.0);
LookupTable table = new ShortLookupTable(0, rootBrighten);
LookupOp rootBrightenOp = new LookupOp(table, null);
```

This lookup operator produces a distinctive result, as shown in Figure C-25.

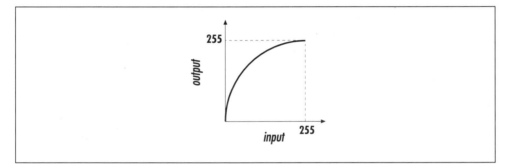

Figure 10-5. A square root brightening function

Color Space Conversion

The last image operator included in the 2D API is used to convert the colors of an image from one color space to another. You might do this to create a version of an image that is optimized for a particular output device. The class that does this conversion is `java.awt.image.ColorConvertOp`. It has four constructors, which are subtly different:

public ColorConvertOp(RenderingHints hints)
> This constructor creates a `ColorConvertOp` that converts from the color space of the source image to the color space of the destination image. Remember that the `filter()` method of `BufferedImageOp` accepts a source image and a destination image. Under normal circumstances, the destination image may be `null`. For a `ColorConvertOp` created using this constructor, however, the destination image must not be `null`—otherwise the operator would not know what color space to convert to.

public ColorConvertOp(ColorSpace cspace, RenderingHints hints)
> A `ColorConvertOp` created using this constructor converts from the source image's color space to the supplied color space. Thus, the destination image may be `null` in calls to `filter()`.

public ColorConvertOp(ColorSpace srcCspace, ColorSpace dstCspace,RenderingHints hints)
> This constructor creates a `ColorConvertOp` that filters from the given source color space to the given destination color space. This constructor is used to create a `ColorConvertOp` for filtering *rasters*. A raster is the part of a `BufferedImage` that holds the image data. See Chapter 11, *Image Guts*, for a full description of raster processing.

public ColorConvertOp(ICC_Profile[] profiles, RenderingHints hints)
> This constructor creates a `ColorConvertOp` that performs the conversions indicated by the supplied color profiles. Each profile represents a color space. Colors in the source image are converted through each of the indicated color spaces.

The following code creates a `ColorConvertOp` that converts any image to grayscale:

```
ColorConvertOp grayOp = new ColorConvertOp(
    ColorSpace.getInstance(ColorSpace.CS_GRAY), null);
```

Figure C-26 shows the effect of this operator.

Roll Your Own

The 2D API comes with a respectable toolbox of image operators. But if you're thirsting for something more exotic, you can write your own operator by implementing the `BufferedImageOp` interface.

The effect I'll implement is a simple one, called *thresholding*. A threshold operator uses three values—a threshold, a minimum, and a maximum—to determine its output. Input values that are less than the threshold are assigned the minimum value. All other input values are changed to the maximum value.* This process is applied, separately, to each color component of each pixel. The mapping from input to output is shown in Figure 10-6.

Our thresholding class will implement the `BufferedImageOp` interface, which has five methods that need to be defined:

public BufferedImage filter(BufferedImage src, BufferedImage dest)
> This is the central method in `BufferedImageOp`. It performs the actual processing on the source image.

public BufferedImage createCompatibleDestImage(BufferedImage src, ColorModel destCM)
> This method is used to create a destination image that is compatible with the given source image and color model. We'll be talking in detail about color models in Chapter 11, *Image Guts*.

---

* You could implement thresholding using a `LookupOp`, too. The purpose of this example is to show how you can implement your own image operators.

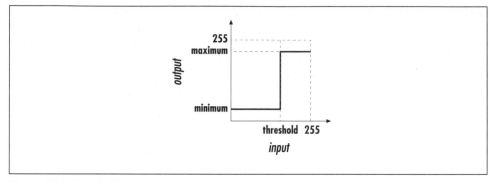

Figure 10-6. Threshold

public Rectangle2D getBounds2D(BufferedImage src)

Some image operators modify the size of the source image. This method tells you how big the destination image will be if you process the given source image.

public Point2D getPoint2D(Point2D srcPt, Point2D dstPt)

This method gives the location of the given source point in the destination image. For image operators that don't geometrically transform the source image in any way, all source and destination points are the same. If the dstPt is not null, it is filled with the correct value. If the parameter is null, a new point will be created and set to the destination point. In either case, the destination point is returned from this method.

public RenderingHints getRenderingHints()

This method returns the rendering hints associated with this image operator. If there are none, this method returns null.

To build a thresholding operator, we really only have to worry about the filter() and createCompatibleDestImage() methods. The thresholding operator doesn't modify the size of the source image, so getBounds2D() can return the size of the source image. Similarly, getPoint2D() will always return a destination point that is the same as the source point. Finally, this class doesn't support rending hints—it always returns null from getRenderingHints().

The strategy in filter() is to go through every pixel in the source image, perform the thresholding algorithm, and set the corresponding pixel in the destination image. I use the getRGB() and setRGB() methods of BufferedImage because they're so convenient. These methods take care of any color conversion that needs to be done.

Don't worry if createCompatibleDestImage() is incomprehensible. I'll be talking about most of the concepts it uses in the next chapter.

Here's the code:

```java
import java.awt.*;
import java.awt.color.*;
import java.awt.geom.Point2D;
import java.awt.geom.Rectangle2D;
import java.awt.image.*;

public class ThresholdOp implements BufferedImageOp {
  protected int mThreshold, mMinimum, mMaximum;

  public ThresholdOp(int threshold, int minimum, int maximum) {
    mThreshold = threshold;
    mMinimum = minimum;
    mMaximum = maximum;
  }

  public final BufferedImage filter (BufferedImage src, BufferedImage dst) {
    if (dst == null) dst = createCompatibleDestImage(src, null);

    for (int y = 0; y < src.getHeight(); y++) {
      for (int x = 0; x < src.getWidth(); x++) {
        int srcPixel = src.getRGB(x, y);
        Color c = new Color(srcPixel);
        int red = threshold(c.getRed());
        int green = threshold(c.getGreen());
        int blue = threshold(c.getBlue());
        dst.setRGB(x, y, new Color(red, green, blue).getRGB());
      }
    }

    return dst;
  }

  public int threshold(int input) {
    if (input < mThreshold) return mMinimum;
    else return mMaximum;
  }

  public BufferedImage createCompatibleDestImage(BufferedImage src,
      ColorModel dstCM) {
    BufferedImage image;
    if (dstCM == null) dstCM = src.getColorModel();

    int width = src.getWidth();
    int height = src.getHeight();
    image = new BufferedImage (dstCM,
        dstCM.createCompatibleWritableRaster(width, height),
        dstCM.isAlphaPremultiplied(), null);
```

```
    return image;
  }

  public final Rectangle2D getBounds2D(BufferedImage src) {
    return src.getRaster().getBounds();
  }

  public final Point2D getPoint2D(Point2D srcPt, Point2D dstPt) {
    if (dstPt == null) dstPt = new Point2D.Float();
    dstPt.setLocation(srcPt.getX(), srcPt.getY());
    return dstPt;
  }

  public final RenderingHints getRenderingHints() { return null; }
}
```

To create one of these operators, use a line of code like the following:

```
ThresholdOp threshold = new ThresholdOp(128, 0, 255);
```

To test this operator in the context of the `Sampler` application from earlier in this chapter, add the following lines to the `createOps()` method:

```
mOps.put("Threshold 64", new ThresholdOp(64, 0, 255));
mOps.put("Threshold 128", new ThresholdOp(128, 0, 255));
mOps.put("Threshold 192", new ThresholdOp(192, 0, 255));
```

Figure C-27 shows the effect of the thresholding operator.

In this chapter:
- *BufferedImage*
- *Color Models*
- *Rasters*
- *Sample Models*
- *Data Buffers*
- *A PNG Decoder*

11

Image Guts

The `java.awt.image.BufferedImage` class is the centerpiece of the 2D API's new image capabilities. Its parent, `java.awt.Image`, represents an image but doesn't offer easy access to the image data. Now, with the addition of `BufferedImage`, applications can twiddle image bits to their hearts' content.

Making image data accessible was no easy task for the designers of the 2D API. There are many strategies for representing the colors in an image and for storing the pixel data in memory. `BufferedImage` was designed to be general enough to support any image data format you could imagine.

In this chapter, I'll start by describing the `BufferedImage` class. Then I'll peel back the layers, one by one, to show you what's inside a `BufferedImage`. Eventually, we'll be staring at the image's data arrays, face-to-face with the raw bits. After that, I'll take you through a practical example that shows how to load data from a Portable Network Graphics (PNG) format file.

This chapter contains the nuts and bolts information you'll need if you're implementing file format encoders or if you're one of those people who'll read it because it's there. If you have passing curiosity about the innards of `BufferedImage`, the first section or two may contain everything you need to know. If you're going to do a lot of pixel-level manipulation, you should read the rest of the chapter.

BufferedImage

The `java.awt.image.BufferedImage` class is the centerpiece of the 2D API's new image capabilities. As a subclass of `java.awt.Image`, you can pass a `BufferedImage` to all of the `drawImage()` methods in `Graphics` and `Graphics2D`. What's so great about `BufferedImage`? You can access the data for the image directly, a task that was awkward previously. In this section, I'll give a quick overview of all the classes that make up a `BufferedImage`. Then I'll talk briefly about how you can use `BufferedImage` directly without worrying about what's inside it. In the remainder of this chapter, I'll burrow deeper and deeper into `BufferedImage`.

Inside BufferedImage

Remember, an image is a rectangular array of colored pixels. That's all it is. As we discuss the innards of `BufferedImage`, it may sound a lot more complicated. It will help to keep the simple picture in your mind.

Figure 11-1 shows what's inside a `BufferedImage`. I'll explain the relationships between all the pieces in this section. In the rest of this chapter, I'll explain each class—`ColorModel`, `Raster`, `SampleModel`, and `DataBuffer`—in detail.

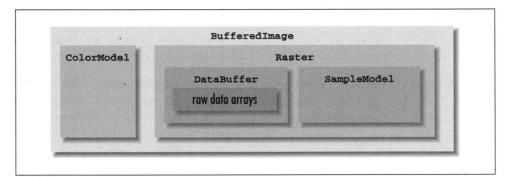

Figure 11-1. BufferedImage from top to bottom

Every `BufferedImage` consists of a *raster* and a *color model*. The image data itself resides in the raster, while the color model knows how to interpret the data as color.

The raster contains the data that determines each pixel's color. Every pixel of the image has one or more values, called *samples*, that represent a color. A grayscale image, for example, would have one sample for each pixel. An RGB image would have three samples per pixel. The raster is the collection of all the samples for every pixel in the image. Inside a raster, a *data buffer* contains the actual pixel samples, stored in arrays of primitive types like `byte` or `int`. The other part of the `Raster`, the *sample model*, knows how to extract the samples for a particular pixel from the data buffer.

The color model's job is to interpret a pixel's samples as a color. In a grayscale image, which has one sample per pixel, the color model interprets the sample as a color between black and white. In an RGB image, the color model uses the three samples in a pixel as the red, green, and blue components of an RGB color.

The color model and raster for an image need to be *compatible*, which means the number of samples per pixel must match the number of components in the color model. In other words, the color model and the raster need to be speaking the same language.

The task of finding the color of a particular pixel in a BufferedImage uses all of the pieces of an image. Suppose, for example, that you ask a BufferedImage for the color of a particular pixel:

1. The image asks its raster for the pixel's samples.

2. The raster asks its sample model to find the pixel's samples.

3. The sample model extracts the pixel's samples from the raster's data buffer. The samples are passed back to the raster; the raster passes them back to the image.

4. The image uses its color model to interpret the pixel's samples as a color.

Setting a pixel's color is basically the same process in reverse:

1. The image asks its color model what samples correspond to a particular color.

2. The image tells its raster to set the samples for the pixel.

3. The raster asks its sample model to set the samples for the pixel.

4. The sample model stores the samples in the raster's data buffer.

An example

Suppose, for instance, you had an RGB image with the following setup:

- Each pixel's color is represented by a three eight-bit samples, one each for red, green, and blue.

- The image data is stored in three byte arrays, one each for red, green, and blue.

- The image is 40 pixels wide and 50 pixels high. Each of the byte arrays has 2000 samples, arranged in row order. (This means that the samples for the first row are stored in elements 0–39, the elements for the second row are stored in elements 40–79, and so on.)

What happens, then, if you ask the BufferedImage for the color of the pixel at 23, 31?

1. The image asks its raster for the pixel's samples.

2. The raster asks its sample model to find the pixel's samples.

3. The sample model extracts the pixel's sample from the raster's data buffer. The sample model knows how the data is laid out in the byte arrays of the data buffer. It also knows that the width of the image is 40 pixels. To find the samples for the pixel at 23, 31, the sample model calculates an appropriate array offset. The offset for the row is $31 \cdot 40 = 1240$. The offset for the column is simply 23. The array offset, then, is $1240 + 23 = 1263$. The sample model extracts element 1263 from each of the byte arrays. The three samples are returned to the raster, which returns them to the image

4. The image uses its color model, an RGB model, to interpret the three samples as a color.

Some useful terminology

A collection of a particular sample is called a *band* or a *channel*. An RGB image, for example, has red, green, and blue samples for each pixel. The red channel refers to the red samples for all the pixels in the image. Some images also have an *alpha channel*, which means that each pixel has an additional sample for alpha. Chapter 2, *The Big Picture*, explains how alpha represents the amount of coverage for a pixel. In other words, the alpha of a pixel expresses its transparency. A pixel with an alpha of 0.0 is entirely transparent, while a pixel with an alpha of 1.0 is opaque. Although the alpha value doesn't define the color of the pixel, it is often treated as an additional color component. An RGB image with an alpha channel, therefore, can be treated as an image with four color components.

Premultiplied alpha is another important concept in image data storage. When an image is composited onto a drawing surface, the alpha value of each of its pixels is multiplied with each of the color components. To optimize this process, you can perform the multiplication for each pixel and store the result as the color components of the image. This is called premultiplied alpha. Premultiplied alpha simplifies the calculations involved in compositing, which should improve performance. For more information on compositing, see Chapter 5, *Rendering*.

Using BufferedImage

You can use `BufferedImage` without knowing too much about what's inside it. `BufferedImage` has three constructors:

public BufferedImage(int width, int height, int imageType)
This constructor creates a new `BufferedImage` with the given width, height, and type. The width and height are specified in pixels. The image type should be one of the `TYPE_` constants defined in the `BufferedImage` class. Table 11-1 describes these constants.

Table 11-1. BufferedImage Types

Constant	Description
TYPE_3BYTE_BGR	8-bit blue, green, and red samples stored in one byte each
TYPE_4BYTE_ABGR	8-bit alpha, blue, green, and red samples in one byte each
TYPE_4BYTE_ABGR_PRE	8-bit alpha and premultiplied blue, green, and red samples
TYPE_BYTE_BINARY	1 bit sample per pixel, packed 8 per byte
TYPE_BYTE_INDEXED	single 8-bit sample per pixel that is an index into a color palette
TYPE_BYTE_GRAY	8-bit gray sample for each pixel stored in a byte
TYPE_USHORT_555_RGB	5-bit red, green, and blue samples packed into a 16-bit short
TYPE_USHORT_565_RGB	5-bit red, 6-bit green, and 5-bit blue samples packed into a short
TYPE_USHORT_GRAY	16-bit gray sample for each pixel stored in a short
TYPE_INT_RGB	8-bit red, green, and blue samples packed into a 32-bit int
TYPE_INT_BGR	8-bit blue, green, and red samples packed into a 32-bit int[a]
TYPE_INT_ARGB	8-bit alpha, red, green, and blue samples packed into an int
TYPE_INT_ARGB_PRE	8-bit alpha and premultiplied red, green, and blue samples

[a] Most display devices pack red, green, and blue color components into integers, but the ordering differs depending on the platform. Some platforms (Windows) use an order that matches Java's default of red, green, blue. Other platforms (Solaris) use an order of blue, green, red. The TYPE_INT_BGR image type, in these cases, is easier to render than a TYPE_INT_RGB image, because no reordering of the color components needs to take place.

public BufferedImage(int width, int height, int imageType, IndexColorModel cm)

This constructor is used for the TYPE_BYTE_INDEXED and TYPE_BYTE_BINARY image types. It allows you to specify the palette you wish to use in the form of an IndexColorModel. If you don't specify a palette (by using the previous constructor) with these image types, a default palette is created for you. For more information on palettes and IndexColorModel, see the next section.

public BufferedImage(ColorModel cm, WritableRaster raster, boolean isRasterPremultiplied, Hashtable properties)

If you create your own ColorModel and WritableRaster, you can make a BufferedImage out of them with this constructor. The isRaster-Premultiplied flag indicates whether the data in the raster is premultiplied with alpha. Finally, the properties parameter contains a list of name and value pairs for storing additional information about the image. You can pass null for this parameter if you wish.

You can find out basic information about a BufferedImage with the following methods:

public int getWidth()
public int getHeight()

These methods return the width and height, in pixels, of this image.

public int getType()

> This method returns one of the types listed in Table 11-1 or `TYPE_CUSTOM` if the image does not have one of the predefined types.

public boolean isAlphaPremultiplied()

> This method returns `true` if the image's samples are premulitplied with alpha.

public ColorModel getColorModel()

> This method returns the color model of this image.

public WritableRaster getRaster()

> This method returns this image's raster.

`BufferedImage` also includes methods for retrieving and setting the color of individual pixels:

public int getRGB(int x, int y)

> This method returns the color of the pixel at `x`, `y`. The color is returned as 8-bit alpha, red, green, and blue components packed into an `int` in the standard format (see Figure 11-3). If the image data is stored with a different color model, the pixel data is converted before being returned from this method.

public int[] getRGB(int startX, int startY, int w, int h, int[] rgbArray, int offset,
*   int scansize)*

> This method returns the colors for an entire rectangle of pixels. The rectangle is described by `startX`, `startY`, `w`, and `h`. If you already have an integer array lying around, you can pass it in as `rgbArray`, and it will be filled with the pixel colors. Alternately, you can pass `null` for `rgbArray`, and a new array will be created for you. Each pixel's color is returned as a packed integer, just as in the previous method. The pixel colors are written into the array starting at `offset`. The `scansize` parameter indicates how many array elements should be in each row of the returned data. Normally this is the same as the width, `w`. The array of pixel colors is returned from this method.

public void setRGB(int x, int y, int rgb)

> Use this method to set the color of a particular pixel. The `rgb` parameter should contain packed alpha, red, green, and blue components in the default format.

public void setRGB(int startX, int startY, int w, int h, int[] rgbArray, int offset,
*   int scansize)*

> This method sets the colors of a rectangle of pixels. The colors are supplied in `rgbArray`. All the other parameters work the same as in the second `getRGB()` method above.

Color Models

A color model knows how to translate between a color and a set of pixel samples. In the 2D API, this concept is encapsulated in the `java.awt.image.ColorModel` class. This class has a dizzying number of poorly named methods. But don't worry—most of these methods fall into two categories. The first group of methods converts from a pixel's samples to a color. The second group performs the opposite conversion, from a color to pixel samples.

A color model uses an underlying color space to describe colors using one or more *components*. An RGB color, for example, has three components: red, green, and blue. A color model based on an RGB color space converts from pixel samples to red, green, and blue components (and vice versa). A color model based on a grayscale color space would convert between pixel samples and a single gray color component. The default color space is sRGB. (For more about color spaces, see Chapter 8, *Color*.)

Don't be misled by `ColorModel`'s method names. Many of these names begin with get, which implies that they retrieve properties of the `ColorModel`. Most of the time, however, this is not the case. Instead, these methods perform a translation. For example, one of the methods that translates from sample values to color components is called `getComponents()`.

An instance of `ColorModel` doesn't really do anything useful, but `ColorModel` has several subclasses that represent common color models. These are described following the general descriptions of `ColorModel`'s methods. Figure 11-2 shows the hierarchy of the color model classes.

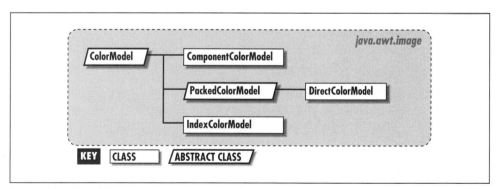

Figure 11-2. The ColorModel posse

Basic Information

The following methods return information about the color model's underlying color space:

public final ColorSpace getColorSpace()
> This method returns the `ColorSpace` that is used to represent colors in this color model.

public int getNumColorComponents()
> This method returns the number of color components (excluding alpha) in this `ColorModel`. It is the same as the number of components in the underlying color space.

Color models may also include an alpha value. Although alpha does not really define the color, strictly speaking, it is treated as an additional color component:

public final boolean hasAlpha()
> This method returns `true` if this color model supports alpha.

public int getNumComponents()
> This method returns the number of components in this `ColorModel`, including alpha. If the color model includes alpha, this method returns one more than `getNumColorComponents()`.

Each of the color components has an associated bit length. The bit length of a component determines its maximum value. For example, if the red component of an RGB color model has a bit length of 8, its value can range from 0 to 255. More generally, a component bit length of n implies a component range of 0 to $2^n - 1$.

These methods let you discover the bit length of each component:

public int[] getComponentSize()
> This method returns an array of the bit lengths of this color model's components.

public int getComponentSize(int componentIdx)
> This method returns the bit length of the color component at the given index.

Integers are used to hold component values. Since integers are 32-bit signed quantities, the maximum bit length for color components is 31 bits.

Color models have a *transfer type*, which is simply a data type. The color model expects to deal with pixel samples expressed as arrays of the transfer type. Currently the 2D API supports `byte`, `short`, and `int` as transfer types. These primitive types are represented by constants in the `DataBuffer` class: `TYPE_BYTE`, `TYPE_USHORT`, and `TYPE_INT`. Usually the transfer type will be the smallest type that will fit all of the bits that define a pixel. `ColorModel` determines a default transfer type using the following code:

```
static int getDefaultTransferType(int pixel_bits) {
    if (pixel_bits <= 8) {
        return DataBuffer.TYPE_BYTE;
    } else if (pixel_bits <= 16) {
        return DataBuffer.TYPE_USHORT;
    } else if (pixel_bits <= 32) {
        return DataBuffer.TYPE_INT;
    } else {
        return DataBuffer.TYPE_UNDEFINED;
    }
}
```

As you'll see later, a raster also has a transfer type. A color model and a raster with the same transfer type are *compatible*. This means that the color model will recognize pixel data it gets from the raster and vice versa.

From Pixel Samples to Color Components

`ColorModel` provides a family of methods, grouped around two central `getComponents()` methods, that convert pixel samples into color components.

public int[] getComponents(Object pixel, int[] components, int offset)

This method converts the pixel samples represented by `pixel` into an array of color components and possibly an alpha component. The input, `pixel`, should be an array of the color model's transfer type. If the supplied `components` array is not `null`, it will be filled with the color and alpha components, starting at `offset`. Otherwise, a new array will be allocated.* Regardless, the array is returned. The color component values are returned before the alpha component, starting at the given `offset` position in the array.

The `pixel` parameter is usually an array of bytes or integers, but this depends on the data format of the image. To use this method, retrieve a pixel's samples using one of the `getDataElements()` methods of `Raster` and pass the results to this method.

public int getRed(Object inData)
public int getGreen(Object inData)
public int getBlue(Object inData)

These convenience methods return specific components of the sRGB color corresponding to the pixel samples described by `inData`. Each of these

---

* If the supplied array is null and the offset is greater than zero, this method does the right thing. It creates a new array of the correct size and fills the array with the color and alpha components, starting at the supplied offset.

methods is equivalent to calling getComponents(), converting the returned color components to sRGB, and extracting the appropriate sRGB component.

public int getAlpha(Object inData)

This method returns the alpha value of the pixel samples described by inData.

public int getRGB(Object inData)

This method returns the sRGB color and alpha components of the pixel represented by inData. The data is returned as red, green, blue, and alpha values packed into an integer in the default format, shown in Figure 11-3.

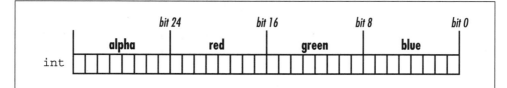

Figure 11-3. The default arrangement of red, green, blue, and alpha in an integer

public float[] getNormalizedComponents(int[] components, int offset,
*   float[] normComponents, int normOffset)*

This method converts an array of components (returned from get-Components(), for example) into an array of *normalized* components. Normalized components are floating-point values ranging from 0.0 to 1.0. This method uses offset to determine where the color components can be found in the components array. If the normComponents parameter is not null, it is filled with the normalized components, starting at normOffset. If normComponents is null, a new array will be created to hold the normalized components. Figure 11-4 shows how the arrays and offsets work for three color components, offset equal to 1, and normOffset equal to 4. This method returns the normalized component array, regardless of whether it was passed in the normComponents parameter or newly created.

public int[] getUnnormalizedComponents(float[] normComponents, int normOffset,
*   int[] components, int offset)*

This method performs the reverse of getNormalizedComponents(). It converts normalized color components to regular, "unnormalized" components. As before, the components array may be null, in which case a new array will be created. The normalized components are taken from the normComponents array, starting at normOffset. The regular color components are written into the components array (or a freshly created array) starting at offset. The color component array is returned.

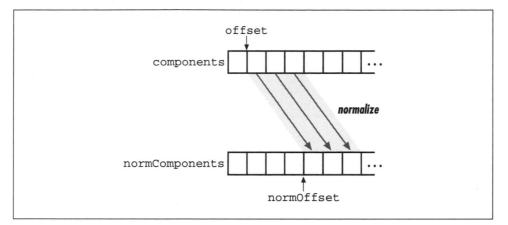

Figure 11-4. Translating color components to normalized components

The methods in this section translate pixel samples to color components. So far, the pixel samples are represented as arrays of `bytes` or `ints` (passed as `Object` references). `ColorModel` includes a matching set of methods that deals with pixel samples packed into a single integer. The color model determines how the samples are packed into an integer. It's up to the `ColorModel` to extract the samples from the integer in order to convert them to color components. These methods are:

public int[] getComponents(int pixel, int[] components, int offset)

    This method takes the pixel samples represented by `pixel` and translates them into color components in the given array, starting at `offset`. A new array is allocated if `components` is `null`.

public int getRed(int pixel)
public int getGreen(int pixel)
public int getBlue(int pixel)

    These convenience methods are equivalent to calling `getComponents` `(pixel, null, 0)`, converting the result to sRGB, and extracting the appropriate component from the result.

public int getAlpha(int pixel)

    This method returns the alpha value of the pixel samples described by `pixel`.

public int getRGB(int pixel)

    This method converts the pixel samples represented by `pixel` to sRGB components and returns them in a packed integer. Although this method accepts a packed integer and returns a packed integer, the formats are not necessarily the same.

Figure 11-5 summarizes `ColorModel`'s capabilities for transforming pixel samples into color components. Pixel samples, represented by either an array (an `Object`) or an `int`, are turned into color components, either in the color model's color space or in sRGB.

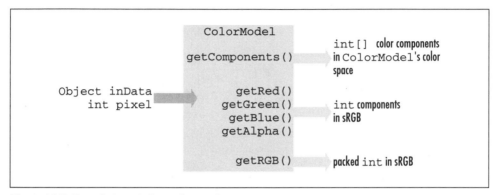

Figure 11-5. Translating pixel samples to color components

From Color Components to Pixel Samples

Color models can convert from pixel samples to colors and back again. As you've seen, the `getComponents()` method and its kin convert pixel samples to color components. `ColorModel` includes three methods that accomplish the opposite transformation, from color components to pixel samples:

public Object getDataElements(int[] components, int offset, Object obj)
> This method converts an array of color and alpha components in this color model's color space to an array of pixel samples. The color and alpha components are assumed to start at `offset` in the `components` array. If `obj` is `null`, a new array will be created to hold the pixel samples. Regardless, the sample array is returned. The type of the array is the transfer type of the color model.

public int getDataElement(int[] components, int offset)
> Like the previous method, this method converts an array of color and alpha components (expressed in this color model's color space) to pixel samples. The color and alpha components are assumed to start at `offset` in `components`. After the conversion, the pixel samples are packed into an integer and returned.

public Object getDataElements(int rgb, Object pixel)
> This method converts a packed integer representing an sRGB color to pixel samples. It works like `setDataElements()`: if `pixel` is `null`, a new array will be created to hold the pixel samples. The array's type is the transfer type of the color model. The pixel sample array is returned.

ComponentColorModel

The simplest case for image data storage is that each pixel's samples correspond exactly to the components of a color in any color space. This case is encapsulated by the `java.awt.image.ComponentColorModel` class. Using an instance of this class, you could convert from an array of pixel samples to an array of color components with the `getComponents(Object, int[], int)` method.

Here is the constructor for `ComponentColorModel`:

public ComponentColorModel(ColorSpace colorSpace, int[] bits, boolean hasAlpha,
   boolean isAlphaPremultiplied, int transparency, int transferType)
> This constructor creates a `ComponentColorModel` that defines colors in the specified color space. The `bits` array contains the bit lengths of each of the sample values. Its length should be the same as the number of components in the color space, or one more if alpha is used. The `hasAlpha` flag indicates whether alpha samples will be present, and `isAlphaPremultiplied` indicates if the color component values are premultiplied with the alpha values. The `transparency` value should be one of the following: `Transparency.OPAQUE`, `Transparency.BITMASK`, or `Transparency.TRANSLUCENT`. Finally, the `transferType` indicates a primitive type for the pixel sample arrays that this color model accepts and creates. It should be one of the constants in the `java.awt.image.DataBuffer` class, either `TYPE_BYTE`, `TYPE_USHORT`, or `TYPE_INT`.

For example, suppose you have an sRGB image with no alpha information. Furthermore, suppose that each pixel has three samples, one each for red, green, and blue. The red and blue samples are each five bits, while the green sample has six bits. Regardless of how the data is actually stored, let's assume that the samples can be extracted as an array of bytes. The `ComponentColorModel` for this image is constructed as follows:

```
ColorSpace cs = ColorSpace.getInstance(ColorSpace.CS_sRGB);
ColorModel cm = new ComponentColorModel(cs, new int[] { 5, 6, 5 },
    false, false, Transparency.OPAQUE, DataBuffer.TYPE_BYTE);
```

The following code shows how to use this color model to convert a color to a pixel sample:

```
Color fifty = new Color(cs, new float[] { 1.0f, 1.0f, 1.0f }, 0);
float[] components = fifty.getComponents(null);
int[] unnormalized = cm.getUnnormalizedComponents(components, 0, null, 0);
Object pixel = cm.getDataElements(unnormalized, 0, (Object)null);
```

First a `Color` (white) is created in the color space.* Then the normalized color components are retrieved using `getComponents()`, which returns a `float` array

---

* This is a little contrived; since sRGB is the default color space, this example is a little more complicated than it really needs to be.

with three elements, all 1.0. Next these components are "unnormalized" using the color model's `getUnnormalizedComponents()`. This method returns an `int` array containing 31, 63, and 31. Note that these values reflect the component bit lengths passed to the color model's constructor. The red and blue components each have five bits, so their maximum value is 31. The green component, on the other hand, has a length of six bits, so its maximum value is 63.

Finally, the unnormalized components are converted to pixel samples using the color model's `getDataElements()` method. This method returns an array of the color model's transfer type (`byte`, in this case) containing the unnormalized component values.

The conversion from pixel samples back to color components looks like this:

```
unnormalized = cm.getComponents(pixel, null, 0);
components = cm.getNormalizedComponents(unnormalized, 0, null, 0);
```

Here's a complete example that prints out the intermediate results:

```
import java.awt.*;
import java.awt.color.*;
import java.awt.image.*;

public class ComponentTest {
  public static void main(String[] args) {
    ColorSpace cs = ColorSpace.getInstance(ColorSpace.CS_sRGB);
    ColorModel cm = new ComponentColorModel(cs, new int[] { 5, 6, 5 },
        false, false, Transparency.OPAQUE, DataBuffer.TYPE_BYTE);

    Color fifty = new Color(cs, new float[] { 1.0f, 1.0f, 1.0f }, 0);
    float[] components = fifty.getComponents(null);
    System.out.print("Original normalized components: ");
    for (int i = 0; i < 3; i++) System.out.print(components[i] + " ");
    System.out.println();
    int[] unnormalized = cm.getUnnormalizedComponents(components,
                                                      0, null, 0);
    System.out.print("Original unnormalized components: ");
    for (int i = 0; i < 3; i++) System.out.print(unnormalized[i] + " ");
    System.out.println();
    Object pixel = cm.getDataElements(unnormalized, 0, (Object)null);
    System.out.print("Pixel samples: ");
    byte[] pixelBytes = (byte[])pixel;
    for (int i = 0; i < 3; i++) System.out.print(pixelBytes[i] + " ");
    System.out.println();

    unnormalized = cm.getComponents(pixel, null, 0);
    System.out.print("Derived unnormalized components: ");
    for (int i = 0; i < 3; i++) System.out.print(unnormalized[i] + " ");
    System.out.println();
    components = cm.getNormalizedComponents(unnormalized, 0, null, 0);
```

```
        System.out.print("Derived normalized components: ");
        for (int i = 0; i < 3; i++) System.out.print(components[i] + " ");
        System.out.println();
    }
}
```

If you run this example, it prints out the following:

```
Original normalized components: 1.0 1.0 1.0
Original unnormalized components: 31 63 31
Pixel samples: 31 63 31
Derived unnormalized components: 31 63 31
Derived normalized components: 1.0 1.0 1.0
```

PackedColorModel

Another of `ColorModel`'s subclasses is `java.awt.image.PackedColorModel`. This color model interprets pixel samples that are packed into a single `byte`, `short`, or `int`. In the previous example, the red, green, and blue samples could be packed into a single 16-bit `short`. A `PackedColorModel` extracts different color components by using a bit mask for each component. The following masks show one way that red, green, and blue samples can be packed into a 16-bit `short`:

    red (5 bits) mask = 0x7c00
    green (5 bits) mask = 0x03e0
    blue (5 bits) mask = 0x001f

Oddly enough, `PackedColorModel` is an abstract class. It has one concrete subclass, `DirectColorModel`, that deals specifically with RGB color spaces. If you want to create a `PackedColorModel` for some other color space type, you'll have to write your own subclass.

DirectColorModel

`java.awt.image.DirectColorModel` is a subclass of `PackedColorModel` that deals specifically with RGB color spaces.

`DirectColorModel` has three constructors. The most general one allows you to specify a color space, color component bit masks, a transfer type, and some information about alpha. The other two constructors use default values for some of these parameters:

public DirectColorModel(ColorSpace space, int bits, int rmask, int gmask, int bmask,
    int aMask, boolean isAlphaPremultiplied, int transferType)
    This constructor creates a `DirectColorModel` for the given color space, which should have the `ColorSpace.TYPE_RGB` type. `bits` is the total number of sample bits. `rmask`, `gmask`, and `bmask` are the bit masks for each of the samples. `amask` is a bit mask for alpha samples, if this color model supports

Who Was That Masked Bit?

PackedColorModel uses *bit masks* to specify where color components are located inside a byte, short, or int. The best way to understand bit masks is to look at some examples. First, think about RGB components packed into a 16-bit short as follows:

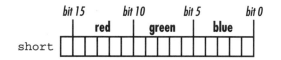

The bit masks are:

- 0111110000000000 or 0x7c00 for the red component

- 0000001111100000 or 0x03e0 for the green component

- 0000000000011111 or 0x001f for the blue component

You can use the bit masks to figure out the value of each component. To do this, combine a pixel value and a mask using the boolean AND operator. Then shift the result to the right until the first 1 bit of the mask is in the lowest bit of the result. For example, a red value would need to be shifted right by 10 bits.

The 1 bits in a mask should always be in a group (contiguous). For example, a bit mask of 01011000 doesn't make any sense.

Here's one more example. Suppose you have red, green, blue, and alpha components packed into an integer in the default format, shown in Figure 11-3. The bit masks are as follows:

- 0xff000000 for the alpha component

- 0x00ff0000 for the red component

- 0x0000ff00 for the green component

- 0x000000ff for the blue component

alpha. If it does not, amask should be zero. Just as in ComponentColorModel, isAlphaPremultiplied is a flag that indicates if the color component values have been premultiplied with alpha. It is ignored if there is no alpha channel. Finally, transferType is the type that will be used for pixel samples. It should be one of the types from java.awt.image.DataBuffer, either TYPE_BYTE, TYPE_USHORT, or TYPE_INT.

public DirectColorModel(int bits, int rmask, int gmask, int bmask, int amask)
> This constructor works the same as the previous constructor. The default sRGB color space is used. If alpha is present (i.e., if `amask` is not zero), the color components are assumed to not be premultiplied. The transfer type is automatically selected as the smallest type that can fit a single pixel (as described by `bits`).

public DirectColorModel(int bits, int rmask, int gmask, int bmask)
> This constructor is just like the previous one, except alpha is not supported.

IndexColorModel

The final `ColorModel` subclass is `java.awt.image.IndexColorModel`. It is used with images that have a color *palette*. A palette is simply a list of colors. Each pixel in the image has a sample value that serves as an index into the palette. For images with a limited number of colors, this is a very efficient way to store color data. In an image with a 256-color palette, for example, each pixel can be described using a single 8-bit sample. An image with only four colors can be described using two bits per pixel.

The `IndexColorModel` class encapsulates a palette of sRGB colors. You can construct an `IndexColorModel` by supplying the colors of the palette and the number of bits that are needed to specify a color.

public IndexColorModel(int bits, int size, byte[] r, byte[] g, byte[] b)
> Use this constructor to create an `IndexColorModel` for samples with the supplied number of bits. The `size` parameter is the number of colors in the palette. The colors are defined by the matching elements of the `r`, `g`, and `b` arrays. Although they are arrays of bytes, the values are treated as unsigned 8-bit quantities. Each array should have at least `size` elements. The transfer type of this color model will be the smallest of `TYPE_BYTE`, `TYPE_USHORT`, or `TYPE_INT` that can hold a color index whose length is `bits`.

public IndexColorModel(int bits, int size, byte[] r, byte[] g, byte[] b, int trans)
> This constructor works just like the previous one, but includes support for a single transparent color. The `trans` parameter is the palette index of a color that will be entirely transparent. All the other colors will be opaque.

public IndexColorModel(int bits, int size, byte[] r, byte[] g, byte[] b, byte[] a)
> This constructor is just like the first one but includes support for alpha. Each palette entry has an alpha component that describes its transparency.

public IndexColorModel(int bits, int size, byte[] cmap, int start, boolean hasalpha)
> Instead of expecting color components in separate arrays, this constructor accepts a single array, `cmap`. This array contains a repeating pattern of red, green, blue, and possibly alpha components. Again, `size` indicates the total

number of palette entries. If alpha is included in the color definitions, hasalpha should be true. The palette entries are assumed to begin at start in the cmap array.

public IndexColorModel(int bits, int size, byte[] cmap, int start, boolean hasalpha, int trans)
This constructor is the same as the previous constructor except it includes support for a single transparent color. Even if the palette colors already include alpha, the designated transparent color will be treated as fully transparent (its alpha will be 0.0).

public IndexColorModel(int bits, int size, int[] cmap, int start, boolean hasalpha, int trans,
int transferType)
This constructor is just like the previous one, but it allows you to explicitly choose the transfer type. The other constructors automatically choose the smallest of TYPE_BYTE, TYPE_USHORT, or TYPE_INT that will fit the given bits of color information.

Here's a slightly contrived example of an IndexColorModel with five colors in its palette:

```
import java.awt.Color;
import java.awt.image.*;

public class IndexTest {
  public static void main(String[] args) {
    byte ff = (byte)0xff;
    byte[] r = { ff, 0, 0, ff, 0 };
    byte[] g = { 0, ff, 0, ff, 0 };
    byte[] b = { 0, 0, ff, ff, 0 };

    ColorModel cm = new IndexColorModel(3, 5, r, g, b);

    Color[] colors = {
        new Color(255, 0, 0),
        new Color(0, 255, 0),
        new Color(0, 0, 255),
        new Color(64, 255, 64),
        new Color(255, 255, 0),
        new Color(0, 255, 255)
    };

    for (int i = 0; i < colors.length; i++) {
      float[] normalizedComponents = colors[i].getComponents(null);
      int[] unnormalizedComponents = cm.getUnnormalizedComponents(
          normalizedComponents, 0, null, 0);
      int rgb = colors[i].getRGB();
      Object pixel = cm.getDataElements(rgb, null);
      System.out.println(colors[i] + " -> " + ((byte[])pixel)[0]);
    }
```

```
      for (byte i = 0; i < 5; i++) {
        int[] unnormalizedComponents = cm.getComponents(i, null, 0);
        System.out.print(i + " -> unnormalized components");
        for (int j = 0; j < unnormalizedComponents.length; j++)
          System.out.print(" " + unnormalizedComponents[j]);
        System.out.println();
      }
    }
  }
```

If you run this example, here's what you will see:

```
java.awt.Color[r=255,g=0,b=0] -> 0
java.awt.Color[r=0,g=255,b=0] -> 1
java.awt.Color[r=0,g=0,b=255] -> 2
java.awt.Color[r=64,g=255,b=64] -> 1
java.awt.Color[r=255,g=255,b=0] -> 0
java.awt.Color[r=0,g=255,b=255] -> 1
0 -> unnormalized components 255 0 0 255
1 -> unnormalized components 0 255 0 255
2 -> unnormalized components 0 0 255 255
3 -> unnormalized components 255 255 255 255
4 -> unnormalized components 0 0 0 255
```

The first part of this example shows how the `IndexColorModel` attempts to match an arbitrary input color to one of the colors in its palette. The last part of the example shows how input bytes, representing pixel samples, are converted to palette colors.

Rasters

Image data is contained in a raster, represented by an instance of `java.awt.image.Raster`. Rasters themselves are composed of two pieces—a sample model and a data buffer. The data buffer contains the raw data, while the sample model describes how the data is organized.

The `Raster` class is useful for two reasons. First, it can retrieve image data by asking its sample model to pull the data out from the data buffer. Second, `Raster` contains many static factory methods that create commonly used `Rasters`.

Basic Information

Remember that an image is a rectangle of colored pixels. A raster is simply a rectangle of pixels, each of which has one or more samples associated with it.

What's a Raster?

In the old days of computers, screen devices came in two varieties: *raster* and *vector*. Both types had one or more electron guns that spewed electrons through a phosphorescent screen. The difference had to do with how the gun was aimed. A vector screen device kept track of a specific list of lines (vectors) that it would draw. You might have seen this type of device in arcade video games from the early 1980s, like Asteroids, Battlezone, and Tempest.

The other type of screen device, raster, is the familiar television-style device. The electron gun (or guns) sweep across horizontal lines (scanlines) of the screen in a left-to-right, top-to-bottom order, changing intensity to indicate different colors.

The difference between vector and raster devices is analogous to the difference between a pen plotter and a dot matrix or laser printer.

Vector screen devices have gone to the great output device in the sky, leaving raster devices as the only widespread screen type. In the 2D API, the terminology persists in names like `TYPE_RASTER_SCREEN` and the `java.awt.image.Raster` class.

The number of samples per pixel is also referred to as the number of *bands* in the raster. A band is a collection of the same sample from each pixel. An RGB image, for example, has three bands.*

The following methods return rudimentary information about a `Raster`:

public Rectangle getBounds()

> Although a `BufferedImage` has only a width and a height, a `Raster` has an entire bounding rectangle. This allows `Rasters` to represent any area of an image.

public final int getMinX()
public final int getMinY()

> These methods return the x and y coordinates of the raster's origin.

public final int getWidth()
public final int getHeight()

> These methods return the width and height of the raster.

---

* The term *band* comes from storing each set of pixel samples in a separate data array. Regardless of the data storage method, though, the term is still useful.

public final int getNumBands()
> This method returns the number of bands (samples per pixel) in this raster.

Sample models have no conception of the origin of the raster. Therefore, pixel coordinates are translated before being passed to a sample model. Generally, the translation is the negative of the raster's origin. You can find out the translation involved with the following pair of methods:

public final int getSampleModelTranslateX()
public final int getSampleModelTranslateY()
> These methods return the translations applied to pixel coordinates before they are passed to a sample model.

Retrieving Pixel Samples

The raster's purpose in life is to retrieve pixel samples. It does this by asking its sample model to pull data out of its data buffer. You can retrieve samples from a single pixel, samples from a rectangle of pixels, a single sample from a single pixel, or a single sample band from a rectangle of pixels. Furthermore, you can perform any of these operations using ints, floats, or doubles, as best suits your application. Here are the methods for retrieving samples:

public int[] getPixel(int x, int y, int[] iArray)
public float[] getPixel(int x, int y, float[] fArray)
public double[] getPixel(int x, int y, double[] dArray)
> These methods return the samples for the pixel located at the given coordinates. Each element of the returned array will contain one of the pixel's samples. If the array parameter is null, a new array will be allocated. The array is filled with the pixel's samples and returned.

public int[] getPixels(int x, int y, int w, int h, int[] iArray)
public float[] getPixels(int x, int y, int w, int h, float[] fArray)
public double[] getPixels(int x, int y, int w, int h, double[] dArray)
> These methods return the samples for the rectangle of pixels described by x, y, w, and h. If the array parameter is null, a new array will be allocated. Each element of the array will contain one pixel sample. The samples are interleaved into the array by reading the pixels in the rectangle in a left-to-right, top-to-bottom fashion, just like reading a book (in English). The array of samples is returned.

public int getSample(int x, int y, int b)
public float getSampleFloat(int x, int y, int b)
public double getSampleDouble(int x, int y, int b)
> These methods return a single sample for the indicated pixel. The b parameter indicates which band the sample should be taken from. These methods are roughly equivalent to calling getPixel(x, y, null)[b].

public int[] getSamples(int x, int y, int w, int h, int b, int[] iArray)
public float[] getSamples(int x, int y, int w, int h, int b, float[] fArray)
public double[] getSamples(int x, int y, int w, int h, int b, double[] dArray)

These methods return a single band of samples for the rectangle of pixels described by x, y, w, and h. The band number is indicated by b. If the array parameter is null, a new array will be allocated. Regardless, the array is filled with the samples from the specified band and returned.

Writable Rasters

The Raster class represents a read-only set of pixel data. A subclass of Raster, java.awt.image.WritableRaster, adds support for writing pixel data. Basically WritableRaster adds a gaggle of "set" methods that match the "get" methods of Raster:

public void setPixel(int x, int y, int[] iArray)
public void setPixel(int x, int y, float[] fArray)
public void setPixel(int x, int y, double[] dArray)

These methods set the samples for the pixel at the given coordinates using the elements of the supplied array.

public void setPixels(int x, int y, int w, int h, int[] iArray)
public void setPixels(int x, int y, int w, int h, float[] fArray)
public void setPixels(int x, int y, int w, int h, double[] dArray)

These methods set the samples for the rectangle of pixels described by x, y, w, and h using the values in the given array. The sample values should be interleaved and ordered in a left-to-right, top-to-bottom fashion.

public void setSample(int x, int y, int b, int s)
public void setSample(int x, int y, int b, float s)
public void setSample(int x, int y, int b, double s)

These methods set a single sample for the pixel at x, y. The band of the sample is given by b and the actual sample value is s.

public void setSamples(int x, int y, int w, int h, int b, int[] iArray)
public void setSamples(int x, int y, int w, int h, int b, float[] fArray)
public void setSamples(int x, int y, int w, int h, int b, double[] dArray)

These methods set an entire band of samples for the rectangle of pixels described by x, y, w, and h. The band number is b, and the given array contains the samples for that band.

Transfer Types

If you're going to be moving a lot of image data around in your application, it may not be very efficient to use the getPixels() and getSamples() methods.

Suppose you have an image that uses four bits to store each of three samples. It doesn't make much sense to cart the samples around in 32-bit ints—that's 28 wasted bits per array element.

Raster supports more efficient data transfer through the use of a *transfer type*. The raster's sample model may choose to pack pixel samples into a single primitive data type or do some other trickiness. Raster has two methods that tell you how to use transfer types:

public final int getTransferType()

This method returns the raster's transfer type. It will be one of the types defined in the DataBuffer class, usually TYPE_BYTE, TYPE_USHORT, or TYPE_INT.

public final int getNumDataElements()

This method tells how many elements of the transfer type are needed to hold a single pixel's samples.

The raster for an RGB image, for example, might be able to pack the samples into a single int. In this case, getTransferType() would return DataBuffer.TYPE_INT, and getNumDataElements() would return 1.

To actually retrieve pixel samples using the transfer type, use one of the getDataElements() methods:

public Object getDataElements(int x, int y, Object outData)

This method retrieves the samples for the pixel at x, y. The returned object is an array of the transfer type with getNumDataElements() elements. If you have already created this array, pass it to this method as outData. Otherwise, pass null for outData, and a new array will be created for you.

public Object getDataElements(int x, int y, int w, int h, Object outData)

This method retrieves the samples for the rectangle of pixels described by x, y, w, and h. If you do not supply an array (that is, if outData is null), a new array will be created and filled with the samples. The array is returned. The length of the array will be w x h x getNumDataElements().

WritableRaster has a corresponding pair of methods for setting pixel samples from an array of the transfer type:

public void setDataElements(int x, int y, Object outData)

This method sets the samples for a single pixel at x, y. The supplied array, outData, should have getNumDataElements() elements of the transfer type.

public void setDataElements(int x, int y, int w, int h, Object outData)

This method sets the samples for an entire rectangle of pixels. It extracts the samples from the supplied array of the transfer type.

It's these methods, `getDataElements()` and `setDataElements()`, that are used with a `BufferedImage`'s color model.

Factory Methods

`Raster` includes many static methods that produce common raster types, saving you the trouble of creating a sample model and data buffer yourself. Because these methods produce fully formed `Raster` instances, they are called *factory methods*. There are four common types of rasters that are supported by `Raster`'s factory methods: interleaved, banded, packed samples, and packed pixels. You might choose to use a certain type of raster because it's compatible with your display device and can be efficiently rendered. Or you may be trying to comply with a file format standard that dictates a certain arrangement of image data.

All of `Raster`'s factory methods have three parameters in common. The w, h, and `location` parameters define the location and size of the new raster. If `location` is `null`, the raster will be positioned at 0, 0. The width and height of the raster are determined by w and h, respectively.

Interleaved

This type of raster stores its pixels' samples in a single array. Each sample is stored in a separate array element. Every band of the image is stored in the same data array. Figure 11-6 shows an interleaved sample data array for a raster with three sample bands. The following methods create interleaved rasters:

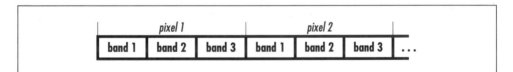

Figure 11-6. Interleaved raster data

public static WritableRaster createInterleavedRaster(int dataType, int w, int h, int bands,
    Point location)
    This method creates an interleaved `WritableRaster` with the given data type: width, height, number of bands, and origin point. The data type should be one of `TYPE_BYTE`, `TYPE_USHORT`, or `TYPE_INT`, as defined in `DataBuffer`.

public static WritableRaster createInterleavedRaster(int dataType, int w, int h,
    int scanlineStride, int pixelStride, int[] bandOffsets, Point location)
    This method gives you more control over creating an interleaved raster. As before, the supplied array type, width, and height will be used for the new raster.

The `scanlineStride` parameter is the number of array elements occupied by each row of the raster. The simplest case (shown in Figure 11-6) is that the scanline stride is the same as the width of the raster times the number of bands. However, there are two possibilities that would make the scanline stride larger. First, the raster's data buffer can contain more bands than the sample model extracts. Some satellite images may have six or seven bands of data. You might want to interleave all the bands into a single data buffer and use different sample models to pull out different bands. The second possibility is that each scanline is padded to some integral number of array elements. Some graphics file formats require this kind of padding. Figure 11-7 shows both of these possibilities.

The `pixelStride` parameter tells how many array elements make up one pixel's samples. Again, you may wish to store more bands of data than your sample model will use. The `bandOffsets` array contains an array of integers that tell where the samples for each band are located. The length of this array is used to determine how many bands are in the newly created raster. In the example shown in Figure 11-7, `bandOffsets` would have three elements: 0, 1, and 3, indicating band 1, band 2, and band 3, respectively.

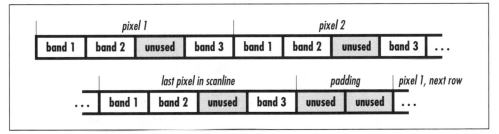

Figure 11-7. Interleaved raster data

public static WritableRaster createInterleavedRaster(DataBuffer dataBuffer, int w, int h, int scanlineStride, int pixelStride, int[] bandOffsets, Point location)
If you already have some interleaved image data in a `DataBuffer`, you can create a `Raster` from it with this method. All of the other parameters work the same as in the last two methods. (There's a section on `DataBuffers` coming up soon. For now, just remember that the data buffer contains arrays of image data.)

Banded

A banded raster stores each sample band in a separate data array. Figure 11-8 shows how this looks for a raster with three bands.

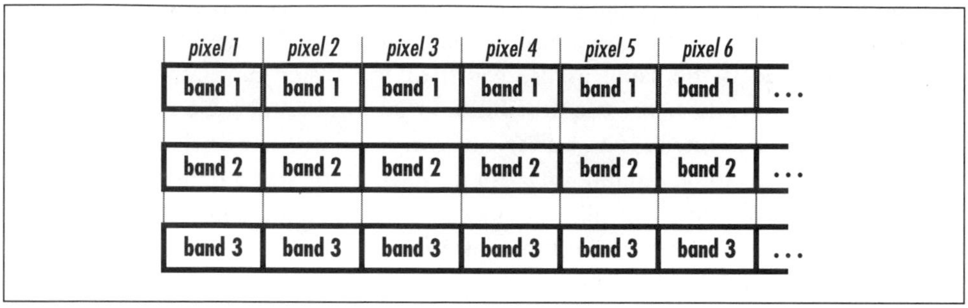

Figure 11-8. Banded raster data

The following methods create banded rasters:

public static WritableRaster createBandedRaster(int dataType, int w, int h, int bands,
    Point location)
This method creates a banded raster using arrays of the given data type. The
supplied width, height, and image origin are used to define the dimensions of
the raster. The number of bands, and consequently the number of data arrays,
is determined by the `bands` parameter.

public static WritableRaster createBandedRaster(int dataType, int w, int h,
    int scanlineStride, int[] bankIndices, int[] bandOffsets, Point location)
This method creates a slightly more sophisticated banded raster. The
`scanlineStride` parameter determines how many array elements make up a
horizontal line of the raster. The `bankIndices` array is a map from bands to
data arrays. The raster's data buffer stores data in arrays, called *banks*. The
`bankIndices` array determines which bank contains which band's data. The
band number serves as an index into the array. The entry should be the bank
number. The `bandOffsets` array contains offsets for each band. The
`bandOffsets` entry for each band should indicate where that band's data
starts in its corresponding data buffer bank. The number of bands in the
raster is determined by the length of the `bankIndices` and `bandOffsets`
arrays, which should be the same length.

public static WritableRaster createdBandedRaster(DataBuffer dataBuffer, int w, int h,
    int scanlineStride, int[] bankIndices, int[] bandOffsets, Point location)
This method is just like the previous one, except it uses the supplied
`DataBuffer` instead of creating a new one.

Packed sample

In this storage scheme, the samples for a single pixel are packed into a single array
element. One possible scenario is packing 8-bit red, green, blue, and alpha
samples into a 32-bit `int`. Figure 11-9 shows an example of packing four sample
bands into each array element.

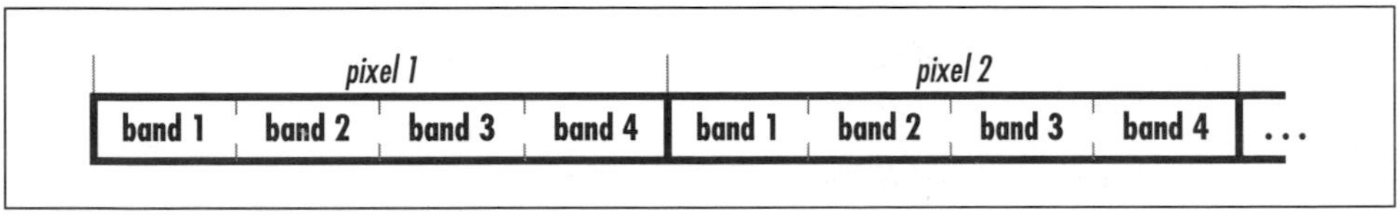

Figure 11-9. Multiple samples packed into array elements

Here are the methods that create packed rasters:

public static WritableRaster createPackedRaster(int dataType, int w, int h, int[] bandMasks, Point location)
This method creates a raster in which every pixel's samples are packed into an array element of type `dataType`. The `bandMasks` array contains bit masks that describe the location of each band inside a data array element. The length of the `bandMasks` array determines the number of bands.

public static WritableRaster createPackedRaster(DataBuffer dataBuffer, int w, int h, int scanlineStride, int[] bandMasks, Point location)
If you already have data in a packed sample format, pass it to this method as a `DataBuffer` to create a `WritableRaster`. All other parameters work the same as in the previous method. `scanlineStride` describes the number of data array elements in each horizontal row. Under normal circumstances, this is the same as the width of the raster, but some data formats may dictate otherwise.

Packed pixel

Rasters with a single band may be able to pack multiple pixels into a single array element. In an image with a 16-color palette, for example, each pixel's color can be expressed with a single 4-bit sample that serves as an index into the palette. You could store two of these 4-bit samples (two pixels) in a single `byte`. Or you could store four of them in a `short`, or eight of them in an `int`. Figure 11-10 shows an example of packing two pixels into each array element.

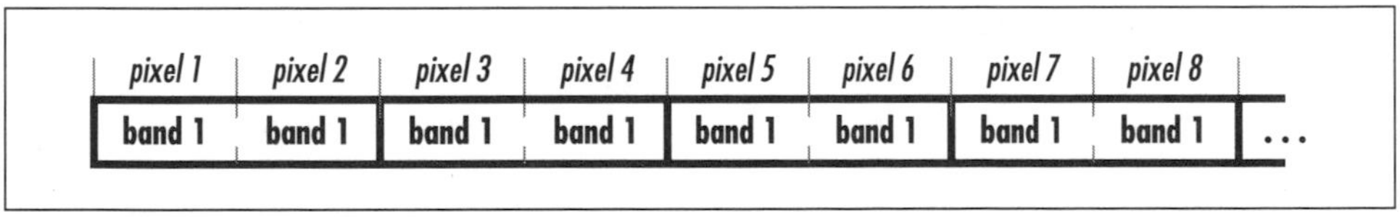

Figure 11-10. Multiple pixels packed into array elements

These methods pack multiple pixels into each array element:

public static WritableRaster createPackedRaster(int dataType, int w, int h, int bands, int bitsPerBand, Point location)
This method creates either a packed pixel or a packed sample `Writable-Raster` using the supplied number of bands and bit length per band. If the

number of bands is 1, this method creates a packed pixel raster. Otherwise, this method creates a packed sample raster using the given number of bands and bits per band.

public static WritableRaster createPackedRaster(DataBuffer dataBuffer, int w, int h, int bitsPerPixel, Point location)
This method works like the last one except the supplied `DataBuffer` is used. The number of bands is assumed to be 1, with the given bits per pixel.

Other Ways to Create Rasters

If you can't find what you want in one of the previously presented factory methods, you can create rasters the hard way. This means creating your own `SampleModel` and `DataBuffer` and passing them to one of the following factory methods in the `Raster` class:

public static Raster createRaster(SampleModel sm, DataBuffer db, Point location)
This method creates a `Raster` from the given sample model and data buffer. The origin of the raster will be the supplied point. If `location` is `null`, the raster's origin will be 0, 0.

public static WritableRaster createWritableRaster(SampleModel sm, DataBuffer db, Point location)
This method works just like the last one, except it creates a `WritableRaster` instead of a `Raster`.

public static WritableRaster createWritableRaster(SampleModel sm, Point location)
This method creates a `WritableRaster` from the given sample model. A suitable `DataBuffer` will be automatically created.

Raster Processing

Back in Chapter 10, *Image Processing*, I showed how you could digitally process entire images using implementations of the `BufferedImageOp` interface. You can perform most of the same operations on the raster that belongs to the image, using an interface called `RasterOp`. `RasterOp` has almost exactly the same methods as `BufferedImageOp`, but its `filter()` method operates on rasters instead of images:

public WritableRaster filter(Raster src, WritableRaster dest)
This method performs some manipulation of the source raster, `src`, and returns the results in a destination `WritableRaster`. If the `dest` parameter is `null`, then `filter()` creates an appropriate destination raster, populates it with the processed raster data, and returns the result. Alternatively, you can create an appropriate `WritableRaster` (perhaps using the create-

`CompatibleRaster()` method, described below) and pass it in as the `dest` parameter. In this case, the writable raster will be populated with the processed data and returned.

You may recall `BufferedImageOp`'s `createCompatibleDestImage()` method, which is handy for creating an image to hold processed data. `RasterOp` has a corresponding method to create a destination raster:

public WritableRaster createCompatibleDestRaster(Raster src)

This method creates a writable destination raster that is compatible with the supplied source raster. Compatible means that the destination raster has the same size and the same number of bands as the source raster. Usually, you won't need to call this method yourself. If you don't have an appropriate destination raster, just pass `null` as the second parameter in `filter()`. The `RasterOp` will call this method to create a compatible destination raster for you.

All of the `BufferedImageOp` image processing classes described in Chapter 10 also implement the `RasterOp` interface. This means that you can perform all the manipulations from Chapter 10 on rasters as well as on images.

Aside from the image processing classes, one additional class implements the `RasterOp` interface. This is `java.awt.image.BandCombineOp`. This class can be used to combine the bands of a raster according to a set of coefficients. The coefficients are contained in a matrix. This matrix is multiplied by each pixel's samples to produce a new set of samples for that pixel. The following formula shows how the matrix modifies the values of a single pixel. The pixel's original samples are s_1, s_2, and s_3:

$$\begin{bmatrix} m_{11} & m_{21} & m_{31} \\ m_{12} & m_{22} & m_{32} \\ m_{13} & m_{23} & m_{33} \end{bmatrix} \cdot \begin{bmatrix} s_1 \\ s_2 \\ s_3 \end{bmatrix} = \begin{bmatrix} m_{11} \cdot s_1 + m_{21} \cdot s_2 + m_{31} \cdot s_3 \\ m_{12} \cdot s_1 + m_{22} \cdot s_2 + m_{32} \cdot s_3 \\ m_{13} \cdot s_1 + m_{23} \cdot s_2 + m_{33} \cdot s_3 \end{bmatrix}$$

The size of the matrix is determined by the number of bands in the raster. A raster with three bands, for example, needs a matrix with three rows and three columns. If you wish, you can add an extra column to the matrix. In this case, an implicit 1 is added to the vector of pixel samples, which affects the computation like this:

$$\begin{bmatrix} m_{11} & m_{21} & m_{31} & m_{41} \\ m_{12} & m_{22} & m_{32} & m_{42} \\ m_{13} & m_{23} & m_{33} & m_{43} \end{bmatrix} \cdot \begin{bmatrix} s_1 \\ s_2 \\ s_3 \\ 1 \end{bmatrix} = \begin{bmatrix} m_{11} \cdot s_1 + m_{21} \cdot s_2 + m_{31} \cdot s_3 + m_{41} \\ m_{12} \cdot s_1 + m_{22} \cdot s_2 + m_{32} \cdot s_3 + m_{42} \\ m_{13} \cdot s_1 + m_{23} \cdot s_2 + m_{33} \cdot s_3 + m_{43} \end{bmatrix}$$

The identity matrix produces no change:

$$\begin{bmatrix} 1 & 0 & 0 \\ 0 & 1 & 0 \\ 0 & 0 & 1 \end{bmatrix} \cdot \begin{bmatrix} s_1 \\ s_2 \\ s_3 \end{bmatrix} = \begin{bmatrix} 1 \cdot s_1 + 0 \cdot s_2 + 0 \cdot s_3 \\ 0 \cdot s_1 + 1 \cdot s_2 + 0 \cdot s_3 \\ 0 \cdot s_1 + 0 \cdot s_2 + 1 \cdot s_3 \end{bmatrix} = \begin{bmatrix} s_1 \\ s_2 \\ s_3 \end{bmatrix}$$

One simple application of `BandCombineOp` is inverting color bands. In an image with three bands, with values that run from 0 to 255, for example, you could invert the first band like this:

$$\begin{bmatrix} -1 & 0 & 0 & 255 \\ 0 & 1 & 0 & 0 \\ 0 & 0 & 1 & 0 \end{bmatrix} \cdot \begin{bmatrix} s_1 \\ s_2 \\ s_3 \\ 1 \end{bmatrix} = \begin{bmatrix} -s_1 + 255 \\ s_2 \\ s_3 \end{bmatrix}$$

To create and use a `BandCombineOp`, you just need to specify the matrix. The matrix is described by a two-dimensional array of floating-point values:

public BandCombineOp(float[][] matrix, RenderingHints hints)

> This constructor creates a `BandCombineOp` using the specified matrix. The first subscript of `matrix` is the row number, while the second subscript is the column number. The `hints` parameter is ignored and may be `null`.

The following example shows how you can use a `BandCombineOp` to invert the red component of an image. It uses the `SplitImageComponent` from Chapter 10, *Image Processing*, to display the original image and the processed image simultaneously. You can click and drag with the mouse to move the split line. The processed image is the same as Figure C-20.

The actual processing is quite simple. First, a `BandCombineOp` is created:

```
float[][] matrix = {
  { -1, 0, 0, 255 },
  {  0, 1, 0, 0 },
  {  0, 0, 1, 0 }
};
BandCombineOp op = new BandCombineOp(matrix, null);
```

Then the raster from the original image is processed using the `BandCombineOp`:

```
Raster source = sourceImage.getRaster();
WritableRaster destination = op.filter(source, null);
```

Finally, the destination image is created from the processed raster. The destination image has the same color model as the source image:

```
    BufferedImage destinationImage = new BufferedImage(
        sourceImage.getColorModel(), destination, false, null);
```

Here is the whole example:

```
import java.awt.*;
import java.awt.event.*;
import java.awt.image.*;

public class Bandito {
  public static void main(String[] args) {
    // Create a frame window to hold everything.
    ApplicationFrame f = new ApplicationFrame("Bandito v1.0");
    // Create a SplitImageComponent with the source image.
    String filename = "Ethol with Roses.small.jpg";
    SplitImageComponent sic = new SplitImageComponent(filename);

    // Create a BandCombineOp.
    float[][] matrix = {
      { -1, 0, 0, 255 },
      {  0, 1, 0, 0 },
      {  0, 0, 1, 0 }
    };
    BandCombineOp op = new BandCombineOp(matrix, null);

    // Process the source image raster.
    BufferedImage sourceImage = sic.getImage();
    Raster source = sourceImage.getRaster();
    WritableRaster destination = op.filter(source, null);

    // Create a destination image using the processed
    //   raster and the same color model as the source image.
    BufferedImage destinationImage = new BufferedImage(
        sourceImage.getColorModel(), destination, false, null);
    sic.setSecondImage(destinationImage);

    // Set up the frame window.
    f.setLayout(new BorderLayout());
    f.add(sic, BorderLayout.CENTER);
    f.setSize(f.getPreferredSize());
    f.center();
    f.setVisible(true);
  }
}
```

BandCombineOp supports in-place processing, which means that the source and destination parameters passed to filter() can be the same. In the example above, the source and destination are distinct so that they can both be shown.

Sample Models

A raster's sample model knows how to pull pixel samples out of a data buffer. In the 2D API, sample models are represented by `java.awt.image.SampleModel` and its subclasses.

The `SampleModel` provides many methods for setting and retrieving pixel sample values. These methods are nearly identical to the methods you've already seen in the `Raster` and `WritableRaster` classes, except that the methods in `SampleModel` also accept a `DataBuffer` that will be used for storing or retrieving the sample data. Because the methods are so similar, I won't list them all here.

Like a `Raster`, a `SampleModel` has both a *data type* and a *transfer type*. The data type is the type of array contained in the matching `DataBuffer`. The transfer type is a type that is used for moving large amounts of pixel data from one place to another. Refer back to the section on rasters for more information.

`SampleModel` has three subclasses that represent common methods of storing image data.

ComponentSampleModel

This class represents a sample model where each pixel sample is stored in a separate array element. It has two subclasses, `BandedSampleModel` and `Pixel-InterleavedSampleModel`.

BandedSampleModel

This class is suitable for use with banded data in a `DataBuffer`. To create a `BandedSampleModel`, use one of its constructors:

public BandedSampleModel(int dataType, int w, int h, int numBands)
> This constructor creates a `BandedSampleModel` suitable for use with the given data type, width, height, and number of bands.

public BandedSampleModel(int dataType, int w, int h, int scanlineStride,
> *int[] bankIndices, int[] bandOffsets)*
> This constructor accepts additional parameters. See `Raster`'s `create-BandedRaster()` factory method for a description of the parameters.

PixelInterleavedSampleModel

This sample model has one constructor:

public PixelInterleavedSampleModel(int dataType, int w, int h, int pixelStride,
> *int scanlineStride, int[] bandOffsets)*
> This constructor's parameters are just like those given in `Raster`'s `createInterleavedRaster()` factory method. See that method,

discussed earlier in this chapter, for a full description of the parameters.

SinglePixelPackedSampleModel

This class is used for packed sample pixel data, where each array element contains multiple pixel samples. It has two constructors:

public SinglePixelPackedSampleModel(int dataType, int w, int h, int[] bitMasks)
This constructor creates a sample model that recognizes packed sample data with the given array type, width, height, and bit masks.

public SinglePixelPackedSampleModel(int dataType, int w, int h, int scanlineStride,
int[] bitMasks)
This constructor is the same as the previous constructor but also allows you to specify a scanline stride.

MultiPixelPackedSampleModel

The `MultiPixelPackedSampleModel` is used to access data in a packed pixel raster. It also has two constructors:

public MultiPixelPackedSampleModel(int dataType, int w, int h, int numberOfBits)
This constructor creates a `MultiPixelPackedSampleModel` for the given data type, width, height, and number of bits per pixel.

public MultiPixelPackedSampleModel(int dataType, int w, int h, int numberOfBits,
int scanlineStride, int dataBitOffset)
This constructor is the same as the previous one but allows you to specify a scanline stride and a data bit offset. The data bit offset is the number of bits from the beginning of the data array to the beginning of the image data. It should be a multiple of `numberOfBits`.

Data Buffers

Now I've peeled back all but one of the layers of `BufferedImage`. The last layer around the actual image data is the `java.awt.image.DataBuffer` class. Instances of this class are containers for one or more data arrays, called *banks*. A `DataBuffer` includes methods for accessing the data contained in its banks. (I won't detail these methods here, however, as you probably won't ever have to use them.)

You may have to construct a `DataBuffer` someday, however, so I'll talk about each of `DataBuffer`'s subclasses and their constructors.

First, take a look at the data type constants that have popped up throughout this chapter. They're defined right here in the DataBuffer class. These constants simply represent different data types. (The same constants are also used in Raster and SampleModel to describe transfer types.)

public static int TYPE_BYTE
public static int TYPE_USHORT
public static int TYPE_SHORT
public static int TYPE_INT
public static int TYPE_FLOAT
public static int TYPE_DOUBLE
public static int TYPE_UNDEFINED

The only types supported in the 2D API are TYPE_BYTE, TYPE_USHORT, and TYPE_INT.

The DataBuffer class has four subclasses that encapsulate byte, short, and int arrays. They are aptly named DataBufferByte, DataBufferShort, DataBuffer-UShort, and DataBufferInt. Because these classes are so similar, I will only describe the constructors for DataBufferByte. You can figure out the constructors for the other classes just by changing the types as appropriate. The six constructors are:

public DataBufferByte(int size)
>   This constructor creates a data buffer with the given number of elements. A single byte array of the given size will be created for you.

public DataBufferByte(int size, int numBanks)
>   This constructor creates a data buffer with numBanks byte arrays with the given size.

public DataBufferByte(byte[] dataArray, int size)
>   Use this constructor to wrap a data buffer around the given byte array. Only the first size elements of the array are used.

public DataBufferByte(byte[] dataArray, int size, int offset)
>   This constructor creates a data buffer around the size elements of the given array, starting at offset.

public DataBufferByte(byte[][] dataArray, int size)
>   This constructor creates a data buffer with the given array data. There will be as many banks as there are arrays. The first size elements of all the arrays will be used as image data.

public DataBufferByte(byte[][] dataArray, int size, int[] offsets)
>   This constructor uses the given arrays for data. You can specify a separate offset for each array to indicate where the data starts. The size parameter tells how many elements can be read from each array.

A PNG Decoder

One reason you might have to know the internal anatomy of `BufferedImage` is if you intend to create images from data contained in files. In this section, I'll present classes that create a `BufferedImage` from information contained in a Portable Network Graphics (PNG) file.* PNG supports many image formats and color depths. This example will load only PNG images with a palette (i.e., only those with indexed color). I won't attempt to describe the PNG format in any detail. If you're interested, a lot more information is available at *http://www.cdrom. com/pub/png/png.html.* If you'd like to learn more about many different file formats, take a look at the *Encyclopedia of Graphics File Formats, Second Edition*, by James D. Murray and William vanRyper (O'Reilly).

This example is comprised of three classes. `PNGDecoder` knows the overall layout of a PNG file and handles the details of loading each part, or *chunk*, of the file. It also includes a `main()` method that will load a PNG file and show it in a frame window. The second class, `PNGChunk`, represents a single chunk of data from the file. The last class is `PNGData`. It represents a collection of chunks and knows how to extract palette and image data from the chunks.

To use a `PNGDecoder`, you just need to create one and give it an `InputStream` that contains a PNG file. The `PNGDecoder` class has only two public methods:

public static BufferedImage decode(InputStream in) throws IOException
> This is the magic method that creates a `BufferedImage` by loading a PNG file from the given input stream. An `IOException` is thrown if anything goes wrong. This method first checks for the signature data which should be at the beginning of every PNG file. Then it loads the file, using a `PNGData`. Then it obtains a color model and a raster from the `PNGData` and creates the `BufferedImage` from them.

public static void main(String[] args) throws Exception
> This method is useful for testing. It decodes an image from the file named on the command line and creates a frame window that displays the image.

The `decode()` method uses several `protected` helper methods. The `read-Signature()` method simply checks for the signature data that should be at the front of every PNG file. To actually read the data, `decode()` calls `readChunks()`. This method creates a `PNGData` that accumulates each chunk of data as it is read. Each data chunk includes a data integrity checksum, called a CRC. Another

---

* The other interpretation of PNG is "PNG is Not GIF." The GIF standard, while popular, has some significant shortcomings. First, it uses LZW compression technology, which is not entirely free; you may need to buy a license in order to write and distribute a GIF encoder or decoder. Furthermore, GIF's maximum color depth is eight bits, which is insufficient for many applications.

method called `verifyCRC()` recalculates the CRC to make sure the image data
has not been damaged.

Here's the `PNGDecoder`:

```java
import java.awt.image.*;
import java.io.*;
import java.util.*;
import java.util.zip.*;

import java.awt.*;
import java.awt.event.*;

public class PNGDecoder {
  public static void main(String[] args) throws Exception {
    String name = "basn3p08.png";
    if (args.length > 0) name = args[0];
    InputStream in = PNGDecoder.class.getResourceAsStream(name);
    final BufferedImage image = PNGDecoder.decode(in);
    in.close();

    // Create a Frame to display the image.
    Frame f = new ApplicationFrame("PNGDecoder v1.0") {
      public void paint(Graphics g) {
        Insets insets = getInsets();
        g.drawImage(image, insets.left, insets.top, null);
      }
    };
    f.setVisible(true);
    Insets insets = f.getInsets();
    f.setSize(image.getWidth() + insets.left + insets.right,
        image.getHeight() + insets.top + insets.bottom);
  }


  public static BufferedImage decode(InputStream in)
      throws IOException {
    DataInputStream dataIn = new DataInputStream(in);
    readSignature(dataIn);
    PNGData chunks = readChunks(dataIn);

    long widthLong = chunks.getWidth();
    long heightLong = chunks.getHeight();
    if (widthLong > Integer.MAX_VALUE || heightLong > Integer.MAX_VALUE)
      throw new IOException("That image is too wide or tall.");
    int width = (int)widthLong;
    int height = (int)heightLong;

    ColorModel cm = chunks.getColorModel();
    WritableRaster raster = chunks.getRaster();
```

```
      BufferedImage image = new BufferedImage(cm, raster, false, null);

    return image;
  }

  protected static void readSignature(DataInputStream in)
      throws IOException {
    long signature = in.readLong();
    if (signature != 0x89504e470d0a1a0aL)
      throw new IOException("PNG signature not found!");
  }

  protected static PNGData readChunks(DataInputStream in)
      throws IOException {
    PNGData chunks = new PNGData();

    boolean trucking = true;
    while (trucking) {
      try {
        // Read the length.
        int length = in.readInt();
        if (length < 0)
          throw new IOException("Sorry, that file is too long.");
        // Read the type.
        byte[] typeBytes = new byte[4];
        in.readFully(typeBytes);
        // Read the data.
        byte[] data = new byte[length];
        in.readFully(data);
        // Read the CRC.
        long crc = in.readInt() & 0x00000000ffffffffL; // Make it unsigned.
        if (verifyCRC(typeBytes, data, crc) == false)
          throw new IOException("That file appears to be corrupted.");

        PNGChunk chunk = new PNGChunk(typeBytes, data);
        chunks.add(chunk);
      }
      catch (EOFException eofe) {
        trucking = false;
      }
    }
    return chunks;
  }

  protected static boolean verifyCRC(byte[] typeBytes, byte[] data,
      long crc) {
    CRC32 crc32 = new CRC32();
    crc32.update(typeBytes);
    crc32.update(data);
```

```
        long calculated = crc32.getValue();
        return (calculated == crc);
    }
}
```

The PNGData class does all the hard work of interpreting the image data. Before we look at it, let's look at the PNGChunk class. After you use a checksum to verify the chunk's integrity, there are just two pieces of information in a chunk: a type and a block of data. The type is a 4-byte identifier. By convention, the four bytes are ASCII characters, but this is a convenience rather than a requirement. PNGChunk has methods that retrieve the type as a String and the data itself as a byte array. PNGChunk also includes some handy utility methods for extracting numerical values from a chunk's data block.

Here's the code for PNGChunk:

```
import java.io.*;

public class PNGChunk {
  private byte[] mType;
  private byte[] mData;

  public PNGChunk(byte[] type, byte[] data) {
    mType = type;
    mData = data;
  }

  public String getTypeString() {
    try { return new String(mType, "UTF8"); }
    catch (UnsupportedEncodingException uee) { return ""; }
  }

  public byte[] getData() { return mData; }

  public long getUnsignedInt(int offset) {
    long value = 0;
    for (int i = 0; i < 4; i++)
      value += (mData[offset + i] & 0xff) << ((3 - i) * 8);
    return value;
  }

  public short getUnsignedByte(int offset) {
    return (short)(mData[offset] & 0x00ff);
  }
}
```

The final class, PNGData, is a box that holds PNGChunks:

```
import java.awt.Transparency;
import java.awt.color.*;
```

```java
import java.awt.image.*;
import java.io.*;
import java.util.zip.*;

public class PNGData {
  private int mNumberOfChunks;
  private PNGChunk[] mChunks;

  public PNGData() {
    mNumberOfChunks = 0;
    mChunks = new PNGChunk[10];
  }

  public void add(PNGChunk chunk) {
    mChunks[mNumberOfChunks++] = chunk;
    if (mNumberOfChunks >= mChunks.length) {
      PNGChunk[] largerArray = new PNGChunk[mChunks.length + 10];
      System.arraycopy(mChunks, 0, largerArray, 0, mChunks.length);
      mChunks = largerArray;
    }
  }

  public long getWidth() { return getChunk("IHDR").getUnsignedInt(0); }
  public long getHeight() { return getChunk("IHDR").getUnsignedInt(4); }
  public short getBitsPerPixel() {
      return getChunk("IHDR").getUnsignedByte(8); }
  public short getColorType() { return getChunk("IHDR").getUnsignedByte(9); }
  public short getCompression() {
      return getChunk("IHDR").getUnsignedByte(10); }
  public short getFilter() { return getChunk("IHDR").getUnsignedByte(11); }
  public short getInterlace() { return getChunk("IHDR").getUnsignedByte(12);
}

  public ColorModel getColorModel() {
    short colorType = getColorType();
    int bitsPerPixel = getBitsPerPixel();

    if (colorType == 3) {
      byte[] paletteData = getChunk("PLTE").getData();
      int paletteLength = paletteData.length / 3;
      return new IndexColorModel(bitsPerPixel,
          paletteLength, paletteData, 0, false);
    }
    System.out.println("Unsupported color type: " + colorType);
    return null;
  }

  public WritableRaster getRaster() {
    int width = (int)getWidth();
```

```
    int height = (int)getHeight();
    int bitsPerPixel = getBitsPerPixel();
    short colorType = getColorType();

    if (colorType == 3) {
      byte[] imageData = getImageData();
      DataBuffer db = new DataBufferByte(imageData, imageData.length);
      WritableRaster raster = Raster.createPackedRaster(db, width, height,
          bitsPerPixel, null);
      return raster;
    }
    else System.out.println("Unsupported color type!");
    return null;
}

public byte[] getImageData() {
  try {
    ByteArrayOutputStream out = new ByteArrayOutputStream();
    // Write all the IDAT data into the array.
    for (int i = 0; i < mNumberOfChunks; i++) {
      PNGChunk chunk = mChunks[i];
      if (chunk.getTypeString().equals("IDAT")) {
        out.write(chunk.getData());
      }
    }
    out.flush();
    // Now deflate the data.
    InflaterInputStream in = new InflaterInputStream(
        new ByteArrayInputStream(out.toByteArray()));
    ByteArrayOutputStream inflatedOut = new ByteArrayOutputStream();
    int readLength;
    byte[] block = new byte[8192];
    while ((readLength = in.read(block)) != -1)
      inflatedOut.write(block, 0, readLength);
    inflatedOut.flush();
    byte[] imageData = inflatedOut.toByteArray();
    // Compute the real length.
    int width = (int)getWidth();
    int height = (int)getHeight();
    int bitsPerPixel = getBitsPerPixel();
    int length = width * height * bitsPerPixel / 8;

    byte[] prunedData = new byte[length];

    // We can only deal with non-interlaced images.
    if (getInterlace() == 0) {
      int index = 0;
      for (int i = 0; i < length; i++) {
        if ((i * 8 / bitsPerPixel) % width == 0) {
```

```
               index++; // Skip the filter byte.
            }
            prunedData[i] = imageData[index++];
          }
        }
        else System.out.println("Couldn't undo interlacing.");

        return prunedData;
      }
      catch (IOException ioe) {}
      return null;
    }

  public PNGChunk getChunk(String type) {
    for (int i = 0; i < mNumberOfChunks; i++)
      if (mChunks[i].getTypeString().equals(type))
        return mChunks[i];
    return null;
  }
}
```

The most important methods in PNGData are as follows:

public void add(PNGChunk chunk)

> This method adds the given chunk to this PNGData. The chunks are managed
> in a member variable array. If the array fills up, a larger one is created.

public ColorModel getColorModel()

> This method examines some fields in an "IHDR" (image header) chunk to
> determine basic characteristics of the image represented by this PNGData. It
> only recognizes files with indexed (palette) color. If the file is the correct type,
> this method reads palette color data from the "PLTE" (palette) chunk and
> creates an appropriate IndexColorModel.

public WritableRaster getRaster()

> This method creates a raster using the image data (see getImageData()
> below) and some information from the "IHDR" chunk about the image itself.

public byte[] getImageData()

> This method builds an array of image data from all available "IDAT" (image
> data) chunks. The data may be split across multiple "IDAT" chunks. Further-
> more, the image data is compressed. This method uses a variety of input and
> output streams to assemble the various pieces of "IDAT" data and decompress
> the data. Finally, PNG image data includes an extra byte (for filtering, which
> this class doesn't recognize) at the beginning of every scanline. This method
> strips out the byte and returns the resulting image data.

public PNGChunk getChunk(String type)

> This method simply searches through the PNGData's list of chunks until it finds the first one with the given type. The first matching chunk is returned.

If you're looking for an appropriate image for testing, *http://www.schaik.com/ pngsuite/pngsuite.html* contains a definitive collection of test images. The PNGDecoder example can recognize only non-interlaced, indexed-color images, so the images you should try are *basn3p01.png*, *basn3p02.png*, *basn3p04.png*, and *basn3p08.png* (in the "Basic formats" page). Run the application by typing the following (assuming you've downloaded the test image):

```
java PNGDecoder basn3p08.png
```

If all goes well, you should see a little window with the test image, shown in Figure C-28.

12

Devices

The 2D API is centered around the task of rendering shapes, text, and images on an output device, usually a monitor or a printer. One of the goals of the API is to make the rendering process the same, regardless of the output device. Sometimes, though, you want information unique to a specific device. For performance reasons, you might want to know the data format of a monitor so you can create compatible images for fast rendering. Whatever the reason, the 2D API has several classes that provide information about the local graphics capabilities. The 2D API describes three concepts:

Environment
> An environment describes the overall graphics capabilities of a particular computer, including the available fonts and screen devices.

Device
> A device is a monitor or printer.

Configuration
> Devices can be set up in more than one way. For example, many video adapters are capable of displaying different screen resolutions and different color resolutions. (Color resolution is the number of bits per pixel (bpp) that are used to represent color.)

The Local Graphics Environment

A graphics environment is represented by an instance of `java.awt.GraphicsEnvironment`. You can get one of these objects representing the local computer using a handy factory method:

public static GraphicsEnvironment getLocalGraphicsEnvironment()
> This method returns a `GraphicsEnvironment` for the local computer.

Font Information

A GraphicsEnvironment knows about fonts that are installed on a computer. There are three methods that provide information about the fonts in a particular environment:

public abstract Font[] getAllFonts()
> This method returns every font in the system in an array.

public abstract String[] getAvailableFontFamilyNames()
> This method returns an array of strings containing the family names of every available font. For more information about how fonts are named, refer back to Chapter 6.

public abstract String[] getAvailableFontFamilyNames(Locale l)
> This method is the same as the previous method, but it returns the names for a particular Locale.

Chapter 6 has examples that show how to use these methods.

Finding Screen Devices

GraphicsEnvironment includes two methods for finding out about screen devices. These are represented by instances of java.awt.GraphicsDevice, which we'll discuss later in this chapter. The two methods are:

public abstract GraphicsDevice[] getScreenDevices()
> This method returns an array containing all the screen devices accessible in this environment.

public abstract GraphicsDevice getDefaultScreenDevice()
> This method returns the default screen device.

The GraphicsDevice Class

Individual devices are represented by instances of java.awt.GraphicsDevice. Currently this class supports three types of devices, represented by integer constants:

public static final int TYPE_RASTER_SCREEN
> This constant represents a monitor.

public static final int TYPE_PRINTER
> This constant represents any kind of printer.

public static final int TYPE_IMAGE_BUFFER
> This constant represents an image. Remember that you can render into an image using a Graphics or Graphics2D object. In this sense, the image is a kind of "virtual device."

To find out the type of a particular device, call the getType() method:

public abstract int getType()
>   This method returns the device type, which should be one of the constants
>   TYPE_RASTER_SCREEN, TYPE_PRINTER, or TYPE_IMAGE_BUFFER.

Devices also have a name, called an *identification string*:

public abstract String getIDstring()
>   This method returns the name of the device. Note the nonstandard capitaliza-
>   tion of this method name.

The following program prints out the ID string of every screen device on your
system:

```
import java.awt.*;

public class ShowDevices {
  public static void main(String[] args) {
    GraphicsEnvironment ge = GraphicsEnvironment.
getLocalGraphicsEnvironment();
    GraphicsDevice[] screenDevices = ge.getScreenDevices();
    for (int i = 0; i < screenDevices.length; i++)
      System.out.println(screenDevices[i].getIDstring());
    System.exit(0);
  }
}
```

On my machine, I only have one screen device:

```
C:\>java ShowDevices
:0.0

C:\>
```

A graphics device may operate in more than one mode, or *configuration*. For
example, a screen device might have the following possible configurations:

*   800 x 600 pixels, 4 bits per pixel color

*   1152 x 864 pixels, 24 bits per pixel color

Device configurations are represented by instances of the java.awt.
GraphicsConfiguration class. (I would have called it DeviceConfiguration,
but nobody asked me.) The GraphicsDevice class has three methods that return
information about configurations:

public abstract GraphicsConfiguration[] getConfigurations()
>   This method returns an array of all possible configurations for a device.

public abstract GraphicsConfiguration getDefaultConfiguration()
>   This method returns the default configuration for a particular device.

public GraphicsConfiguration getBestConfiguration(GraphicsConfigTemplate gct)
>   This method is provided for use by the 3D API. It's not currently useful in 2D.

Device Configurations

A `java.awt.GraphicsConfiguration` represents a specific setup of a specific graphics device. There are a few interesting things that a Graphics-Configuration can do.

Configuration Information

Most of `GraphicsConfiguration`'s methods return information about the configuration itself:

public abstract GraphicsDevice getDevice()
>   This method returns the `GraphicsDevice` associated with this particular configuration.

public abstract ColorModel getColorModel()
>   This method returns the color model used by the device in this configuration. Physical devices are entirely opaque, so the color model returned by this method doesn't support transparency (alpha values).

public abstract ColorModel getColorModel(int transparency)
>   This method is the same as above, but returns a color model that supports the requested transparency mode. (If you're wondering what a color model is, take a look back at Chapter 11, *Image Guts*.) The transparency parameter should be one of the constants from the `java.awt.Transparency` interface—either OPAQUE, BITMASK, or TRANSLUCENT.

Here's a simple program that displays the color model of the default screen device in its available configurations:

```
import java.awt.*;

public class ShowConfigurations {
  public static void main(String[] args) {
    GraphicsEnvironment ge =
      GraphicsEnvironment.getLocalGraphicsEnvironment();
    GraphicsDevice defaultScreen = ge.getDefaultScreenDevice();
    GraphicsConfiguration[] configurations = defaultScreen.
getConfigurations();
```

```
        System.out.println("Default screen device: " +
          defaultScreen.getIDstring());
        for (int i = 0; i < configurations.length; i++) {
          System.out.println("  Configuration " + (i + 1));
          System.out.println("    " + configurations[i].getColorModel());
        }
        System.exit(0);
      }
    }
```

On my system, this is the output:

```
Default screen device: :0.0
  Configuration 1
  DirectColorModel: rmask=ff0000 gmask=ff00 bmask=ff amask=0
```

This corresponds to the settings I have chosen on my Windows system. The
DirectColorModel reflects my choice of color depth, 24 bits (called "True Color"
in the Windows control panel). As you can see from the band masks, Microsoft
orders its color bytes in the same way as Java. On a Solaris system, the red and blue
are reversed. It doesn't really matter; the 2D API takes care of the details of swap-
ping color bytes when it's necessary.

The last type of information about a device configuration has to do with transformations. Remember that the 2D API provides an automatic transformation from
User Space to Device Space so that the results of rendering are the same size,
regardless of the output device. The methods that return transformations are:

public abstract AffineTransform getDefaultTransform()
> This method returns a transformation that places the origin of User Space at
> the upper left corner of the device, with the x axis increasing to the right and
> the y axis increasing downward.

public abstract AffineTransform getNormalizingTransform()
> The transformation returned by this method can be concatenated with the
> default transformation to make 72 User Space units equal to one inch in the
> real world.

Creating Images

One of the really useful things you can do with a GraphicsConfiguration is to
create an image that is *compatible* with the device configuration. Compatible means
that the image has a color model and data layout that is the same as the underlying device configuration. This allows the image to be quickly rendered on the
device. Using a compatible image won't make much difference in your
programming—after all, you're just dealing with a BufferedImage, and you don't
usually care what data format it uses. However, using compatible images may

improve the speed of your application. The following methods create compatible
`BufferedImages`:

public abstract BufferedImage createCompatibleImage(int width, int height)

This method creates a new `BufferedImage` of the specified width and height.
The new image has the same color model and data layout as this device
configuration.

public abstract BufferedImage createCompatibleImage(int width, int height, int transparency)

This method works just like the previous method except the new image
supports the specified transparency mode. The `transparency` parameter
should be one of `OPAQUE`, `BITMASK`, or `TRANSLUCENT` as defined in the
`Transparency` interface.

13

Printing

It used to be that making pretty pictures on a computer was nothing unless you could put the results on paper or transparencies. These days, paper is not as important as it used to be, with images and graphics migrating to the Web. Transparencies, which used to be *de rigueur* for business presentations, are now old-fashioned. Now a laptop computer attached to a video display is the standard equipment for presentations. But don't give up on paper yet. The paperless society hasn't arrived, and I'm not going to hold my breath waiting for it.

The Java 2 platform offers a clean, compact Printing API. If you've been struggling to get JDK 1.0 or JDK 1.1 to produce nice printed output, you'll be really happy to see the Printing API.[*] The basic concept is very simple: the Printing API can give you a `Graphics2D` that represents a printer. You can perform the same rendering, regardless of whether the output device is the screen or a printer. Java 2 unleashes the full power of the 2D API is on your printer. Whee!

The classes and interfaces involved in printing are neatly tucked away in the `java.awt.print` package. It's a small package, easy to understand and easy to use. The secret of this simplicity is that an application can use the same code to render on a screen or on a printer. Printing is simply a matter of obtaining a `Graphics2D` that corresponds to the printer and rendering away.

Aside from rendering, there are two issues that are important in printing:

Job control

It's up to your application to start printing and to display printing dialogs. The 2D API can show the standard print and page setup dialogs for you.

---

[*] JDK 1.0 didn't include any printing support, so you may have turned to third-party native code solutions.

Pagination

Each page consists of some finite printable area. Your application should break its data into page-sized pieces for printing.

How Printing Works

The Printing API uses a *callback* model, which means that the printing system calls your application when it needs something to be drawn. But it's more complicated than that. The following is a typical sequence of events:

1. The user of your application requests printed output, usually by clicking on a button or choosing a menu item.

2. Your application displays a print dialog box that is appropriate for the underlying operating system. The Windows print dialog is shown in Figure 13-1. From this dialog, users can choose a printer, change the number of copies that will be printed, and fiddle with other options.

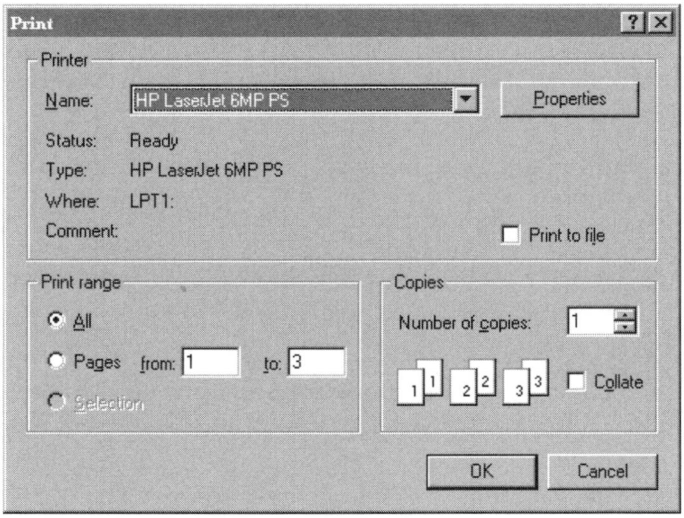

Figure 13-1. The print dialog in Windows

3. If the user clicks on the **OK** button in the print dialog, your application can tell the system to begin a printing job.

4. The system will call back your rendering code at the appropriate time to render your picture on the printer.

The Players

One class and one interface form the crux of the Printing API:

java.awt.print.PrinterJob

> The `PrinterJob` class controls the printing process.* You can use this class to kick off printing or to cancel a job in progress. This class also includes methods for displaying a print dialog and a page setup dialog.

java.awt.print.Printable

> The `Printable` interface represents something that can be printed. It contains a single method, `print()`.

Let's get something on paper right away to illustrate how `PrinterJob` and `Printable` work together. Here's a simple example that displays a print dialog and prints a single page:

```java
import java.awt.*;
import java.awt.print.*;

public class HelloNurse {
  public static void main(String[] args) {
    PrinterJob pj = PrinterJob.getPrinterJob();
    pj.setPrintable(new HelloNursePrintable());
    if (pj.printDialog()) {
      try { pj.print(); }
      catch (PrinterException e) {
        System.out.println(e);
      }
    }
  }
}


class HelloNursePrintable
    implements Printable {
  public int print(Graphics g, PageFormat pf, int pageIndex) {
    if (pageIndex != 0) return NO_SUCH_PAGE;
    Graphics2D g2 = (Graphics2D)g;
    g2.setFont(new Font("Serif", Font.PLAIN, 36));
    g2.setPaint(Color.black);
    g2.drawString("Hello, nurse!", 144, 144);
    return PAGE_EXISTS;
  }
}
```

---

* Don't confuse this with `java.awt.PrintJob`, which was part of JDK 1.1's printing solution.

Let's look at the sequence of events in this small application:

1. First, a `PrinterJob` is instantiated by calling the `getPrinterJob()` factory method:

   ```
   PrinterJob pj = PrinterJob.getPrinterJob();
   ```

2. The thing to be printed, `HelloNursePrintable`, is passed to the `PrinterJob`'s `setPrintable()` method:

   ```
   pj.setPrintable(new HelloNursePrintable());
   ```

3. Then the example shows a print dialog:

   ```
   if (pj.printDialog()) {
   ```

4. If the user pressed **OK** in the print dialog, the `printDialog()` method returns `true`. In this case, the printing job is started by calling `print()`:

   ```
   try { pj.print(); }
   ```

5. The job is now in the hands of the Printing API. It calls our `Hello-NursePrintable`'s `print()` method as appropriate to render the page on the printer. Control is returned to the `HelloNurse` application once the entire printing job has been sent to the underlying operating system. Since `HelloNurse` doesn't have anything else to do, it exits right away.

Don't worry about the parts of this example that don't make sense yet. I'll cover everything in detail in this chapter.

The Printable Interface

Let's take a closer look at the `Printable` interface, which contains one method:

public int print(Graphics g, PageFormat pf, int pageIndex) throws PrinterException
   This method is called by the Printing API to render a page on a printer. The `Graphics` object represents the drawing surface of the page. You can cast it to a `Graphics2D` to take advantage of the 2D API's features. The `PageFormat` object describes the size and orientation of the paper. I'll describe the `PageFormat` class in detail later. The `pageIndex` parameter is the number of the page that will be printed. It is zero-based; that is, the first page is 0.

   It's possible that this method will be called multiple times to render the same page. Usually this doesn't affect how you write the method—just make sure you're not expecting only one call to `print()` per page.

   If your `Printable` implementation is able to print the requested page, it should do its rendering and return `PAGE_EXISTS`, a constant in the `Printable` interface. If the requested page does not exist, return `NO_SUCH_PAGE`.*

---

* You don't have to declare that the method throws a `PrinterException` if you don't plan to throw one yourself.

The `HelloNursePrintable` class, presented above, only prints one page. If any other page index is passed to `print()`, it returns `NO_SUCH_PAGE`:

```
public int print(Graphics g, PageFormat pf, int pageIndex) {
    if (pageIndex != 0) return NO_SUCH_PAGE;
```

Otherwise, `HelloNursePrintable` goes ahead and renders the page. In this case, it just draws a single string. Having successfully rendered the page, it returns `PAGE_EXISTS`:

```
Graphics2D g2 = (Graphics2D)g;
g2.setFont(new Font("Serif", Font.PLAIN, 36));
g2.drawString("Hello, nurse!", 144, 144);
return PAGE_EXISTS;
}
```

You've probably noticed that the `print()` method in the `Printable` interface looks a lot like a `paint()` method. If you want to render the same thing on the screen and on a printer, you should take advantage of this similarity. Instead of doing any rendering in the `print()` method, just call a `paint()` method from the `print()` method. You'll see examples of this later.

The PageFormat Class

Instances of `java.awt.print.PageFormat` describe a sheet of paper and its orientation. The origin of User Space is always placed at the corner of the paper. However, the page's *orientation* determines which corner is considered the User Space origin and how the coordinate axes are aligned. Printers, furthermore, usually cannot print right up to the edges of paper. The *imageable area* is the part of the paper on which the printer can print. Figure 13-2 shows how portrait and landscape orientations look, while Figure 13-3 shows how they appear as they come out of the printer.

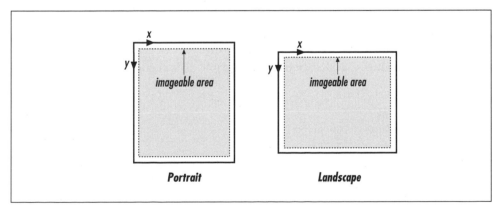

Figure 13-2. Orientation and imageable area

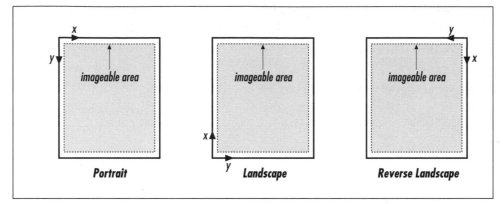

Figure 13-3. Different orientations, as they come out of the printer

`PageFormat` defines three constants that represent orientations:

public static int PORTRAIT
public static int LANDSCAPE
public static int REVERSE_LANDSCAPE

You can find out the orientation and size of a `PageFormat` with the following methods:

public int getOrientation()
> This method returns the paper orientation. The returned value will be one of the orientation constants, either PORTRAIT, LANDSCAPE, or REVERSE_LANDSCAPE.

public double getWidth()
public double getHeight()
> These methods return the width and height of the paper, in units of 1/72 inch. A standard 8.5" by 11" piece of paper in portrait orientation will have a width and height of 612 and 792, respectively, as returned from these methods.

The imageable area is the rectangle on which the printer can print. The following methods return values that describe the imageable area rectangle:

public double getImageableX()
public double getImageableY()
public double getImageableWidth()
public double getImageableHeight()
> These methods return the origin, width, and height of this `PageFormat`'s imageable area. These values are also returned in units of 1/72 inch.

Let's modify our original example to take advantage of this new information. The new example draws a rectangle around the imageable area:

```java
import java.awt.*;
import java.awt.geom.*;
import java.awt.print.*;

public class OutlineImageableArea {
  public static void main(String[] args) {
    PrinterJob pj = PrinterJob.getPrinterJob();
    pj.setPrintable(new OutlinePrintable());
    if (pj.printDialog()) {
      try { pj.print(); }
      catch (PrinterException e) {
        System.out.println(e);
      }
    }
  }
}

class OutlinePrintable
    implements Printable {
  public int print(Graphics g, PageFormat pf, int pageIndex) {
    if (pageIndex != 0) return NO_SUCH_PAGE;
    Graphics2D g2 = (Graphics2D)g;
    Rectangle2D outline = new Rectangle2D.Double(
        pf.getImageableX(), pf.getImageableY(),
        pf.getImageableWidth(), pf.getImageableHeight());
    g2.setPaint(Color.black);
    g2.draw(outline);
    return PAGE_EXISTS;
  }
}
```

Any rendering that you do outside the imageable area of the page will be clipped.

You can set the orientation of a `PageFormat` with the following method:

public void setOrientation(int orientation) throws IllegalArgumentException

> Use this method to change the orientation of this `PageFormat`. The orientation parameter should be `PORTRAIT`, `LANDSCAPE`, or `REVERSE_LANDSCAPE`. If you pass any other value, an `IllegalArgumentException` is thrown.

If you want to use a paper size other than the default, you'll need the following method. The `Paper` class is discussed in the following section.

public void setPaper(Paper paper)

> Use this method to set the paper size and imageable area. Normally, you won't ever need to call this method from your application. Users choose the paper

size from the printing or page setup dialogs. Usually, your application has to deal with the paper size but doesn't choose it.

The Paper Class

The `PageFormat` class, as you've seen, describes a piece of paper and its orientation. `PageFormat` uses a simpler class, `java.awt.print.Paper`, to represent the paper itself. If you want to define your own paper sizes, you'll have to create your own `Paper` instances. If you just want your users to be able to choose different page sizes, they can use the page setup dialog to do that. (I'll talk about the page setup dialog later in this chapter.)

To programmatically create a `Paper` object, use the following constructor:

public Paper()
> This constructor creates a default-sized `Paper`, 8.5" by 11". The imageable area is 6.5" by 9" with 1" margins on all sides.

To change the imageable area or the size of the paper, use the following methods:

public void setSize(double width, double height)
> This method sets the paper size in units of 1/72 inch.

public void setImageableArea(double x, double y, double width, double height)
> This method sets the imageable origin, width, and height for this `Paper`.

Controlling Printing

The `PrinterJob` class is the boss of the printing process. As you've seen, you can obtain an instance of `PrinterJob` with the following factory method:

public static PrinterJob getPrinterJob()
> This method returns a `PrinterJob` instance. You can use this `PrinterJob` to show a print dialog and a page setup dialog, and to start and cancel a print job.

PrinterJob Basics

There are two essential steps to using a `PrinterJob`. You have to give it something to print, and you have to tell it to start printing.

The "something to print" may be a `Printable`, as you saw in the examples above:

public abstract void setPrintable(Printable painter)
> This method sets this `PrinterJob` to print the supplied object.

public abstract void setPrintable(Printable painter, PageFormat format)
> Use this method to supply a `Printable` and an associated `PageFormat` to the `PrinterJob`.

`PrinterJob` also knows how to print instances of `Printable`'s more capable cousin, `java.awt.print.Pageable`. But don't be confused—`Pageable` is really just a container for `Printable` objects anyhow. I'll talk about the `Pageable` interface later in this chapter. This method gives a `PrinterJob` a `Pageable` object to print:

public abstract void setPageable(Pageable document)
> This method tells this `PrinterJob` to print the supplied `Pageable`.

Once the `PrinterJob` knows what it's supposed to print, you just need to kick off the job:

public abstract void print() throws PrinterException
> This method begins the printer job. This method does not return until the entire job has been queued to the printer in your operating system.

NOTE   There are two methods named `print()`. The first, in the `Printable` interface, is a method that renders a single page on a printer. It is called by the Printing API; you will probably never have to call it yourself. The second `print()` method, in the `PrinterJob` class, is used to start a printing job. You must call it explicitly to begin the printing process. Eventually, the `print()` method in `PrinterJob` will end up calling the `print()` method in `Printable`, but you don't have to worry about exactly how this happens.

If you need to stop a print job for any reason, call the `cancel()` method:

public abstract void cancel()
> This method cancels a print job in progress. You can cancel a job only between the time that `print()` is called and when it returns. Therefore, if you want to call `cancel()`, you'll have to do it from another thread. The job may not be canceled immediately; the documentation merely states that the job will be canceled as soon as possible.

Print jobs have a name. This name may allow a user to identify a print job in printing queues displayed by the operating system. You can retrieve the print job's name or set it as follows:

public abstract String getJobName()
> This method returns the name of this `PrinterJob`.

public abstract void setJobName(String jobName)
> Use this method to set the name of the print job.

A `PrinterJob` can also supply you with a default `PageFormat`:

public PageFormat defaultPage()
> This method returns the default `PageFormat` for this `PrinterJob`.

Showing Dialogs (or Not!)

To show the familiar print dialog, use the following method:

public abstract boolean printDialog()
> This method displays the print dialog for this `PrinterJob`. Using this dialog, you can change the printer that will be used, the number of copies, the page range that will be printed, and other parameters. This method returns `true` if the user clicked on the **OK** button to leave the dialog and `false` otherwise. Note that after this method returns, you don't have to do anything to retrieve the parameters the user selected. The `PrinterJob` is automatically updated with the user's selections.

You can also show a standard page setup dialog:

public abstract PageFormat pageDialog(PageFormat page)
> This method shows a page setup dialog using the underlying operating system. It uses the supplied `PageFormat` to initialize the controls in the dialog. If the user clicks **OK** in the dialog, a new `PageFormat` containing the appropriate parameters is returned. Otherwise, the original `PageFormat` will be returned.

Figure 13-4 shows a page setup dialog in Windows.

It is possible to print something without showing any dialogs whatsoever. This sneaky technique is called *silent printing*. Except for some specific applications, it's not a good idea to print something without letting the user know about it. If you really want to print silently, however, you can just set up a `PrinterJob` and call `print()`. The job will be sent to the user's default printer.

The following example pulls together a few of the things you've been learning recently. It demonstrates how to change the imageable area of your paper using the `setPaper()` method of `PageFormat`:

```
import java.awt.*;
import java.awt.geom.*;
import java.awt.print.*;

public class PageFormatMania {
  public static void main(String[] args) {
    PrinterJob pj = PrinterJob.getPrinterJob();

    PageFormat pf = pj.defaultPage();
    Paper paper = new Paper();
```

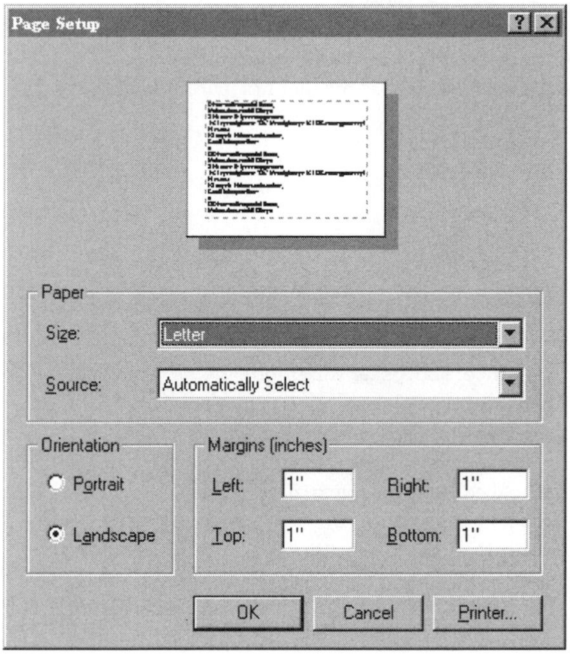

Figure 13-4. The page setup dialog in Windows

```
      double margin = 36; // half inch
      paper.setImageableArea(margin, margin,
          paper.getWidth() - margin * 2,
          paper.getHeight() - margin * 2);
      pf.setPaper(paper);

      pj.setPrintable(new ManiaPrintable(), pf);
      if (pj.printDialog()) {
        try { pj.print(); }
        catch (PrinterException e) {
          System.out.println(e);
        }
      }
    }
  }

class ManiaPrintable
    implements Printable {
  public int print(Graphics g, PageFormat pf, int pageIndex) {
    if (pageIndex != 0) return NO_SUCH_PAGE;
    Graphics2D g2 = (Graphics2D)g;
    g2.setFont(new Font("Serif", Font.PLAIN, 36));
```

```
      g2.setPaint(Color.black);
      g2.drawString("ManiaPrintable", 100, 100);
      Rectangle2D outline = new Rectangle2D.Double(
          pf.getImageableX(), pf.getImageableY(),
          pf.getImageableWidth(), pf.getImageableHeight());
      g2.draw(outline);
      return PAGE_EXISTS;
    }
  }
```

This example uses a custom `Paper` with an imageable area that is 1/2-inch from each side of the page. It uses this `Paper` in a `PageFormat` by calling the `setPaper()` method:

```
PrinterJob pj = PrinterJob.getPrinterJob();
PageFormat pf = pj.defaultPage();
Paper paper = new Paper();
double margin = 36; // half inch
paper.setImageableArea(margin, margin,
    paper.getWidth() - margin * 2,
    paper.getHeight() - margin * 2);
pf.setPaper(paper);
```

When it's time to print, the `PageFormat` is passed to `PrinterJob`'s `setPrintable()` method:

```
pj.setPrintable(new ManiaPrintable(), pf);
```

The printing proceeds as usual, except that the custom `Paper` is used.

Power Printing

In this section, I'll cover two important printing topics:

Integrating printing into an existing application

I'll show how to add printing support to a simple Swing application. Along the way, I'll develop a simple class that can print any screen component.[*]

Printing more than one page

If you know that all the pages you'll print have the same `PageFormat`, you can use the `Printable` interface to print more than one page. If your needs are more sophisticated, the `java.awt.print.Pageable` interface keeps track of multiple pairs of `PageFormats` and `Printables`. It can be used to associate a different `PageFormat` with each page of a print job. The `java.awt.print.Book` class is a convenient implementation of the `Pageable` interface.

---

[*] Well, it prints any screen component that defines a `paint()` method. Heavyweight components cannot be printed this way.

Printing User Interface Components

The Printing API makes it easy to add printing capabilities to an existing application. After all, the `print()` method in the `Printable` interface can easily call the `paint()` method of a user interface component.

It's so simple that it can be done in 36 lines of code:

```
import java.awt.*;
import java.awt.print.*;

import javax.swing.JComponent;

public class ComponentPrintable
    implements Printable {
  private Component mComponent;

  public ComponentPrintable(Component c) {
    mComponent = c;
  }

  public int print(Graphics g, PageFormat pageFormat, int pageIndex) {
    if (pageIndex > 0) return NO_SUCH_PAGE;
    Graphics2D g2 = (Graphics2D)g;
    g2.translate(pageFormat.getImageableX(), pageFormat.getImageableY());
    boolean wasBuffered = disableDoubleBuffering(mComponent);
    mComponent.paint(g2);
    restoreDoubleBuffering(mComponent, wasBuffered);
    return PAGE_EXISTS;
  }

  private boolean disableDoubleBuffering(Component c) {
    if (c instanceof JComponent == false) return false;
    JComponent jc = (JComponent)c;
    boolean wasBuffered = jc.isDoubleBuffered();
    jc.setDoubleBuffered(false);
    return wasBuffered;
  }

  private void restoreDoubleBuffering(Component c, boolean wasBuffered) {
    if (c instanceof JComponent)
      ((JComponent)c).setDoubleBuffered(wasBuffered);
  }
}
```

This class wraps an existing `Component` and implements the `Printable` interface. When asked to print, this class simply translates the `Graphics2D`'s origin to the imageable area of the page and renders the component:

```
g2.translate(pageFormat.getImageableX(), pageFormat.getImageableY());
// ...
mComponent.paint(g2);
```

But there's a catch. Swing containers automatically implement double buffering, a technique that is described in Chapter 9, *Images*. A double buffered component draws its contents into an offscreen image; then the offscreen image is rendered on the screen. This is a nice technique for reducing flicker in animations or user interface components; however, it has a very undesirable effect on printing. The problem is that the offscreen image that is used for double buffering has the same resolution as the screen, typically 72 dots per inch (dpi). If you attempt to print a Swing component on a higher-resolution device (like a 300 dpi laser printer), the 72 dpi offscreen image will be rendered on the device. The end result is that your 300 dpi or 600 dpi printer will carefully render a 72 dpi image. The extra resolution of the printer will be wasted.

Fortunately, there's a way around this dilemma. It's possible to disable double buffering in Swing components. You should do this before you attempt to print them. With double buffering disabled, the Swing component will draw directly to the printer, taking full advantage of the printer's resolution. In the `Component-Printable` class, the `disableDoubleBuffering()` and `restoreDouble-Buffering()` methods take care of this.

How would you use such a class? Let's look at a very simple Swing application, called `SwingPrinter`.[*] This application consists of a `JFrame`, which contains a component that does some fancy drawing. The frame also contains a menu with **Print** and **Page setup** items. When the user chooses to print, a `Component-Printable` is wrapped around the frame's contents and printed:

```java
import java.awt.*;
import java.awt.event.*;
import java.awt.print.*;

import javax.swing.*;
import javax.swing.event.*;

public class SwingPrinter
    extends JFrame {
  public static void main(String[] args) {
    new SwingPrinter();
  }

  private PageFormat mPageFormat;
```

---

[*] For more information on Swing programming, see *Java Swing*, by Bob Eckstein, Marc Loy, and Dave Wood (O'Reilly).

```
public SwingPrinter() {
  super("SwingPrinter v1.0");
  createUI();
  PrinterJob pj = PrinterJob.getPrinterJob();
  mPageFormat = pj.defaultPage();
  setVisible(true);
}

protected void createUI() {
  setSize(300, 300);
  center();

  // Add the menu bar.
  JMenuBar mb = new JMenuBar();
  JMenu file = new JMenu("File", true);
  file.add(new FilePrintAction()).setAccelerator(
      KeyStroke.getKeyStroke(KeyEvent.VK_P, Event.CTRL_MASK));
  file.add(new FilePageSetupAction()).setAccelerator(
      KeyStroke.getKeyStroke(KeyEvent.VK_P,
          Event.CTRL_MASK | Event.SHIFT_MASK));
  file.addSeparator();
  file.add(new FileQuitAction()).setAccelerator(
      KeyStroke.getKeyStroke(KeyEvent.VK_Q, Event.CTRL_MASK));
  mb.add(file);
  setJMenuBar(mb);

  // Add the contents of the window.
  getContentPane().add(new PatchworkComponent());

  // Exit the application when the window is closed.
  addWindowListener(new WindowAdapter() {
    public void windowClosing(WindowEvent e) {
      System.exit(0);
    }
  });
}

protected void center() {
  Dimension screen = Toolkit.getDefaultToolkit().getScreenSize();
  Dimension us = getSize();
  int x = (screen.width - us.width) / 2;
  int y = (screen.height - us.height) / 2;
  setLocation(x, y);
}

public class FilePrintAction
    extends AbstractAction {
  public FilePrintAction() { super("Print"); }
  public void actionPerformed(ActionEvent ae) {
```

```
        PrinterJob pj = PrinterJob.getPrinterJob();
        ComponentPrintable cp = new ComponentPrintable(getContentPane());
        pj.setPrintable(cp, mPageFormat);
        if (pj.printDialog()) {
          try { pj.print(); }
          catch (PrinterException e) {
            System.out.println(e);
          }
        }
      }
    }

    public class FilePageSetupAction
        extends AbstractAction {
      public FilePageSetupAction() { super("Page setup..."); }
      public void actionPerformed(ActionEvent ae) {
        PrinterJob pj = PrinterJob.getPrinterJob();
        mPageFormat = pj.pageDialog(mPageFormat);
      }
    }

    public class FileQuitAction
        extends AbstractAction {
      public FileQuitAction() { super("Quit"); }
      public void actionPerformed(ActionEvent ae) {
        System.exit(0);
      }
    }
  }
```

Let's take a closer look at the interesting parts of this example. SwingPrinter
stores a PageFormat as a member variable called mPageFormat. This variable is
initialized with a default page setup in SwingPrinter's constructor:

```
PrinterJob pj = PrinterJob.getPrinterJob();
mPageFormat = pj.defaultPage();
```

If the user chooses the **Page setup** menu item, mPageFormat will be modified by
the page setup dialog. This is buried in the FilePageSetupAction inner class:

```
PrinterJob pj = PrinterJob.getPrinterJob();
mPageFormat = pj.pageDialog(mPageFormat);
```

Finally, SwingPrinter uses the stored page format when printing actually takes
place, in the FilePrintAction inner class:

```
PrinterJob pj = PrinterJob.getPrinterJob();
ComponentPrintable cp = new ComponentPrintable(getContentPane());
pj.setPrintable(cp, mPageFormat);
```

Notice how the ComponentPrintable is used here. It is simply wrapped around
the frame's content pane and passed to the PrinterJob.

To run this example, you'll need the `PatchworkComponent` class, which renders some visually interesting stuff. You could use any component; this one renders some gradient-filled rectangles and text:

```java
import java.awt.*;
import java.awt.font.*;
import java.awt.geom.*;
import java.awt.print.*;

import javax.swing.*;

public class PatchworkComponent
    extends JComponent
    implements Printable {

  private float mSide = 36;
  private float mOffset = 36;
  private int mColumns = 8;
  private int mRows = 4;
  private String mString = "Captivated";
  private Font mFont = new Font("Serif", Font.PLAIN, 64);

  private Paint mHorizontalGradient, mVerticalGradient;

  public PatchworkComponent() {
    float x = mOffset;
    float y = mOffset;
    float halfSide = mSide / 2;
    float x0 = x + halfSide;
    float y0 = y;
    float x1 = x + halfSide;
    float y1 = y + (mRows * mSide);
    mVerticalGradient = new GradientPaint(
      x0, y0, Color.darkGray, x1, y1, Color.lightGray, true);
    x0 = x;
    y0 = y + halfSide;
    x1 = x + (mColumns * mSide);
    y1 = y + halfSide;
    mHorizontalGradient = new GradientPaint(
      x0, y0, Color.darkGray, x1, y1, Color.lightGray, true);
  }

  public PatchworkComponent(String s) { this(); mString = s; }

  public void paintComponent(Graphics g) {
    Graphics2D g2 = (Graphics2D)g;

    g2.rotate(Math.PI / 24, mOffset, mOffset);

    for (int row = 0; row < mRows; row++) {
```

```
      for (int column = 0; column < mColumns; column++) {
        float x = column * mSide + mOffset;
        float y = row * mSide + mOffset;

        if (((column + row) % 2) == 0) g2.setPaint(mVerticalGradient);
        else g2.setPaint(mHorizontalGradient);

        Rectangle2D r = new Rectangle2D.Float(x, y, mSide, mSide);
        g2.fill(r);
      }
    }

    FontRenderContext frc = g2.getFontRenderContext();
    float width = (float)mFont.getStringBounds(mString, frc).getWidth();
    LineMetrics lm = mFont.getLineMetrics(mString, frc);
    float x = ((mColumns * mSide) - width) / 2 + mOffset;
    float y = ((mRows * mSide) + lm.getAscent()) / 2 + mOffset;
    g2.setFont(mFont);
    g2.setPaint(Color.white);
    g2.drawString(mString, x, y);
  }

  public int print(Graphics g, PageFormat pageFormat, int pageIndex) {
    if (pageIndex != 0) return NO_SUCH_PAGE;
    paintComponent(g);
    return PAGE_EXISTS;
  }
}
```

Figure 13-5 shows the SwingPrinter example in action.

It's just as simple to print user interface components. In the last example, PatchworkComponent did all the rendering. What if, instead of Patchwork-Component, the frame window contained some user interface elements, like radio buttons and combo boxes?

To see how this works, remove the following line in the createUI() method of SwingPrinter:

```
getContentPane().add(new PatchworkComponent());
```

Replace it with the following:

```
JPanel panel = new JPanel();
JButton printButton = new JButton("Print");
panel.add(printButton);
panel.add(new JList(new Object[] { "One", "Two", "Three" }));
panel.add(new JButton("Push me"));
panel.add(new JCheckBox("Chess", true));
panel.add(new JComboBox(new Object[] { "Eins", "Zwei", "Drei" }));
setContentPane(panel);
```

Figure 13-5. A Swing application that prints

That's all there is to it! This time, the `SwingPrinter` frame window looks like Figure 13-6. Printing is just as simple as before.

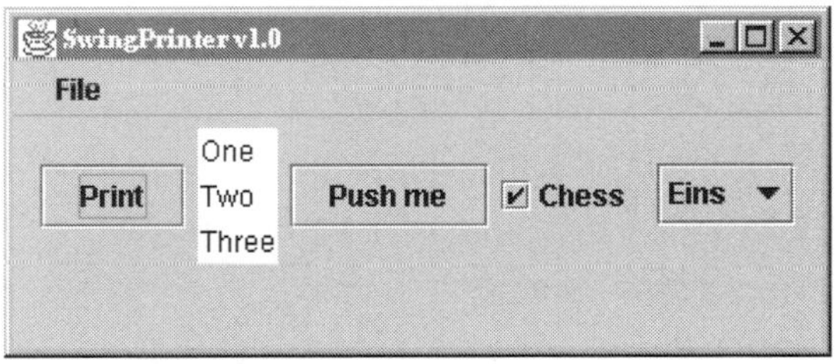

Figure 13-6. Printing Swing components is just as easy

NOTE This technique won't work for AWT components. The reason has to do with *lightweight* and *heavyweight* components. The old AWT components were all heavyweight, which means that they had *peers*, or counterparts, in the native windowing system. The native windowing system was responsible for rendering these components on the screen. If you call the `paint()` method of heavyweight components, it may not do anything. By contrast, Swing components are all lightweight, which means they have no native counterpart and must render themselves. Whenever you call `paint()` on a lightweight component, you're sure to get a representation of the component.

Printing Multiple Pages

In the real world, printing jobs usually span more than one page. The Printing API offers two ways to handle printing on multiple pages. The first solution is based on `Printable`. This section includes an example that demonstrates this technique. The other solution uses the `Pageable` interface, which serves as a container for `Printables`. I'll talk about `Pageable` in the next section.

A `Printable`'s `print()` method is called every time the Printing API wants to print a new page. The Printing API doesn't know in advance how many pages will be printed. It just blindly calls the `print()` until the return value is NO_SUCH_PAGE. In the previous examples in this chapter, the `print()` methods return NO_SUCH_PAGE for every page except the very first. Thus, these examples only print out one page.

Printing multiple pages can be a little tricky. Your application needs to be savvy about what gets rendered on each page. The following example demonstrates how to handle multiple pages with a single `Printable` instance. It lists the contents of a file. The example is divided into two pieces:

FilePrinter

> This `JFrame` subclass runs the application. It has a menu that you can use to load a file, print the file, or change the page setup. You can also view different pages of a file, just as they will appear when they are printed. Figure C-29 shows a snapshot of this class as it is running.

FilePageRenderer

> This class renders a page of a file, either on the screen or on the printer. It reads the entire file into memory and figures out how the file should be paginated.

The `FilePrinter` application is mostly concerned with the details of being a nice Swing application. It's an expanded version of the `SwingPrinter` class that's presented above. The `FilePrintAction` and `FilePageSetupAction` inner classes should look very familiar.

`FilePrinter` keeps track of a `FilePageRenderer` in an instance variable called `mPageRenderer`. This object is responsible for displaying a page on the screen or on the printer. When you choose the **Next page** or **Previous page** menu items, `FilePrinter` notifies its `FilePageRenderer` to change the current page. `FilePrinter` shows the name of the file and the current page in the title bar of its frame window.

Here's the code for the `FilePrinter` class:

```
import java.awt.*;
import java.awt.event.*;
```

```java
import java.awt.print.*;

import javax.swing.*;
import javax.swing.event.*;

public class FilePrinter
    extends JFrame {
  public static void main(String[] args) {
    new FilePrinter();
  }

  private PageFormat mPageFormat;
  private FilePageRenderer mPageRenderer;
  private String mTitle;

  public FilePrinter() {
    super("FilePrinter v1.0");
    createUI();
    PrinterJob pj = PrinterJob.getPrinterJob();
    mPageFormat = pj.defaultPage();
    setVisible(true);
  }

  protected void createUI() {
    setSize(350, 300);
    center();
    Container content = getContentPane();
    content.setLayout(new BorderLayout());

    // Add the menu bar.
    JMenuBar mb = new JMenuBar();
    JMenu file = new JMenu("File", true);
    file.add(new FileOpenAction()).setAccelerator(
        KeyStroke.getKeyStroke(KeyEvent.VK_O, Event.CTRL_MASK));
    file.add(new FilePrintAction()).setAccelerator(
        KeyStroke.getKeyStroke(KeyEvent.VK_P, Event.CTRL_MASK));
    file.add(new FilePageSetupAction()).setAccelerator(
        KeyStroke.getKeyStroke(KeyEvent.VK_P,
            Event.CTRL_MASK | Event.SHIFT_MASK));
    file.addSeparator();
    file.add(new FileQuitAction()).setAccelerator(
        KeyStroke.getKeyStroke(KeyEvent.VK_Q, Event.CTRL_MASK));
    mb.add(file);
    JMenu page = new JMenu("Page", true);
    page.add(new PageNextPageAction()).setAccelerator(
        KeyStroke.getKeyStroke(KeyEvent.VK_PAGE_DOWN, 0));
    page.add(new PagePreviousPageAction()).setAccelerator(
        KeyStroke.getKeyStroke(KeyEvent.VK_PAGE_UP, 0));
    mb.add(page);
```

```
      setJMenuBar(mb);

    // Add the contents of the window.
    getContentPane().setLayout(new BorderLayout());

    // Exit the application when the window is closed.
    addWindowListener(new WindowAdapter() {
      public void windowClosing(WindowEvent e) {
        System.exit(0);
      }
    });
  }

  protected void center() {
    Dimension screenSize = Toolkit.getDefaultToolkit().getScreenSize();
    Dimension frameSize = getSize();
    int x = (screenSize.width - frameSize.width) / 2;
    int y = (screenSize.height - frameSize.height) / 2;
    setLocation(x, y);
  }

  public void showTitle() {
    int currentPage = mPageRenderer.getCurrentPage() + 1;
    int numPages = mPageRenderer.getNumPages();
    setTitle(mTitle + " - page " + currentPage + " of " + numPages);
  }

  public class FileOpenAction
      extends AbstractAction {
    public FileOpenAction() { super("Open..."); }
    public void actionPerformed(ActionEvent ae) {
      // Pop up a file dialog.
      JFileChooser fc = new JFileChooser(".");
      int result = fc.showOpenDialog(FilePrinter.this);
      if (result != 0) { return; }
      java.io.File f = fc.getSelectedFile();
      if (f == null) { return; }
      // Load the specified file.
      try {
        mPageRenderer = new FilePageRenderer(f, mPageFormat);
        mTitle = "[" + f.getName() + "]";
        showTitle();
        JScrollPane jsp = new JScrollPane(mPageRenderer);
        getContentPane().removeAll();
        getContentPane().add(jsp, BorderLayout.CENTER);
        validate();
      }
      catch (java.io.IOException ioe) {
        System.out.println(ioe);
```

```
      }
    }
  }

  public class FilePrintAction
      extends AbstractAction {
    public FilePrintAction() { super("Print"); }
    public void actionPerformed(ActionEvent ae) {
      PrinterJob pj = PrinterJob.getPrinterJob();
      pj.setPrintable(mPageRenderer, mPageFormat);
      if (pj.printDialog()) {
        try { pj.print(); }
        catch (PrinterException e) {
          System.out.println(e);
        }
      }
    }
  }

  public class FilePageSetupAction
      extends AbstractAction {
    public FilePageSetupAction() { super("Page setup..."); }
    public void actionPerformed(ActionEvent ae) {
      PrinterJob pj = PrinterJob.getPrinterJob();
      mPageFormat = pj.pageDialog(mPageFormat);
      if (mPageRenderer != null) {
        mPageRenderer.paginate(mPageFormat);
        showTitle();
      }
    }
  }

  public class FileQuitAction
      extends AbstractAction {
    public FileQuitAction() { super("Quit"); }
    public void actionPerformed(ActionEvent ae) {
      System.exit(0);
    }
  }

  public class PageNextPageAction
      extends AbstractAction {
    public PageNextPageAction() { super("Next page"); }
    public void actionPerformed(ActionEvent ae) {
      if (mPageRenderer != null) mPageRenderer.nextPage();
      showTitle();
    }
  }
```

```
     public class PagePreviousPageAction
         extends AbstractAction {
       public PagePreviousPageAction() { super("Previous page"); }
       public void actionPerformed(ActionEvent ae) {
         if (mPageRenderer != null) mPageRenderer.previousPage();
         showTitle();
       }
     }
   }
```

The `FilePageRenderer` class does the work of rendering each page. It's a subclass of `JComponent` that also implements the `Printable` interface. The `paint()` method does all of the page rendering. The `print()` method adjusts the origin of the `Graphics2D` to coincide with the paper's imageable area and then calls `paint()` to render the page.

A `FilePageRenderer` is created with a `File` and a `PageFormat`. It initializes itself in two steps:

1. The entire file is read, line by line. The lines are stored in a `Vector` member variable, `mLines`.

2. The `FilePageRenderer` paginates itself using the supplied `PageFormat`. It goes through the `mLines` vector and figures out how many lines will fit on each page. Each page is stored as a `Vector` of `Strings`. The pages themselves are stored in a `Vector` called `mPages`. This algorithm is contained in the `paginate()` method.

If the current `PageFormat` changes (i.e., if the user chooses the **Page setup** menu item), the `FilePageRenderer` can be repaginated with another call to `paginate()`.

To render a single page, `FilePageRenderer` simply looks in `mPages` to find the current page. Then it renders all of the strings for the current page, not really caring whether it's rendering to the screen or the printer. Here's an example:

```
import java.awt.*;
import java.awt.print.*;
import java.io.*;
import java.util.Vector;

import javax.swing.*;

public class FilePageRenderer
    extends JComponent
    implements Printable {
  private int mCurrentPage;
  // mLines contains all the lines of the file.
  private Vector mLines;
```

```
// mPages is a Vector of Vectors. Each of its elements
//   represents a single page. Each of its elements is
//   a Vector containing Strings that are the lines for
//   a particular page.
private Vector mPages;
private Font mFont;
private int mFontSize;
private Dimension mPreferredSize;

public FilePageRenderer(File file, PageFormat pageFormat)
    throws IOException {
  mFontSize = 12;
  mFont = new Font("Serif", Font.PLAIN, mFontSize);
  // Open the file.
  BufferedReader in = new BufferedReader(
      new FileReader(file));
  // Read all the lines.
  String line;
  mLines = new Vector();
  while ((line = in.readLine()) != null)
    mLines.addElement(line);
  // Clean up.
  in.close();
  // Now paginate, based on the PageFormat.
  paginate(pageFormat);
}

public void paginate(PageFormat pageFormat) {
  mCurrentPage = 0;
  mPages = new Vector();
  float y = mFontSize;
  Vector page = new Vector();
  for (int i = 0; i < mLines.size(); i++) {
    String line = (String)mLines.elementAt(i);
    page.addElement(line);
    y += mFontSize;
    if (y + mFontSize * 2 > pageFormat.getImageableHeight()) {
      y = 0;
      mPages.addElement(page);
      page = new Vector();
    }
  }
  // Add the last page.
  if (page.size() > 0) mPages.addElement(page);
  // Set our preferred size based on the PageFormat.
  mPreferredSize = new Dimension((int)pageFormat.getImageableWidth(),
      (int)pageFormat.getImageableHeight());
  repaint();
}
```

```java
  public void paintComponent(Graphics g) {
    Graphics2D g2 = (Graphics2D)g;
    // Make the background white.
    java.awt.geom.Rectangle2D r = new java.awt.geom.Rectangle2D.Float(0, 0,
        mPreferredSize.width, mPreferredSize.height);
    g2.setPaint(Color.white);
    g2.fill(r);
    // Get the current page.
    Vector page = (Vector)mPages.elementAt(mCurrentPage);
    // Draw all the lines for this page.
    g2.setFont(mFont);
    g2.setPaint(Color.black);
    float x = 0;
    float y = mFontSize;
    for (int i = 0; i < page.size(); i++) {
      String line = (String)page.elementAt(i);
      if (line.length() > 0) g2.drawString(line, (int)x, (int)y);
      y += mFontSize;
    }
  }

  public int print(Graphics g, PageFormat pageFormat, int pageIndex) {
    if (pageIndex >= mPages.size()) return NO_SUCH_PAGE;
    int savedPage = mCurrentPage;
    mCurrentPage = pageIndex;
    Graphics2D g2 = (Graphics2D)g;
    g2.translate(pageFormat.getImageableX(), pageFormat.getImageableY());
    paint(g2);
    mCurrentPage = savedPage;
    return PAGE_EXISTS;
  }

  public Dimension getPreferredSize() { return mPreferredSize; }

  public int getCurrentPage() { return mCurrentPage; }
  public int getNumPages() { return mPages.size(); }

  public void nextPage() {
    if (mCurrentPage < mPages.size() - 1)
      mCurrentPage++;
    repaint();
  }

  public void previousPage() {
    if (mCurrentPage > 0)
      mCurrentPage--;
    repaint();
  }
}
```

WARNING   The initial release of Java 2 (JDK 1.2) contains printing bugs in
             Graphics2D's `drawString()` methods. Specifically, the `draw-`
             `String(String, float, float)` and `drawString(Attributed-`
             `CharacterIterator, float, float)` methods do not work when
             printing. These bugs are fixed in JDK 1.2.1. If `FilePrinter` doesn't
             work the first time you try, make sure you're running JDK 1.2.1.

Advanced Page Control

You can use `Printable` to print as many pages as you want, but they all will have
the same page setup. In complex documents, you may want to mix different paper
orientations and sizes. To accomplish this, you need the `java.awt.print.`
`Pageable` interface. This interface specifies a way to associate a `PageFormat` and a
`Printable` with each page of a print job. Most likely, you will use the `java.awt.`
`print.Book` class, which implements the `Pageable` interface. `Pageable` defines
three simple methods:

public int getNumberOfPages()
> This method returns the total number of pages in this `Pageable`.

public PageFormat getPageFormat(int pageIndex)
> This method returns the `PageFormat` that corresponds to the given page.

public Printable getPrintable(int pageIndex)
> This method returns the `Printable` that should be used to render the given
> page.

The `Book` class supports the three methods described above and adds three more:

public void append(Printable painter, PageFormat page)
> This method adds a single page to the end of this `Book`. The page will have the
> given `PageFormat` and be rendered using the supplied `Printable`.

public void append(Printable painter, PageFormat page, int numPages)
> This method adds `numPages` new pages to the end of this `Book`. Each of the
> new pages will use the supplied `Printable` and `PageFormat`.

public void setPage(int pageIndex, Printable painter, PageFormat page)
> Use this method to change an existing page in this `Book`. The page will use the
> supplied `Printable` and `PageFormat`.

The following example shows how to use a `Book`. It uses the `Patchwork-`
`Component` from earlier in this chapter. Two of these components are created and
wrapped with `BookComponentPrintable` instances. The `BookComponent-`
`Printable` class is just like the `ComponentPrintable` presented earlier, with one
important difference. While the `ComponentPrintable` class was only designed to

print the first page of a print job, BookComponentPrintable is capable of printing any page. Thus, its print() method never returns NO_SUCH_PAGE.

The other important thing to notice is that instead of calling setPrintable() on the PrinterJob, this example creates a Book and passes it to the setPageable() method.

When you run this example, you should get two pages of output. The first page is in portrait orientation and contains the string "printable1," while the second page is in landscape orientation with the string "printable2."

```java
import java.awt.*;
import java.awt.print.*;

public class Booker {
  public static void main(String[] args) {
    PrinterJob pj = PrinterJob.getPrinterJob();
    // Create two Printables.
    Component c1 = new PatchworkComponent("printable1");
    Component c2 = new PatchworkComponent("printable2");
    c1.setSize(500, 400);
    c2.setSize(500, 400);
    BookComponentPrintable printable1 = new BookComponentPrintable(c1);
    BookComponentPrintable printable2 = new BookComponentPrintable(c2);
    // Create two PageFormats.
    PageFormat pageFormat1 = pj.defaultPage();
    PageFormat pageFormat2 = (PageFormat)pageFormat1.clone();
    pageFormat2.setOrientation(PageFormat.LANDSCAPE);
    // Create a Book.
    Book book = new Book();
    book.append(printable1, pageFormat1);
    book.append(printable2, pageFormat2);
    // Print the Book.
    pj.setPageable(book);
    if (pj.printDialog()) {
      try { pj.print(); }
      catch (PrinterException e) {
        System.out.println(e);
      }
    }
  }
}

class BookComponentPrintable
    implements Printable {
  private Component mComponent;

  public BookComponentPrintable(Component c) {
    mComponent = c;
  }
```

```
public int print(Graphics g, PageFormat pageFormat, int pageIndex) {
  Graphics2D g2 = (Graphics2D)g;
  g2.translate(pageFormat.getImageableX(), pageFormat.getImageableY());
  mComponent.paint(g2);
  return PAGE_EXISTS;
}
}
```

14

In this chapter:
• *It's Tougher Than You Might Think*
• *See for Yourself*
• *Memory*
• *Optimizations*

Animation and Performance

Performance is a term that refers to how fast an application runs. If someone says that an application has "performance issues," it means the application is too slow. Computer chips double in speed every eighteen months or so, but software increases proportionately in size and complexity. There's a lot of stuff between your application and the silicon. If you're a Java developer, there's an extra layer—the Java Virtual Machine (JVM). All developers, and especially Java developers, have to be careful to make sure that their applications run fast enough to be useful.

What does this have to do with the 2D API? Many developers have expressed interest in using the 2D API in animations, where each frame of the animation is generated on the fly. While the 2D API wasn't designed specifically for animation, it can be used in this way.

This chapter includes a flexible framework for building animation applications. It also includes three applications, built from the framework, that allow you to examine the effects of various 2D operations on the animation rate.

It's Tougher Than You Might Think

Whether 2D can render frames at a smooth animation rate depends on many factors, including the following:

*   the application itself
*   the JVM implementation
*   the 2D API implementation, which may vary in different JDK releases
*   the operating system
*   the operating system configuration

- the display hardware (i.e. a video card)
- the system processor speed
- the system bus speed
- available memory

To make things more complicated, the 2D API may perform different operations depending on the display hardware and software that's available.

Finally, the initial release of the 2D API may not be particularly fast. Sun was concentrating hard on getting the API design correct, which means they weren't worrying as much about fixing bugs or making it run fast. Subsequent releases of the JDK should get better and better. And the elusive vaporware called HotSpot is supposed to improve performance dramatically some time in the Java 2 era. See *http://java.sun.com/products/hotspot/* for more information.

The bottom line is that it's extremely difficult to pin down exactly what will make an application run quickly or slowly. As you read this chapter, keep your wits about you. Performance analysis and tuning is as much an art as a science. A healthy dose of common sense will take you a long way.

There are tools that will help you analyze your application to find out what parts take the most time. These are called *profilers*. But as of this writing, profilers aren't available for the Java 2 platform yet.

See for Yourself

To see the effect of 2D operations on animation speeds, let's develop an animation application framework. Through the rest of the chapter, I'll develop classes that plug in to this framework to perform animation.

The framework is composed of two classes, `AnimationComponent` and `AnimationFrame`. `AnimationFrame` serves as a container for `Animation-Component` and displays the current animation rate.

AnimationComponent

The `AnimationComponent` class is an abstract subclass of `java.awt.Component`. It contains one additional method, `timeStep()`, that is called every time the animation should be moved ahead by a single frame. Creating a subclass of `AnimationComponent` is as simple as defining two methods:

public void timeStep()

> This method is called before every frame of the animation. Your subclass should update its internal state appropriately. For a bouncing ball animation, for example, this method might update the position of the ball.

public void paint(Graphics g)

This is the `paint()` method defined in `Component`. This method should render the component's current state. For the bouncing ball animation, this method should draw the ball in its current location.

`AnimationComponent` is a `Runnable`, which means it can be placed in its own thread. The `run()` method is a tight loop that renders the current frame (by calling `render()`) and prepares for the next frame (by calling `timeStep()`). It also calculates a frame rate. I'll explain how that works a little later.

```
public void run() {
  while (mTrucking) {
    render();
    timeStep();
    calculateFrameRate();
  }
}
```

You may be wondering what `render()` does. Why not just call `repaint()`? The reason has to do with how `repaint()` works. The problem is that `repaint()` doesn't do the drawing right away. That is, it doesn't call the component's `paint()` method directly. Instead, it tells AWT to redraw the component the next time it gets a chance. In a tight animation loop like this one, AWT doesn't ever get a chance to redraw the window.* Because of this, the `render()` method actually does the drawing directly. The `render()` method implements one other nice feature: double buffering. It draws the component into an offscreen image and then renders the image on the screen.

```
protected void render() {
  Graphics g = getGraphics();
  if (g != null) {
    Dimension d = getSize();
    if (checkImage(d)) {
      Graphics imageGraphics = mImage.getGraphics();
      // Clear the image background.
      imageGraphics.setColor(getBackground());
      imageGraphics.fillRect(0, 0, d.width, d.height);
      imageGraphics.setColor(getForeground());
      // Draw this component offscreen.
      paint(imageGraphics);
      // Now put the offscreen image on the screen.
      g.drawImage(mImage, 0, 0, null);
      // Clean up.
      imageGraphics.dispose();
    }
```

---

* Be careful if you decide to port this class to Swing. Threading in Swing is a bit more subtle; for more details, see *Java Swing*, by Robert Eckstein, Marc Loy, and Dave Wood (O'Reilly).

```
        g.dispose();
      }
   }
```

There are two `Graphics` objects involved. The first, `g`, is the drawing surface of the onscreen component. The second, `imageGraphics`, is the drawing surface of the offscreen image. All the painting is performed on `imageGraphics`. Then the offscreen image is rendered to `g` to put it on the screen.

`AnimationComponent` also calculates the frame rate of the animation. The basic algorithm for calculating the frame rate is to find the amount of time between two adjacent frames and take the reciprocal. Because the times are measured in milliseconds, the result is multiplied by 1000 to get frames per second:

$$\text{frameRate} = \frac{1000}{\text{currentTime} - \text{previousTime}}$$

This result, however, fluctuates wildly depending on the current state of the system. It is also subject to the resolution of the clock.* For more stable results, `AnimationComponent` calculates an average frame rate. It keeps an array of frame times in the `mPreviousTimes` array and calculates the frame rate based on the oldest entry in that array. Until this array is filled, however, `AnimationComponent` uses the previous method. Here's the code for `calculateFrameRate()`:

```
    protected void calculateFrameRate() {
      // Measure the frame rate
      long now = System.currentTimeMillis();
      int numberOfFrames = mPreviousTimes.length;
      double newRate;
      // Use the more stable method if a history is available.
      if (mPreviousFilled)
        newRate = (double)numberOfFrames /
            (double)(now - mPreviousTimes[mPreviousIndex]) *
            1000.0;
      else
        newRate = 1000.0 /
            (double)(now - mPreviousTimes[numberOfFrames - 1]);
      firePropertyChange("frameRate", mFrameRate, newRate);
      mFrameRate = newRate;
      // Update the history.
      mPreviousTimes[mPreviousIndex] = now;
      mPreviousIndex++;
      if (mPreviousIndex >= numberOfFrames) {
        mPreviousIndex = 0;
        mPreviousFilled = true;
      }
    }
```

---

* On my Windows NT system, for example, I only get readings in multiples of ten milliseconds.

Sharp-eyed readers will have noticed that `calculateFrameRate()` fires off a property event when the rate changes. What's that all about? `Animation-Component` allows other objects that are interested in the frame rate to receive notification when it changes. This is done through the use of the `java.beans.PropertyChangeSupport` class.

Without further ado, here is the entire `AnimationComponent` class:

```
import java.awt.*;

public abstract class AnimationComponent
    extends Container
    implements Runnable {
  private boolean mTrucking = true;
  private long[] mPreviousTimes; // milliseconds
  private int mPreviousIndex;
  private boolean mPreviousFilled;
  private double mFrameRate; // frames per second
  private Image mImage;

  public AnimationComponent() {
    mPreviousTimes = new long[128];
    mPreviousTimes[0] = System.currentTimeMillis();
    mPreviousIndex = 1;
    mPreviousFilled = false;
  }

  public abstract void timeStep();

  public void run() {
    while (mTrucking) {
      render();
      timeStep();
      calculateFrameRate();
    }
  }

  protected void render() {
    Graphics g = getGraphics();
    if (g != null) {
      Dimension d = getSize();
      if (checkImage(d)) {
        Graphics imageGraphics = mImage.getGraphics();
        // Clear the image background.
        imageGraphics.setColor(getBackground());
        imageGraphics.fillRect(0, 0, d.width, d.height);
        imageGraphics.setColor(getForeground());
        // Draw this component offscreen.
        paint(imageGraphics);
```

```
          // Now put the offscreen image on the screen.
          g.drawImage(mImage, 0, 0, null);
          // Clean up.
          imageGraphics.dispose();
        }
        g.dispose();
      }
    }


    // Offscreen image.
    protected boolean checkImage(Dimension d) {
      if (d.width == 0 || d.height == 0) return false;
      if (mImage == null || mImage.getWidth(null) != d.width
          || mImage.getHeight(null) != d.height) {
        mImage = createImage(d.width, d.height);
      }
      return true;
    }


    protected void calculateFrameRate() {
      // Measure the frame rate
      long now = System.currentTimeMillis();
      int numberOfFrames = mPreviousTimes.length;
      double newRate;
      // Use the more stable method if a history is available.
      if (mPreviousFilled)
        newRate = (double)numberOfFrames /
            (double)(now - mPreviousTimes[mPreviousIndex]) *
            1000.0;
      else
        newRate = 1000.0 /
            (double)(now - mPreviousTimes[numberOfFrames - 1]);
      firePropertyChange("frameRate", mFrameRate, newRate);
      mFrameRate = newRate;
      // Update the history.
      mPreviousTimes[mPreviousIndex] = now;
      mPreviousIndex++;
      if (mPreviousIndex >= numberOfFrames) {
        mPreviousIndex = 0;
        mPreviousFilled = true;
      }
    }


    public double getFrameRate() { return mFrameRate; }


    // Property change support.
    private transient AnimationFrame mRateListener;


    public void setRateListener(AnimationFrame af) {
```

```
    mRateListener = af;
}

protected void firePropertyChange(String name, double oldValue,
    double newValue) {
  mRateListener.rateChanged(newValue);
}
}
```

AnimationFrame

The `AnimationFrame` class is considerably simpler. It displays a single `AnimationComponent` in the main part of a frame window. It registers itself to be notified when the `AnimationComponent`'s frame rate changes, and it displays the frame rate in the bottom part of the window.

Here's the `AnimationFrame` class:

```
import java.awt.*;
import java.text.NumberFormat;

public class AnimationFrame
    extends ApplicationFrame {
  private Label mStatusLabel;
  private NumberFormat mFormat;

  public AnimationFrame(AnimationComponent ac) {
    super("AnimationFrame v1.0");
    setLayout(new BorderLayout());
    add(ac, BorderLayout.CENTER);
    add(mStatusLabel = new Label(), BorderLayout.SOUTH);
    // Create a number formatter.
    mFormat = NumberFormat.getInstance();
    mFormat.setMaximumFractionDigits(1);
    // Listen for the frame rate changes.
    ac.setRateListener(this);
    // Kick off the animation.
    Thread t = new Thread(ac);
    t.start();
  }

  public void rateChanged(double frameRate) {
    mStatusLabel.setText(mFormat.format(frameRate) + " fps");
  }
}
```

Animated Shapes

Let's take this animation framework out for a test drive. The following class, `Bouncer`, uses the framework to animate a curvy shape made from a series of cubic curves. Each of the endpoints and control points of the curves moves around the window, bouncing off the edges. The rendered shape is constantly changing as the endpoints and control points of its segments move around the window. Figure C-30 shows a snapshot of this example in action.

The options are as follows:

Anti

    This checkbox controls whether antialiasing is used to render the shape.

Trans

    When checked, this option causes the entire shape to rotate slowly.

Gradient

    When this option is checked, the shape is filled with a color gradient. Otherwise, the shape is filled with a solid color.

Outline

    This option controls whether the outline of the shape is stroked.

Dotted

    If the **Outline** option is checked, this checkbox determines whether the outline is a solid or a dashed line.

Axes

    If this checkbox is checked, coordinate axes will be drawn. The axes are useful in observing the effects of the **Trans** option.

Clip

    When this option is checked, all rendering is clipped to a text shape.

Bouncer follows the conventions for an AnimationComponent subclass: it updates its state in timeStep() and renders itself in paint(). Notice, however, that a lot of the rendering depends on boolean member variables. Bouncer's main() method wires checkboxes to these boolean variables, so you can adjust what Bouncer renders and how it's rendered as it's running.

The curvy shape is stored as an array of floating point coordinates called mPoints. Each of these coordinates has a corresponding delta value, stored in mDeltas. For each new frame, timeStep() adds the deltas to the coordinates. If any coordinates are at the edges of the component, the delta value is negated so that the point appears to bounce off the edges of the component.

The paint() method, at its core, is very simple. It creates the curvy shape, using the createShape() method, then fills it. It uses a handful of helper methods to accomplish all the other neat features, like turning on antialiasing or using a gradient paint. Here's the code for Bouncer:

```
import java.awt.*;
import java.awt.event.*;
```

```java
import java.awt.font.*;
import java.awt.geom.*;
import java.util.Random;

public class Bouncer
    extends AnimationComponent {
  public static void main(String[] args) {
    final Bouncer bouncer = new Bouncer();
    Frame f = new AnimationFrame(bouncer);
    f.setFont(new Font("Serif", Font.PLAIN, 12));

    Panel controls = new Panel();
    controls.add(bouncer.createCheckbox("Anti.", Bouncer.ANTIALIASING));
    controls.add(bouncer.createCheckbox("Trans.", Bouncer.TRANSFORM));
    controls.add(bouncer.createCheckbox("Gradient", Bouncer.GRADIENT));
    controls.add(bouncer.createCheckbox("Outline", Bouncer.OUTLINE));
    controls.add(bouncer.createCheckbox("Dotted", Bouncer.DOTTED));
    controls.add(bouncer.createCheckbox("Axes", Bouncer.AXES));
    controls.add(bouncer.createCheckbox("Clip", Bouncer.CLIP));
    f.add(controls, BorderLayout.NORTH);

    f.setVisible(true);
  }

  // Tweakable variables
  private boolean mAntialiasing, mGradient, mOutline;
  private boolean mTransform, mDotted, mAxes, mClip;
  // ...and the constants that represent them. See setSwitch().
  public static final int ANTIALIASING = 0;
  public static final int GRADIENT = 1;
  public static final int OUTLINE = 2;
  public static final int TRANSFORM = 3;
  public static final int DOTTED = 4;
  public static final int AXES = 5;
  public static final int CLIP = 6;

  private float[] mPoints;
  private float[] mDeltas;
  private float mTheta;
  private int mN;
  private Shape mClipShape;

  public Bouncer() {
    mN = 38;
    mPoints = new float[mN];
    mDeltas = new float[mN];
    Random random = new Random();
    for (int i = 0; i < mN; i++) {
      mPoints[i] = random.nextFloat() * 500;
```

```
        mDeltas[i] = random.nextFloat() * 3;
      }
      // Make sure points are within range.
      addComponentListener(new ComponentAdapter() {
        public void componentResized(ComponentEvent ce) {
          Dimension d = getSize();
          for (int i = 0; i < mN; i++) {
            int limit = ((i % 2) == 0) ? d.width : d.height;
            if (mPoints[i] < 0) mPoints[i] = 0;
            else if (mPoints[i] >= limit) mPoints[i] = limit - 1;
          }
        }
      });
    }

    public void setSwitch(int item, boolean value) {
      switch(item) {
        case ANTIALIASING: mAntialiasing = value; break;
        case GRADIENT: mGradient = value; break;
        case OUTLINE: mOutline = value; break;
        case TRANSFORM: mTransform = value; break;
        case DOTTED: mDotted = value; break;
        case AXES: mAxes = value; break;
        case CLIP: mClip = value; break;
        default: break;
      }
    }

    protected Checkbox createCheckbox(String label, final int item) {
      Checkbox check = new Checkbox(label);
      check.addItemListener(new ItemListener() {
        public void itemStateChanged(ItemEvent ie) {
          setSwitch(item, (ie.getStateChange() == ie.SELECTED));
        }
      });
      return check;
    }

    public void timeStep() {
      Dimension d = getSize();
      for (int i = 0; i < mN; i++) {
        float value = mPoints[i] + mDeltas[i];
        int limit = ((i % 2) == 0) ? d.width : d.height;
        if (value < 0 || value > limit) {
          mDeltas[i] = -mDeltas[i];
          mPoints[i] += mDeltas[i];
        }
        else mPoints[i] = value;
      }
```

```
    mTheta += Math.PI / 192;
    if (mTheta > (2 * Math.PI)) mTheta -= (2 * Math.PI);
  }

  public void paint(Graphics g) {
    Graphics2D g2 = (Graphics2D)g;
    setAntialiasing(g2);
    setClip(g2);
    setTransform(g2);
    Shape shape = createShape();
    setPaint(g2);
    // Fill the shape.
    g2.fill(shape);
    // Maybe draw the outline.
    if (mOutline) {
      setStroke(g2);
      g2.setPaint(Color.blue);
      g2.draw(shape);
    }
    drawAxes(g2);
  }

  protected void setAntialiasing(Graphics2D g2) {
    if (mAntialiasing == false) return;
    g2.setRenderingHint(RenderingHints.KEY_ANTIALIASING,
        RenderingHints.VALUE_ANTIALIAS_ON);
  }

  protected void setClip(Graphics2D g2) {
    if (mClip == false) return;
    if (mClipShape == null) {
      Dimension d = getSize();
      FontRenderContext frc = g2.getFontRenderContext();
      Font font = new Font("Serif", Font.PLAIN, 144);
      String s = "Spoon!";
      GlyphVector gv = font.createGlyphVector(frc, s);
      Rectangle2D bounds = font.getStringBounds(s, frc);
      mClipShape = gv.getOutline((d.width - (float)bounds.getWidth()) / 2,
          (d.height + (float)bounds.getHeight()) / 2);
    }
    g2.clip(mClipShape);
  }

  protected void setTransform(Graphics2D g2) {
    if (mTransform == false) return;
    Dimension d = getSize();
    g2.rotate(mTheta, d.width / 2, d.height / 2);
  }
```

```
   protected Shape createShape() {
     GeneralPath path = new GeneralPath(GeneralPath.WIND_EVEN_ODD,
         mPoints.length);
     path.moveTo(mPoints[0], mPoints[1]);
     for (int i = 2; i < mN; i += 6)
       path.curveTo(mPoints[i], mPoints[i + 1],
           mPoints[i + 2], mPoints[i + 3],
           mPoints[i + 4], mPoints[i + 5]);
     path.closePath();
     return path;
   }

   protected void setPaint(Graphics2D g2) {
     if (mGradient) {
       GradientPaint gp = new GradientPaint(0, 0, Color.yellow,
           50, 25, Color.red, true);
       g2.setPaint(gp);
     }
     else g2.setPaint(Color.orange);
   }

   protected void setStroke(Graphics2D g2) {
     if (mDotted == false) return;
     // Create a dotted stroke.
     Stroke stroke = new BasicStroke(1, BasicStroke.CAP_BUTT,
         BasicStroke.JOIN_ROUND, 10,
         new float[] { 4, 4 }, 0);
     g2.setStroke(stroke);
   }

   protected void drawAxes(Graphics2D g2) {
     if (mAxes == false) return;
     g2.setPaint(getForeground());
     g2.setStroke(new BasicStroke());
     Dimension d = getSize();
     int side = 20;
     int arrow = 4;
     int w = d.width / 2, h = d.height / 2;
     g2.drawLine(w - side, h, w + side, h);
     g2.drawLine(w + side - arrow, h - arrow, w + side, h);
     g2.drawLine(w, h - side, w, h + side);
     g2.drawLine(w + arrow, h + side - arrow, w, h + side);
   }
 }
```

You can learn quite a bit from this application. Table 14-1 shows some results when testing under the following conditions:

- JDK 1.2 build V

- Windows NT 4.0 with Service Pack 3

316 · CHAPTER 14: ANIMATION AND PERFORMANCE

- 266 MHz Pentium II processor
- Matrox Millenium II display card, set to "True Color" and 1152 by 864 pixels
- 64 MB physical memory

The frame rates are approximate, as they fluctuate based on the size of the rendered shape as well as changing system conditions.

Table 14-1. Frame Rates for the Bouncer Animation

Antialiasing	Transform	Gradient	Outline	Dotted	Axes	Clip	Frame Rate (fps)
							70
					x		70
	x				x		70
	x		x		x		66
	x		x	x	x		21
x	x		x	x	x		15
x	x	x	x	x	x		12
						x	42
					x	x	37
	x				x	x	37
	x		x		x	x	32
	x		x	x	x	x	15
x	x		x	x	x	x	17
x	x	x	x	x	x	x	14

There are a few interesting tidbits to be gleaned from Table 14-1:

- The rotational transformation costs almost nothing at all.
- Drawing the dotted outline is much slower than drawing a solid outline. This makes sense, since each dot of the outline is a separate shape. The solid outline could be one shape.
- The combination of a clipping shape and a dotted outline actually performs faster when antialiasing is on.

Animated Text

This section contains an application, structurally similar to Bouncer, which will help you examine the performance properties of rendering text. Figure C-31 shows the application, TextBouncer.

TextBouncer is a lot like Bouncer, but it adds support for choosing the font that will be used to display the text. It also includes separate checkboxes for shearing and rotational transformations. Here's the example application:

```java
import java.awt.*;
import java.awt.event.*;
import java.awt.font.*;
import java.awt.geom.*;
import java.util.Random;

public class TextBouncer
    extends AnimationComponent {
  public static void main(String[] args) {
    String s = "Firenze";
    final int size = 64;
    if (args.length > 0) s = args[0];

    Panel controls = new Panel();
    final Choice choice = new Choice();
    GraphicsEnvironment ge =
        GraphicsEnvironment.getLocalGraphicsEnvironment();
    Font[] allFonts = ge.getAllFonts();
    for (int i = 0; i < allFonts.length; i++)
      choice.addItem(allFonts[i].getName());
    Font defaultFont = new Font(allFonts[0].getName(), Font.PLAIN, size);

    final TextBouncer bouncer = new TextBouncer(s, defaultFont);
    Frame f = new AnimationFrame(bouncer);
    f.setFont(new Font("Serif", Font.PLAIN, 12));
    controls.add(bouncer.createCheckbox("Antialiasing",
        TextBouncer.ANTIALIASING));
    controls.add(bouncer.createCheckbox("Gradient", TextBouncer.GRADIENT));
    controls.add(bouncer.createCheckbox("Shear", TextBouncer.SHEAR));
    controls.add(bouncer.createCheckbox("Rotate", TextBouncer.ROTATE));
    controls.add(bouncer.createCheckbox("Axes", TextBouncer.AXES));

    Panel fontControls = new Panel();
    choice.addItemListener(new ItemListener() {
      public void itemStateChanged(ItemEvent ie) {
        Font font = new Font(choice.getSelectedItem(), Font.PLAIN, size);
        bouncer.setFont(font);
      }
    });
    fontControls.add(choice);

    Panel allControls = new Panel(new GridLayout(2, 1));
    allControls.add(controls);
    allControls.add(fontControls);
    f.add(allControls, BorderLayout.NORTH);
```

```
      f.setVisible(true);
  }

  private boolean mAntialiasing = false, mGradient = false;
  private boolean mShear = false, mRotate = false, mAxes = false;
  public static final int ANTIALIASING = 0;
  public static final int GRADIENT = 1;
  public static final int SHEAR = 2;
  public static final int ROTATE = 3;
  public static final int AXES = 5;

  private float mDeltaX, mDeltaY;
  private float mX, mY, mWidth, mHeight;
  private float mTheta;
  private float mShearX, mShearY, mShearDeltaX, mShearDeltaY;
  private String mString;

  public TextBouncer(String s, Font f) {
    mString = s;
    setFont(f);
    Random random = new Random();
    mX = random.nextFloat() * 500;
    mY = random.nextFloat() * 500;
    mDeltaX = random.nextFloat() * 3;
    mDeltaY = random.nextFloat() * 3;
    mShearX = random.nextFloat() / 2;
    mShearY = random.nextFloat() / 2;
    mShearDeltaX = mShearDeltaY = .05f;
    FontRenderContext frc = new FontRenderContext(null, true, false);
    Rectangle2D bounds = getFont().getStringBounds(mString, frc);
    mWidth = (float)bounds.getWidth();
    mHeight = (float)bounds.getHeight();
    // Make sure points are within range.
    addComponentListener(new ComponentAdapter() {
      public void componentResized(ComponentEvent ce) {
        Dimension d = getSize();
        if (mX < 0) mX = 0;
        else if (mX + mWidth >= d.width) mX = d.width - mWidth - 1;
        if (mY < 0) mY = 0;
        else if (mY + mHeight >= d.height) mY = d.height - mHeight - 1;
      }
    });
  }

  public void setSwitch(int item, boolean value) {
    switch(item) {
      case ANTIALIASING: mAntialiasing = value; break;
      case GRADIENT: mGradient = value; break;
      case SHEAR: mShear = value; break;
```

```
      case ROTATE: mRotate = value; break;
      case AXES: mAxes = value; break;
      default: break;
  }
}

protected Checkbox createCheckbox(String label, final int item) {
  Checkbox check = new Checkbox(label);
  check.addItemListener(new ItemListener() {
    public void itemStateChanged(ItemEvent ie) {
      setSwitch(item, (ie.getStateChange() == ie.SELECTED));
    }
  });
  return check;
}

public void timeStep() {
  Dimension d = getSize();
  if (mX + mDeltaX < 0) mDeltaX = -mDeltaX;
  else if (mX + mWidth + mDeltaX >= d.width) mDeltaX = -mDeltaX;
  if (mY + mDeltaY < 0) mDeltaY = -mDeltaY;
  else if (mY + mHeight + mDeltaY >= d.height) mDeltaY = -mDeltaY;
  mX += mDeltaX;
  mY += mDeltaY;

  mTheta += Math.PI / 192;
  if (mTheta > (2 * Math.PI)) mTheta -= (2 * Math.PI);

  if (mShearX + mShearDeltaX > .5) mShearDeltaX = -mShearDeltaX;
  else if (mShearX + mShearDeltaX < -.5) mShearDeltaX = -mShearDeltaX;
  if (mShearY + mShearDeltaY > .5) mShearDeltaY = -mShearDeltaY;
  else if (mShearY + mShearDeltaY < -.5) mShearDeltaY = -mShearDeltaY;
  mShearX += mShearDeltaX;
  mShearY += mShearDeltaY;
}

public void paint(Graphics g) {
  Graphics2D g2 = (Graphics2D)g;
  setAntialiasing(g2);
  setTransform(g2);
  setPaint(g2);
  // Draw the string.
  g2.setFont(getFont());
  g2.drawString(mString, mX, mY + mHeight);
  drawAxes(g2);
}

protected void setAntialiasing(Graphics2D g2) {
  if (mAntialiasing == false) return;
```

```
    g2.setRenderingHint(RenderingHints.KEY_ANTIALIASING,
        RenderingHints.VALUE_ANTIALIAS_ON);
}

protected void setTransform(Graphics2D g2) {
    Dimension d = getSize();
    int cx = d.width / 2;
    int cy = d.height / 2;
    g2.translate(cx, cy);
    if (mShear) g2.shear(mShearX, mShearY);
    if (mRotate) g2.rotate(mTheta);
    g2.translate(-cx, -cy);
}

protected void setPaint(Graphics2D g2) {
    if (mGradient) {
        GradientPaint gp = new GradientPaint(0, 0, Color.blue,
            50, 25, Color.green, true);
        g2.setPaint(gp);
    }
    else g2.setPaint(Color.orange);
}

protected void drawAxes(Graphics2D g2) {
    if (mAxes == false) return;
    g2.setPaint(getForeground());
    g2.setStroke(new BasicStroke());
    Dimension d = getSize();
    int side = 20;
    int arrow = 4;
    int w = d.width / 2, h = d.height / 2;
    g2.drawLine(w - side, h, w + side, h);
    g2.drawLine(w + side - arrow, h - arrow, w + side, h);
    g2.drawLine(w, h - side, w, h + side);
    g2.drawLine(w + arrow, h + side - arrow, w, h + side);
}
}
```

Table 14-2 summarizes some relevant frame rates for TextBouncer, as measured on my computer.

Table 14-2. Frame Rates for TextBouncer

Antialiasing	Gradient	Shear	Rotate	Axes	Font	Frame Rate (fps)
					Arial	94
x					Arial	82
x				x	Arial	73

Table 14-2. Frame Rates for TextBouncer (continued)

Antialiasing	Gradient	Shear	Rotate	Axes	Font	Frame Rate (fps)
x			x	x	Arial	29
x		x		x	Arial	66
x		x	x	x	Arial	28
x	x	x	x	x	Arial	32
x	x	x	x	x	Times New Roman	36
x	x	x	x	x	Lucida Bright Regular	32

What can you learn from this application? The results of this application are counter-intuitive:

- Using the gradient paint actually speeds things up when antialiasing is being used.

- The font used is significant, especially with complex rendering. Although you might expect serif fonts like Times New Roman to be slower than sans serif fonts, this is not the case.

- Although the shearing transformation costs very little, the rotation is expensive.

Remember, performance is likely to vary from one system to another and from one release to another. I suggest you try these applications out for yourself.

Animated Images

I've discussed how shapes and text perform under different circumstances. Now let's take a look at the third graphic type—images. There aren't quite as many variables to fiddle with, mostly because the image contains its own color data. The current `Paint` of the `Graphics2D` doesn't affect how images are drawn. Even antialiasing isn't a factor.

Several aspects of images are important for performance. The following example animates an image, in the same spirit as `Bouncer` and `TextBouncer`. The running application is shown in Figure C-32. A small image bounces around the window. You can choose to transform the image as it is rendered, and you can choose from a short list of image storage types.

The transformation is a simple rotation, performed at the center of the image. You can, however, choose the interpolation algorithm that is used when the image is rotated. This algorithm specifies how the colors of the rotated image are determined. The default is the "nearest neighbor" algorithm, which is fast but sloppy. As the example runs, you can see the "jaggies" that result from this algorithm in the borders between the hair on my head and the background of the image. If you instead use "bilinear interpolation" (by checking the **Bilinear** checkbox), the rotated picture will be higher quality, but the animation will be slower.

The combo box lets you choose what basic image type will be rendered. Some image types require color conversions before the image can be rendered on your screen. For example, if the base type is TYPE_BYTE_GRAY and you have a color display, the grayscale pixels of the image will have to be converted to red, green, and blue values before the image can be displayed on the screen.

Here's the code for the ImageBouncer example:

```java
import java.awt.*;
import java.awt.event.*;
import java.awt.geom.*;
import java.awt.image.*;
import java.util.Random;

public class ImageBouncer
    extends AnimationComponent {
  public static void main(String[] args) {
    String filename = "knudsen.gif";
    if (args.length > 0) filename = args[0];

    Image image = Utilities.blockingLoad(filename);

    final ImageBouncer bouncer = new ImageBouncer(image);
    Frame f = new AnimationFrame(bouncer);
    f.setFont(new Font("Serif", Font.PLAIN, 12));
    Panel controls = new Panel();
    controls.add(bouncer.createCheckbox("Bilinear", ImageBouncer.BILINEAR));
    controls.add(bouncer.createCheckbox("Transform",ImageBouncer.TRANSFORM));
    final Choice typeChoice = new Choice();
    typeChoice.add("TYPE_INT_RGB");
    typeChoice.add("TYPE_INT_ARGB");
    typeChoice.add("TYPE_INT_ARGB_PRE");
    typeChoice.add("TYPE_3BYTE_BGR");
    typeChoice.add("TYPE_BYTE_GRAY");
    typeChoice.add("TYPE_USHORT_GRAY");
    typeChoice.add("TYPE_USHORT_555_RGB");
    typeChoice.add("TYPE_USHORT_565_RGB");
    controls.add(typeChoice);
    f.add(controls, BorderLayout.NORTH);

    typeChoice.addItemListener(new ItemListener() {
      public void itemStateChanged(ItemEvent ie) {
        String type = typeChoice.getSelectedItem();
        bouncer.setImageType(type);
      }
```

```
      });

      f.setVisible(true);
    }

    private boolean mBilinear = false;
    private boolean mTransform = false;
    public static final int BILINEAR = 1;
    public static final int TRANSFORM = 3;

    private float mDeltaX, mDeltaY;
    private float mX, mY, mWidth, mHeight;
    private float mTheta;
    private Image mOriginalImage;
    private BufferedImage mImage;

    public ImageBouncer(Image image) {
      mOriginalImage = image;
      setImageType("TYPE_INT_RGB");

      Random random = new Random();
      mX = random.nextFloat() * 500;
      mY = random.nextFloat() * 500;
      mWidth = mImage.getWidth();
      mHeight = mImage.getHeight();
      mDeltaX = random.nextFloat() * 3;
      mDeltaY = random.nextFloat() * 3;
      // Make sure points are within range.
      addComponentListener(new ComponentAdapter() {
        public void componentResized(ComponentEvent ce) {
          Dimension d = getSize();
          if (mX < 0) mX = 0;
          else if (mX + mWidth >= d.width) mX = d.width - mWidth - 1;
          if (mY < 0) mY = 0;
          else if (mY + mHeight >= d.height) mY = d.height - mHeight - 1;
        }
      });
    }

    public void setSwitch(int item, boolean value) {
      switch(item) {
        case BILINEAR: mBilinear = value; break;
        case TRANSFORM: mTransform = value; break;
        default: break;
      }
    }

    public void setImageType(String s) {
      int type = BufferedImage.TYPE_CUSTOM;
```

```java
    if (s.equals("TYPE_INT_RGB"))
      type = BufferedImage.TYPE_INT_RGB;
    else if (s.equals("TYPE_INT_ARGB"))
      type = BufferedImage.TYPE_INT_ARGB;
    else if (s.equals("TYPE_INT_ARGB_PRE"))
      type = BufferedImage.TYPE_INT_ARGB_PRE;
    else if (s.equals("TYPE_3BYTE_BGR"))
      type = BufferedImage.TYPE_3BYTE_BGR;
    else if (s.equals("TYPE_BYTE_GRAY"))
      type = BufferedImage.TYPE_BYTE_GRAY;
    else if (s.equals("TYPE_USHORT_GRAY"))
      type = BufferedImage.TYPE_USHORT_GRAY;
    else if (s.equals("TYPE_USHORT_555_RGB"))
      type = BufferedImage.TYPE_USHORT_565_RGB;
    else if (s.equals("TYPE_USHORT_565_RGB"))
      type = BufferedImage.TYPE_USHORT_565_RGB;
    else {
      System.out.println("Unrecognized type.");
      return;
    }
    mImage = Utilities.makeBufferedImage(mOriginalImage, type);
  }

  protected Checkbox createCheckbox(String label, final int item) {
    Checkbox check = new Checkbox(label);
    check.addItemListener(new ItemListener() {
      public void itemStateChanged(ItemEvent ie) {
        setSwitch(item, (ie.getStateChange() == ie.SELECTED));
      }
    });
    return check;
  }

  public void timeStep() {
    Dimension d = getSize();
    if (mX + mDeltaX < 0) mDeltaX = -mDeltaX;
    else if (mX + mWidth + mDeltaX >= d.width) mDeltaX = -mDeltaX;
    if (mY + mDeltaY < 0) mDeltaY = -mDeltaY;
    else if (mY + mHeight + mDeltaY >= d.height) mDeltaY = -mDeltaY;
    mX += mDeltaX;
    mY += mDeltaY;

    mTheta += Math.PI / 192;
    if (mTheta > (2 * Math.PI)) mTheta -= (2 * Math.PI);
  }

  public void paint(Graphics g) {
    Graphics2D g2 = (Graphics2D)g;
    setTransform(g2);
    setBilinear(g2);
```

```
          // Draw the image.
          g2.drawImage(mImage, AffineTransform.getTranslateInstance(mX, mY), null);
      }

      protected void setTransform(Graphics2D g2) {
        if (mTransform == false) return;
        float cx = mX + mWidth / 2;
        float cy = mY + mHeight / 2;
        g2.rotate(mTheta, cx, cy);
      }

      protected void setBilinear(Graphics2D g2) {
        if (mBilinear == false) return;
        g2.setRenderingHint(RenderingHints.KEY_INTERPOLATION,
            RenderingHints.VALUE_INTERPOLATION_BILINEAR);
      }
  }
```

Table 14-3 lists some frame rates for the ImageBouncer example.

Table 14-3. Frame Rates for ImageBouncer

Bilinear	Transform	Image type	Frame Rate (fps)
		TYPE_INT_RGB	80
		TYPE_INT_ARGB	72
		TYPE_INT_ARGB_PRE	72
		TYPE_3BYTE_BGR	82
		TYPE_BYTE_GRAY	80
		TYPE_USHORT_GRAY	80
		TYPE_USHORT_555_RGB	79
		TYPE_USHORT_565_RGB	79
x	x	TYPE_INT_RGB	37
x	x	TYPE_INT_ARGB	38
x	x	TYPE_INT_ARGB_PRE	26
x	x	TYPE_3BYTE_BGR	24
x	x	TYPE_BYTE_GRAY	10
x	x	TYPE_USHORT_GRAY	10
x	x	TYPE_USHORT_555_RGB	36
x	x	TYPE_USHORT_565_RGB	36

When you run ImageBouncer, you'll probably notice the following:

- It's expensive to transform the image. Animating the transformed image using bilinear interpolation runs at about 50% of the untransformed image frame rate.

- Bilinear interpolation yields nicer-looking transformed images, but it takes longer than the "nearest neighbor" algorithm. In this respect, it's a lot like antialiasing for shapes and text: a trade-off of quality for speed.

- The rendering engine is optimized for some operations and not for others. For example, the TYPE_3BYTE_BGR image type performs best when the image is not transformed. But when the image is transformed, it's a terrible performer. Subsequent releases of Java 2 should contain more optimizations.

Memory

One aspect of performance tuning is making your application handle memory nicely. It's very awkward for your support staff if the only answer they have for some problems is "buy more memory." An ideal application doesn't use much memory and doesn't crash if it can't get enough memory.

In 2D applications, images are the biggest area of concern for memory usage. If your application does any image handling, including double-buffered drawing, you should probably be thinking about memory.

Images

Any image in your application uses some memory. The formula is pretty simple:

$$memoryUsed = width \cdot height \cdot bytesPerPixel$$

This formula gives you a minimum size for the image. Of course, there's some additional memory for the Image or BufferedImage object itself, but this is small compared to the raw image data. The actual memory used also depends on how the image data is stored. Suppose you had an image with a 16-color palette. Each pixel can be represented with four bits. An inefficient way to store this image would be to put the four bits of each pixel into an 8-bit byte. In this case, the image data would actually occupy twice as much memory as given in the formula above.

The following method calculates the memory usage for a BufferedImage. It retrieves the actual DataBuffer for the image and calculates the size accordingly. Note that this calculates the full size of the image's data buffers, which is a little more realistic measure of memory usage than the minimum size given by the formula above:

```
public static long getImageSize(BufferedImage image) {
    DataBuffer db = image.getRaster().getDataBuffer();
    int dataType = db.getDataType();
    int elementSizeInBits = DataBuffer.getDataTypeSize(dataType);
    return db.getNumBanks() * db.getSize() * elementSizeInBits / 8;
}
```

Managing image memory may be as simple as throwing away images that you don't need any more.* Furthermore, if you have several images that represent different parts of the same data set, you should share a single `DataBuffer` among the images. `DataBuffer`s really take up space, not `Image`s.

Double Buffering

Double buffering is a technique that is described fully in Chapter 9, *Images*. It's a technique for avoiding image flickering. Basically, your application draws into an offscreen image instead of drawing directly on the screen. The image is then drawn onscreen.

Double buffering doubles an application's memory consumption. Think of it this way: instead of just needing some display memory for a window or component, your application now needs memory for a corresponding offscreen image.

You should be especially worried about this if you perform double buffering for a resizeable window. Suppose, for example, that your application has a frame window with a default size of 300 by 200 pixels. An offscreen image for double buffering will be 240K, assuming you use 32 bits per pixel. Suppose the user maximizes the window, to 800 by 600 pixels. The size of the offscreen image jumps to 1.92M. But that's not the worst of it. Many users have systems that allow for much higher screen resolutions. It's very possible that a user could maximize your application to his or her 1600 by 1200 desktop. This makes the size of the offscreen image a whopping 7.68M!

The moral of the story is to be careful about double buffering. Try to double buffer only small, size-controlled parts of your application. If you have to use double buffering on an entire window, consider making the window a fixed size, or add code to enforce a maximum size for the window.

Swing Components

Swing components perform double buffering by default. If you use Swing components, you are already paying the memory penalty that double buffering imposes, and you should be careful about the size of these components, as discussed previously. The good news is that Swing is intelligent about its double buffering. If a component is part of a container that already has an offscreen image, the child component will paint itself into its parent's offscreen image without creating its own offscreen image.

---

* Of course, you can't actually free up the memory yourself. You have to `null` out references; it's up to the garbage collector to free up the memory.

If you'd rather not use this feature, you can disable it with a call to the following method in the JComponent class:

public void setDoubleBuffered(boolean aFlag)

> This method determines whether double buffering will be used for this component or not. If aFlag is true, then drawing will be performed in an offscreen buffer belonging to either this component or one of its visual parents. If aFlag is false, this component's drawing will be performed directly on the screen.

Optimizations

Performance tuning is a complex subject—I've really only scratched the surface in this chapter. The example programs show the relative "cost" of different kinds of operations, but there are several techniques you can use to optimize your applications. Two of these techniques are listed below:

prerendering

> For some applications it makes sense to render transformed shapes, images, or text into offscreen buffers. These can be selectively transferred to the screen during an animation. In many cases, this technique is significantly faster than doing the rendering in real time. It's a trade-off—you buy speed by using more memory.

smart update

> The examples in this chapter erase the offscreen buffer and render the whole thing at every time step. In some applications, it's possible to redraw just a portion of the entire onscreen component. For example, this technique would be helpful in animating a small character over a large background.

Other optimization techniques exist, but they are out of the scope of this book. This chapter gives you the tools you need to examine the cost of different operations in the 2D API.

Index

About the Author

"Java" Jonathan Knudsen is a staff writer for O'Reilly & Associates. He is the author of *Java Cryptography* and has contributed to *Java Swing, Java AWT Reference,* and the second and third editions of *Exploring Java.* Currently he is working on a book about LEGO® MINDSTORMS™. He also writes a monthly online column called "Bite-Size Java."

Jonathan graduated cum laude from Princeton in 1993 with a degree in mechanical engineering. However, it was the non-engineering courses he really enjoyed, including Italian Renaissance art, Russian literature, and epic poetry. Jonathan is one of perhaps a dozen engineers in the world who has read Spenser's *Faerie Queene* cover to cover.

Jonathan's current interests include inline skating and music, both popular and operatic. (A recording of Puccini's "Tosca" fueled much of the finishing touches for this book. Also, you can see echoes of Seal in Chapter 6.) Jonathan works at home with his wife, Kristen, and their children, Daphne, Luke, and Andrew.

Colophon

Our look is the result of reader comments, our own experimentation, and feedback from distribution channels. Distinctive covers complement our distinctive approach to technical topics, breathing personality and life into potentially dry subjects.

The image on the cover of *Java 2D Graphics* is a watercolor paint set.

Nicole Arigo was the copyeditor and production editor for *Java 2D Graphics*. Sarah Jane Shangraw was the proofreader. Maureen Dempsey, Melanie Wang, and Sheryl Avruch provided quality control reviews. Nancy Crumpton wrote the index.

The cover was designed by Hanna Dyer using a series design by Edie Freedman. The image was photographed by Kevin Thomas and manipulated in Adobe Photoshop by Michael Snow. The cover layout was produced by Kathleen Wilson with Quark XPress 3.3 using the Bodoni Black font from URW Software and Bodoni BT Bold Italic from Bitstream. The color insert was designed by Hanna Dyer. The inside text layout was designed by Nancy Priest.

Text was produced in FrameMaker 5.5 using a template implemented by Mike Sierra. The heading font is Bodoni BT; the text font is New Baskerville. The illustrations that appear in the book were created in Macromedia Freehand 8 and Adobe Photoshop 5 by Robert Romano.

Whenever possible, our books use RepKover™, a durable and flexible lay-flat binding. If the pagecount exceeds RepKover's limit, perfect binding is used.

How to stay in touch with O'Reilly

1. Visit Our Award-Winning Web Site

http://www.oreilly.com/

★ "Top 100 Sites on the Web" —*PC Magazine*
★ "Top 5% Web sites" —*Point Communications*
★ "3-Star site" —*The McKinley Group*

Our web site contains a library of comprehensive product information (including book excerpts and tables of contents), downloadable software, background articles, interviews with technology leaders, links to relevant sites, book cover art, and more. File us in your Bookmarks or Hotlist!

2. Join Our Email Mailing Lists

New Product Releases
To receive automatic email with brief descriptions of all new O'Reilly products as they are released, send email to:
listproc@online.oreilly.com
Put the following information in the first line of your message (*not* in the Subject field):
subscribe oreilly-news

O'Reilly Events
If you'd also like us to send information about trade show events, special promotions, and other O'Reilly events, send email to:
listproc@online.oreilly.com
Put the following information in the first line of your message (*not* in the Subject field):
subscribe oreilly-events

3. Get Examples from Our Books via FTP

There are two ways to access an archive of example files from our books:

Regular FTP
- ftp to:
  ftp.oreilly.com
  (login: anonymous
  password: your email address)
- Point your web browser to:
  ftp://ftp.oreilly.com/

FTPMAIL
- Send an email message to:
  ftpmail@online.oreilly.com
  (Write "help" in the message body)

4. Contact Us via Email

order@oreilly.com
To place a book or software order online. Good for North American and international customers.

subscriptions@oreilly.com
To place an order for any of our newsletters or periodicals.

books@oreilly.com
General questions about any of our books.

software@oreilly.com
For general questions and product information about our software. Check out O'Reilly Software Online at **http://software.oreilly.com/** for software and technical support information. Registered O'Reilly software users send your questions to: **website-support@oreilly.com**

cs@oreilly.com
For answers to problems regarding your order or our products.

booktech@oreilly.com
For book content technical questions or corrections.

proposals@oreilly.com
To submit new book or software proposals to our editors and product managers.

international@oreilly.com
For information about our international distributors or translation queries. For a list of our distributors outside of North America check out:
http://www.oreilly.com/www/order/country.html

O'Reilly & Associates, Inc.
101 Morris Street, Sebastopol, CA 95472 USA
TEL   707-829-0515 or 800-998-9938
          (6am to 5pm PST)
FAX   707-829-0104

International Distributors

UK, EUROPE, MIDDLE EAST AND AFRICA (EXCEPT FRANCE, GERMANY, AUSTRIA, SWITZERLAND, LUXEMBOURG, LIECHTENSTEIN, AND EASTERN EUROPE)

INQUIRIES

O'Reilly UK Limited
4 Castle Street
Farnham
Surrey, GU9 7HS
United Kingdom
Telephone: 44-1252-711776
Fax: 44-1252-734211
Email: josette@oreilly.com

ORDERS

Wiley Distribution Services Ltd.
1 Oldlands Way
Bognor Regis
West Sussex PO22 9SA
United Kingdom
Telephone: 44-1243-779777
Fax: 44-1243-820250
Email: cs-books@wiley.co.uk

FRANCE

ORDERS

GEODIF
61, Bd Saint-Germain
75240 Paris Cedex 05, France
Tel: 33-1-44-41-46-16 (French books)
Tel: 33-1-44-41-11-87 (English books)
Fax: 33-1-44-41-11-44
Email: distribution@eyrolles.com

INQUIRIES

Éditions O'Reilly
18 rue Séguier
75006 Paris, France
Tel: 33-1-40-51-52-30
Fax: 33-1-40-51-52-31
Email: france@editions-oreilly.fr

GERMANY, SWITZERLAND, AUSTRIA, EASTERN EUROPE, LUXEMBOURG, AND LIECHTENSTEIN

INQUIRIES & ORDERS

O'Reilly Verlag
Balthasarstr. 81
D-50670 Köln
Germany
Telephone: 49-221-973160-91
Fax: 49-221-973160-8
Email: anfragen@oreilly.de (inquiries)
Email: order@oreilly.de (orders)

CANADA (FRENCH LANGUAGE BOOKS)

Les Éditions Flammarion ltée
375, Avenue Laurier Ouest
Montréal (Québec) H2V 2K3
Tel: 00-1-514-277-8807
Fax: 00-1-514-278-2085
Email: info@flammarion.qc.ca

HONG KONG

City Discount Subscription Service, Ltd.
Unit D, 3rd Floor, Yan's Tower
27 Wong Chuk Hang Road
Aberdeen, Hong Kong
Tel: 852-2580-3539
Fax: 852-2580-6463
Email: citydis@ppn.com.hk

KOREA

Hanbit Media, Inc.
Sonyoung Bldg. 202
Yeksam-dong 736-36
Kangnam-ku
Seoul, Korea
Tel: 822-554-9610
Fax: 822-556-0363
Email: hant93@chollian.dacom.co.kr

PHILIPPINES

Mutual Books, Inc.
429-D Shaw Boulevard
Mandaluyong City, Metro
Manila, Philippines
Tel: 632-725-7538
Fax: 632-721-3056
Email: mbikikog@mnl.sequel.net

TAIWAN

O'Reilly Taiwan
No. 3, Lane 131
Hang-Chow South Road
Section 1, Taipei, Taiwan
Tel: 886-2-23968990
Fax: 886-2-23968916
Email: benh@oreilly.com

CHINA

O'Reilly Beijing
Room 2410
160, FuXingMenNeiDaJie
XiCheng District
Beijing, China PR 100031
Tel: 86-10-86631006
Fax: 86-10-86631007
Email: frederic@oreilly.com

INDIA

Computer Bookshop (India) Pvt. Ltd.
190 Dr. D.N. Road, Fort
Bombay 400 001 India
Tel: 91-22-207-0989
Fax: 91-22-262-3551
Email: cbsbom@giasbm01.vsnl.net.in

JAPAN

O'Reilly Japan, Inc.
Kiyoshige Building 2F
12-Bancho, Sanei-cho
Shinjuku-ku
Tokyo 160-0008 Japan
Tel: 81-3-3356-5227
Fax: 81-3-3356-5261
Email: japan@oreilly.com

ALL OTHER ASIAN COUNTRIES

O'Reilly & Associates, Inc.
101 Morris Street
Sebastopol, CA 95472 USA
Tel: 707-829-0515
Fax: 707-829-0104
Email: order@oreilly.com

AUSTRALIA

WoodsLane Pty., Ltd.
7/5 Vuko Place
Warriewood NSW 2102
Australia
Tel: 61-2-9970-5111
Fax: 61-2-9970-5002
Email: info@woodslane.com.au

NEW ZEALAND

Woodslane New Zealand, Ltd.
21 Cooks Street (P.O. Box 575)
Waganui, New Zealand
Tel: 64-6-347-6543
Fax: 64-6-345-4840
Email: info@woodslane.com.au

LATIN AMERICA

McGraw-Hill Interamericana
Editores, S.A. de C.V.
Cedro No. 512
Col. Atlampa
06450, Mexico, D.F.
Tel: 52-5-547-6777
Fax: 52-5-547-3336
Email: mcgraw-hill@infosel.net.mx

O'REILLY®